SMART BALL

SMART BALL

MARKETING THE MYTH AND
MANAGING THE REALITY OF
MAJOR LEAGUE BASEBALL

ROBERT F. LEWIS II

UNIVERSITY PRESS OF MISSISSIPPI / JACKSON

www.upress.state.ms.us

The University Press of Mississippi is a member
of the Association of American University Presses.

Copyright © 2010 by University Press of Mississippi
All rights reserved
Manufactured in the United States of America

First printing 2010

∞

Library of Congress Cataloging-in-Publication Data

Lewis, Robert F.
 Smart ball : marketing the myth and managing the reality
of major league baseball / Robert F. Lewis II.
   p. cm.
 Includes bibliographical references and index.
 ISBN 978-1-60473-207-8 (cloth : alk. paper) 1. Baseball—
Economic aspects—United States. 2. Baseball—United
States—Marketing. 3. Baseball—United States—Manage-
ment. I. Title.
 GV880.L55 2010
 796.3570973—dc22   2009019920

British Library Cataloging-in-Publication Data available

Frederic V. Lewis
Robert F. Lewis
Brian R. Lewis
Grandfather, Father, Son

Baseball is the mythical game of fathers and sons.

CONTENTS

ix   LIST OF ABBREVIATIONS

xi   ON DECK

3   **AT BAT**

9   **FIRST BASE**   BASEBALL AS A SPORT: CREATING POWER

36   **SECOND BASE**   BASEBALL AS A DOMESTIC MONOPOLY: DEVELOPING POWER

70   **THIRD BASE**   BASEBALL AS A NEOCOLONIALIST: ABUSING POWER

104   **HOME PLATE**   BASEBALL AS A GLOBAL BUSINESS: BALANCING POWER

133   **FINAL SCORE**

139   NOTES

153   BIBLIOGRAPHY

163   INDEX OF MAJOR LEAGUE BASEBALL NAMES

ABBREVIATIONS

AL	American League
CBA	Collective Bargaining Agreement
ChBA	China Baseball Association
FL	Federal League
IBAF	International Baseball Federation
IOC	International Olympic Committee
LL	Little League
MiLB	Minor League Baseball
MLB	Major League Baseball
MLBAM	Major League Baseball Advanced Media
MNC	multinational corporation
MLBPA	Major League Baseball Players Association
NL	National League
NPB	Nippon Professional Baseball
WBC	World Baseball Classic

ON DECK

This book probably began in spirit in 1948, when I, at the time a seven-year-old boy inspired by my father and grandfather to become a baseball fan, fortuitously chose to root for the Cleveland Indians and their player-manager, Lou Boudreau. The Indians won the World Series that year (but haven't since), and Boudreau was the Most Valuable Player in the American League (and later joined the Hall of Fame). From that Frank Merriwell beginning, through the ensuing six decades, I first followed Boudreau to the Boston Red Sox and to the Kansas City A's, then stayed with the A's as he migrated to the National League Chicago Cubs. I persevered through the "Yankee farm club" years in Kansas City and moved emotionally with Charlie Finley's team to Oakland, and I have steadfastly remained loyal despite the ups and downs of a "small market" team.

From that experience, I have developed what poet Robert Frost called "a lover's quarrel" with my world of baseball. Frost, a baseball fan, was the subject of my Princeton senior thesis nearly fifty years ago. He had a recurring argument with his New England world, but it was solidly grounded on a foundation of genuine love. My relationship with baseball has run the gamut of emotions from joy and pride to sorrow and disappointment but has always maintained that base of love. This book articulates my lover's quarrel.

I gratefully acknowledge the changing cast of people who have offered supportive suggestions and criticism as I developed the ideas for this volume. Beth Bailey and David Farber, now at Temple University, were vital in the launch of this project, and Amanda Cobb was helpful in transition. Ron Briley, Jake

Kosek, Enrique Sanabria, and Rebecca Schreiber skillfully and compassionately guided me to completion.

The staff at the National Baseball Hall of Fame Museum and Library were very responsive, and the annual Cooperstown Symposium on Baseball and American Culture was a fertile venue for gathering and testing ideas. Selected Society of American Baseball Research members offered useful insights, as did attendees at Society of American Baseball Research, American Culture Association, American Studies Association, and Popular Culture Association conferences, where I presented papers. Major League Baseball (MLB), notably Paul Archey Jr. in International Operations, offered helpful information and insight. Steven A. Riess let me contribute a chapter on the A's to his encyclopedia of Major League teams and encouraged me in this effort. David Ogden and Joel Nathan Rosen, whose book, *Falling from Grace*, includes my chapter on Branch Rickey, provided helpful feedback on that important figure as well as criticism of parts of this work.

Faculty members and students at the University of New Mexico's Department of American Studies not only tolerated an aged associate but provided numerous ideas, sources, and supportive comments. My family—son Brian, daughter Jennifer, and especially wife and best friend Dianna—were cheerleaders who humored me, propped me up, or left me alone as needed during the process.

It indeed takes a village to produce a book.

SMART BALL

AT BAT

Some baseball is the fate of us all.
—ROBERT FROST

In 1999, economists James Quirk and Rodney Fort published *Hard Ball: The Abuse of Power in Pro Team Sports*. A sequel to their generic 1992 treatment of sports economics, *Pay Dirt: The Business of Professional Team Sports*, *Hard Ball* argues that professional sports should be more competitive and that government should act as a principal corrective of monopoly abuses. By using an analogue to an international political crisis, one could conclude that Quirk and Fort view the four major U.S. professional sports—baseball, football, basketball, and hockey—as possessing domestic "weapons of mass destruction" in the forms of monopoly license, media leverage, union power, and celebrity player influence. As abusers of power, these sports organizations, in Quirk and Fort's opinion, deserve a combined public and private economic counterattack to deprive them of their autocratic controls and convert them to more democratic forms of governance.

One of these professional sports, Major League Baseball (MLB), is now more productively serving itself and both its traditional domestic and growing international markets by channeling its strengths into a more collaborative strategy that significantly utilizes soft power, comparable to that described by Joseph S. Nye Jr., dean of the Kennedy School of Government at Harvard, in his 2004 geopolitical analysis bearing that name. Nye has developed a "smart power" model that seems generally applicable to any leadership evaluation and frames this book.

Nye first defines *power* as "the ability to influence the behavior of others to get the outcomes one wants."[1] He then simply divides power into two contrasting subcategories, hard and soft, and applies them to nations that venture alone unilaterally or work together multilaterally. For him, hard power is typically military or economic in the form of inducements (carrots) or threats (sticks). He observes that unilateral nations, such as the United States, tend to consider themselves exceptional and to rely primarily on hard power military or economic forces to accomplish their national objectives. Nye contends that twenty-first-century U.S. foreign policy has combined "unilateralism, arrogance, and parochialism."[2] The early Obama administration actions, however, suggest a shift toward multilateralism.

Outside Nye's geopolitical context, hard power tends to be economic. Its dominant use also correlates more—but not exclusively—with organizations self-defined as unilateral and exceptional. MLB's hard power generally has economic elements but can also simply reflect an autocratic adherence to the contrived mythology of baseball, without material economic implications.

Soft power, Nye observes, is "the ability to get what you want through attraction rather than coercion or payments. It builds upon the attractiveness of a country's culture, political ideals, and policies and co-opts others."[3] In his view, it "rests on the ability to set the political agenda in a way that shapes the preferences of others." Soft power is not the same as influence but is a source of it. Soft power is more than cultural power because it includes values and behaviors.[4] Therefore, he notes, nations that rely primarily on soft power tend to be multilateral and collaborative in their approach to issues.

In MLB "country," supported by its own culture, ideals, and policies, leaders have a multilateral option to persuade owners, players, fans, and media by improving the attraction of the game. Co-optative rather than coercive marketing has become a significant element of soft power in MLB as it has increasingly allied with various corporate sponsors and charitable organizations. Credibility, Nye observes, is a crucial resource and an important source of soft power. Historically, therefore, it has been important for MLB to maintain its credibility while addressing such challenging issues as gambling and steroids. Nye acknowledges that unilateral nations can and should use soft power and that multilateral nations can and should use hard power when appropriate. "Smart power," he writes, is "neither hard nor soft. It is both," an optimal blend of the two strategies.[5]

Since introducing his concept of power in *Bound to Lead: The Changing Nature of American Power* (1990) and differentiating the benign soft power concept of influence through attractive promotion of culture and ideology with the more adversarial commanding or coercive military and economic forces of hard power, Nye has tracked U.S. power practices with increasing alarm.[6] He contends that both hard and soft power are necessary in varying degrees depending on the geopolitical context of the situation at hand. Power is paradoxical, he notes, because increasing reliance on hard power reduces the potential effectiveness of soft power and eventually of overall power. He argues that American global leadership today increasingly depends more on an ability to persuade and attract than on commanding and coercing. The optimal balance now generally needs more soft and less hard power.

Nye acknowledges that popular culture is often a resource that produces global soft power.[7] While MLB, representing our "national pastime," is becoming an international popular culture element, it is only a minor player on the geopolitical stage. Therefore, the book focuses on the use of smart power for MLB's interests, not those of the United States. MLB, which has historically relied primarily on economic hard power in establishing, preserving, and expanding its domain, is now more skillfully using the soft power of its traditional ideology and cultural attraction to collaborate with its various constituents. It is utilizing Nye's macro thesis to develop a smart power formula to enhance its multinational as well as domestic appeal.

This volume is divided into four reinforcing and cumulative aspects ("bases") of baseball: as a sport, as a domestic monopoly, as a neocolonial power, and as an international business. While the sequence has a general chronological progression, the elements overlap and influence each other, thereby demonstrating that all remain present and important to varying degrees in MLB today. MLB has historically faced the challenges of preserving and enhancing its mythical mystique while managing and growing a business that complicates and contradicts its mythology. While MLB continues to possess the elements of sport, domestic monopoly, and neocolonialism, the book ultimately focuses on MLB's policies and practices in its current global context.

The first chapter ("First Base") interrogates baseball through theories of modern sport and social construction. Included are MLB's soft power efforts to establish baseball's pastoral mythology, reinforced by its Cooperstown "creation," as a stabilizing and uplifting influence in nineteenth-century urban America. In doing so, baseball incorporates premodern, modern, and postmodern elements. As MLB emerged as the controlling organization for the sport, it reinforced its soft power mythology through links to religion, nationalism, militarism, and popular culture.

Early in its history, the sport positioned itself as an exclusively American secular religion built on moral and patriotic principles. It obsessively reinforced its indigenous creation and fabricated rural background to appeal to Americans' nostalgic yearnings for a pastoral life that individuals may not have actually experienced. Throughout its history, however, MLB has complicated and contradicted its simply constructed mythology. It has destructively abused as well as productively used its influence, often as a result of its overemphasis on hard power economic tactics as it evolved into and continued as an essentially unchallenged monopoly until the 1970s. While providing an attractive escape for Americans from the stresses of modern urban life, it exploited fans as well as players. Nevertheless, MLB's mythical mystique has endured in America as a result of continuous self-promotion and popular fantasy acceptance. While reinforcing its appeal, its self-reinforced exceptional role as the national pastime presents a potentially divisive challenge to MLB's international strategy unless it pursues a collaborative soft power approach.

From a domestic business perspective, described in the second chapter ("Second Base"), MLB both complements and contradicts its sport role as the national pastime. Its unique monopoly status, affirmed by the Supreme Court in 1922, enabled MLB almost from its inception to control its labor supply and costs and to establish local market exclusivity. The absence of labor, consumer, and government counterforces, however, removed traditional free-market challenges that would have pushed it to improve its overall business performance. As a protected monopoly, it therefore lagged other businesses in the development of professional management because of its virtual insulation from normal competitive business stimuli. Supportive media and iconic players such as Ty Cobb and Babe Ruth enhanced MLB's mythical appeal. They helped MLB withstand negative events such as the 1919 Black Sox gambling scandal.

While using the soft power of culture and ideology to sell its product, MLB owners bullied players, fans, and local government with hard power economic tactics. That sustained hegemonic application of its versions of hard power inevitably produced effective resistances through unions, governments, alternative entertainment vehicles, and public backlash, thereby opening the competitive playing field to other professional sports, most notably football and basketball, as well as other forms of leisure. The growing competition and opposition forced MLB to become a more effective marketer and manager of its business.

On the labor side, the successful counterattack of the Major League Baseball Players Association (MLBPA), led by former United Steelworkers executive Marvin Miller, also demanded that MLB operate more like a competitive business that values its employees. The resultant hostility between the two parties has posed a continuing threat to the viability of the game. The prolonged and acrimonious 1994–95 strike significantly reduced MLB's popularity for several years. The more recent steroid issue, which has publicly shamed both MLB and particularly the MLBPA, increased the inherent challenges for these enemies to exercise soft power collaboration for mutual benefit.

Chapter 3 ("Third Base") traces MLB's historical racial and class biases, primarily on the labor side, to argue that its illogical and unwarranted monopoly status enabled it to function both domestically and internationally like neocolonial nations and multinational corporations (MNCs) in the global political and economic arenas. Although the United States lauded MLB for crossing the color line with the signing of Jackie Robinson in 1945, when black-white relations in this country needed a breakthrough event, baseball's motives were primarily economic. MLB continued racially prejudicial practices, albeit less overtly and less consistently, for several more decades. It continues to publicize its racial achievement despite (and/or because of) losing the black athlete and fan market to other sports, most notably basketball and football.

MLB's primary motivation in recruiting players has always been economic. It has taken financial advantage of immigrant and rural white as well as domestic and foreign minority athletes while emphasizing the game's diversity. Financial treatment of minority players conformed to the biased split-labor theory that extended beyond salaries to field positions and management opportunities. The most abusive behavior has occurred in the Caribbean, which the U.S. government and corporations had already politically and economically colonized. MLB teams took unfair advantage of that leverage to exploit Caribbean youth as the cost of recruiting domestic talent increased.

There, its cultural hegemony reinforced resistance that produced a regional "small ball" variation of the game, *béisbol romántico*, that emphasized pitching, speed, and defense. The resultant nationalistic passion not only improved the quality of play but also tempered MLB's exploitation. Evidence suggests that MLB now operates more like the meritocracy it has always purported to be. It has become the most racially and nationally diverse professional sport. Although racial parity has not been complete, signing bonuses, salaries, and management opportunities have disproportionately increased for domestic and foreign minorities, particularly in the past decade. In 2008, seven of the top thirteen salaried players (earning more than sixteen million dollars per year) were Latinos. The Oakland A's signed a sixteen-year old Dominican pitcher, Michel Ynoa, for $4.25 million. Only three U.S. amateur pitchers had received higher bonuses at that time.[8]

The final chapter ("Home Plate") describes MLB's emergence as an international business pursuing the geographic expansion of labor and consumer markets for their own sakes. MLB's global strategy also enhances the sport's domestic appeal in a United States that reveres its immigrant roots and increasingly values racial diversity. MLB's implementation of Nye's soft power approach is becoming productive at home as well as abroad, albeit disproportionately so in the Caribbean and Asia. The strategy has met with only minimal success in Europe, perhaps because of that continent's more entrenched sports legacies and its strained geopolitical relations with the United States.

Evolving from a hard power neocolonial to a soft power "glocalization" (think global, act local) strategy, MLB has become more respectful of Caribbean countries and their talent. Japan has become a collaborative rival in developing its small ball version of the game, *yakyû*, more extensively in Asia. These are hopeful signs of success in a competitive international sports environment that does not provide the monopolistic insulation MLB previously enjoyed domestically. While not the global sports giant that soccer is, baseball in the aggregate more than holds its own with the other U.S. exports, basketball and football, through the International Baseball Federation (IBAF) and its 113 member countries.

The MLB-initiated 2006 World Baseball Classic (WBC), including a sixteen-country competition, provided a major though risky soft power opportunity to market the game globally. Implementing the event demanded soft power skills to achieve collaboration among the participating country organizations as well as cooperation from the U.S. players' union and team owners. A March format, however, prompted many MLB players to opt out to prepare traditionally for the regular season. Nevertheless, since baseball is no longer an Olympic sport, the initial and subsequent WBC ventures are giving MLB an international event base on which to build. With IBAF support and 220-plus countries receiving MLB-televised games, MLB has a significant potential global market. The WBC also represents a recurring opportunity to collaborate more effectively with the IBAF, which now has an executive director from the United States, and the affiliated International Olympic Committee (IOC).

While this more intensive and extensive MLB "smart ball" strategy is only a minor blip on the world screen, its execution can once again, as U.S. baseball has often done, offer an educational mirror to its nation, which is retooling its global strategy in light of increased competition and resentment. American geopolitical leadership, ironically headed for much of the early twenty-first century by George W. Bush, a former MLB team owner turned hard power president, could see in MLB a small example of the value of attractive soft power collaboration in a smart power formula. The United States could do worse than play ball the way MLB does.

More pointedly, however, smart power appears to be an improved means for both preserving MLB's challenged position as the national pastime in a diverse United States and enhancing the country's role in a global market.

FIRST BASE

BASEBALL AS A SPORT: CREATING POWER

Whoever wants to know the hearts and minds of America had
better learn baseball, the rules and the realities of the game.
—JACQUES BARZUN

THE BIRTH AND THE "CREATION"

In the beginning was the ball. But no one knew when the beginning was. In *Baseball before We Knew It*, David Block contends, "The roots of baseball were planted the moment the first cave kid hit a stone with a club. Since then, the game's progression has been a little more difficult to figure out." He observes that baseball's origin can be claimed by a handful of nations on three different continents but that there is neither a single, conclusive beginning nor a traceable confluence of influences that chart the history—"an ironic (if not embarrassing) predicament for a sport that has been dissected and studied like no other."

His research reveals baseball-like games mentioned in English town records dating to the thirteenth century, portrayed in a fourteenth-century French illuminated manuscript, and recalled in a memoir by a Polish worker who was in the Jamestown settlement in 1609. Block records eight different attempts to describe baseball before 1845, when the New York Knickerbockers club established rules that formed the basis of the U.S. game. From those disparate findings, he concludes that "baseball evolved from a matrix of early English folk games, and it follows that baseball's rules were borrowed and shaped from those, considered the "father traditional pastimes."[1] Native American sports such as lacrosse and shinny appear to have had no causal relationship with baseball.

In North America, baseball coalesced from separate initiatives undertaken in the 1830s and 1840s not only in the New York area but also in Philadelphia, Boston, and southern Ontario. The game progressed differently in each area, but the varieties developed similarities as they matured. The New York game prevailed because of that city's growing importance and the Knickerbockers' formalized rules documentation attributed to by Alexander Joy Cartwright, considered the father of baseball for that act and enshrined in the Hall of Fame.[2] Americans were calling baseball the national pastime as early as 1856.[3]

This chapter focuses on baseball as a sport and its creation of power and specifically on how it developed as the national pastime and a quasi-religion in the Progressive Era. The game combined an adherence to the mythology of traditional agrarian values with an exploitation of reality-driven urban opportunities. In the process, it identified itself with America's emerging national culture. This development has enabled baseball to preserve a unique and self-sustaining mythical quality among Americans despite a recent decline in its relative popularity among sports and alternative entertainments in the domestic marketplace. The soft power attraction derived from its mythological foundation enhances its importance beyond its current competitive position among major sports.

French cultural linguist Roland Barthes offers perceptive insight on mythology through a collection of essays written a half century ago. His observations are generally applicable to the creation of Major League Baseball (MLB) and the promotion of its game mythologies. Barthes's observation that "men do not have with myth a relationship based on truth but on use; they depoliticize according to their needs" captures MLB's relationship with mythology, particularly the Cooperstown myth. He further notes that "myth essentially aims at causing an immediate impression—it does not matter if one is later allowed to see through the myth, its action is assumed to be stronger than the rational explanation which may later belie it." As if speaking about Cooperstown, he concludes, "Myth does not deny things, on the contrary, its function is to talk about them; simply, it purifies them, it makes them innocent, it gives them a natural and eternal justification, it gives them a clarity which is not that of an explanation but that of a statement of fact."[4]

The game's dominant early proponent, Albert B. Spalding, was one of the first great players and later a successful owner of the Chicago White Sox as well as a sports equipment manufacturer and retailer. His *Spalding's Official Base Ball Guide*, an annual publication begun in 1877, shaped public and institutional opinion about the game. A self-declared historian of the game, he noted that the British Museum houses a small leather-covered ball that Egyptians played with more than forty centuries ago.[5] Befitting a commitment to America's self-declared exceptionalism, however, he initiated a formal effort to establish baseball as an exclusively indigenous sport. In so doing, he helped to create a lasting mythology that has romanticized and popularized the game despite its often contradictory progression.

Described by S. W. Pope as "baseball's leading power broker" at the time,[6] Spalding persuaded MLB to create a commission led by A. G. Mills, a former National League president and head of the Amateur Athletic Union, for the allegedly neutral purpose of determining its origins. Presumably influenced by Spalding's desire to affirm an indigenous creation, the commission concluded in its December 30, 1907, report that the formalized game of baseball originated with the Knickerbockers club in 1845 but that the sport was initially created in 1839 by Abner Doubleday, then a cadet at the U.S. Military Academy, in the upstate village of Cooperstown, New York. An old ball later discovered in a local field was used to substantiate this conclusion.[7]

In this "immaculate conception," which has long since been disproved, MLB established a rural, heroic mythology of baseball as the indigenous sport. The National Baseball Hall of Fame and Museum in Cooperstown, opened a century after Doubleday's "creation," remains a continuing tangible tribute to the game's mythological foundation and a dynamic symbol of its soft power, even though Doubleday was not elected to the Hall. In 1923, the Village of Cooperstown bought Doubleday Field, built in 1920 on the pasture site allegedly used by Abner and his friends for the first baseball game, to commemorate the myth. It upgraded the field and expanded the stands to 9,791 seats in time for a May 6, 1939, game preceding the Cooperstown Baseball Centennial and the Hall of Fame and Museum dedication the following month. Currently, various groups play some 350 games annually on the field, paying a fee of three hundred dollars per game to the village.[8]

"Doubleday didn't invent baseball, baseball invented Doubleday," asserts Block, noting that the "the age-old debate over baseball's ancestry has always been long on bluster and short on facts."[9] A further refutation of the Cooperstown myth was the May 2004 discovery of a 1791 Pittsfield, Massachusetts, ordinance banning the playing of a game called baseball within eighty yards of the big church in the town square. As the most recent city to claim origin, Pittsfield is now calling itself baseball's Garden of Eden.[10] Despite a lack of agreement on its creation, MLB continues to use folklore to preserve baseball's position as the national pastime and thus maintain a degree of influence beyond the impact of actual participants and spectators.

Complementing the Cooperstown "birthplace" is the baseball field constructed for the 1989 film *Field of Dreams* in rural Dyersville, Iowa. The field, which was built on two adjacent farms, remains a tourist attraction and a visual tribute to baseball's rural connection. Noting that these two mythologized venues, symbolically linked by U.S. Highway 20, are in a "dialogic relationship," Charles Fruehling Springwood observes that both locations are part of the pastoral "heritage industry" that commodifies nostalgia in America and thereby criticizes its urbanization. Nostalgia, he notes, is "a paramount cultural semiotic" in the contemporary world.[11] Baseball's history is one of exploiting nostalgia.

The Cooperstown and Dyersville sites differ in their critiques of modern urban America. Cooperstown, Springwood concludes, is a well-crafted corporate project that supports the contrived national historical narrative. Its field is an artfully constructed replica of a late-nineteenth-century town ballpark, enhanced with a permanent grandstand and outfield fence in the middle of a commercially quaint lakeside village. Dyersville's diamond is laid out on a plowed-over portion of a cornfield that borders the unfenced outfield and has a small set of temporary bleachers. Though built for a commercial movie set, it is less constrained, more ludic and pastoral, and more directly connected to traditional family values signified by the nearby farmhouse. Both locales conform to what Barthes calls the very principle of myth: "It transforms history into nature."[12]

Shoeless Joe Jackson, a premier player banished in the 1919 Black Sox gambling scandal and thus denied entry into the Hall of Fame at Cooperstown, reemerges in the W. P. Kinsella novel that forms the basis of the Dyersville movie. Jackson's "second chance" participation in the film's game contrasts rural Dyersville with Cooperstown, which rejected him for the Hall of Fame. It also reminds the reader/viewer of his fate in Chicago and protests his expulsion from his urban "home."

"For many Americans," Howard Good observes, "the Black Sox scandal marked the end of innocence."[13] Gambling and oppressive owner treatment of players had been a part of professional baseball since its inception a half century earlier. This scandal, in which eight White Sox players, feeling underpaid by notoriously cheap owner Charles Comiskey, allegedly threw the World Series against the less talented Cincinnati Reds, became known as MLB's "original sin." In his cultural history of the scandal, Daniel A. Nathan called it an ideal news piece, "constructed by the press as a labyrinthine story of deception, betrayal, and moral disorder." He asserts that it affected Americans' view not only of the national pastime but also of the country itself as it moved from World War I into the turbulent 1920s.[14]

Ironically, the press had earlier played a significant role in establishing baseball's mythical moral certainty. In assessing baseball in the Progressive Era, Steven A. Riess asserts, "A substantial disparity existed between the ideology of baseball, which sought to present the sport in the best possible context, and the realities of the game. The baseball creed constituted a cultural fiction; that is, the baseball ideology was regarded as an accurate description of the sport, and even though it was inaccurate, the conventional wisdom influenced the way people behaved and thought. It did not matter that the ideology strayed from the truth."[15] Sportswriters marketed the mythology of the sport simplistically and continuously until the Black Sox scandal, then complicated it thereafter. While writers continued to promote the game generally, the scandal fostered an element of criticism that has continued to grow as media became more provocative and less objective in their reporting.

The *Shoeless Joe* book and its essentially faithful *Field of Dreams* movie were 1980s attempts to recapture the myth, portraying the iconic Jackson more as a victim than a sinner because of his illiteracy and strong World Series performance. Wes Gehring observes that "second chance" is a populist theme reinforced in *Field of Dreams* through Jackson and his fellow Black Sox returnees. The 1980s represented a revival of late-nineteenth–early-twentieth-century populism in America. Other characters also get second chances as they come to this Eden. Terrance Mann, a black activist author (and ardent baseball fan), appears to remind farm owners Ray and Annie Kinsella of their 1960s Los Angeles college protest days. Joining him at the field is Archie "Moonlight" Graham, who played only one inning in a 1905 Major League game, never got to bat, and retired to become a doctor. For them as well as the Kinsellas, the field represents home, that most populist of baseball metaphors, and a coming to terms with one's life.[16]

In *Eight Men Out* (1988), released a year before *Field of Dreams*, director John Sayles provides a more complicated and pessimistic interpretation of the Black Sox scandal. Set in Chicago and filmed in shadows, the movie portrays a city and nation in moral darkness but also shows the players as victims of circumstances. Although critical of the business of baseball, the film does not absolve the players. Based on Eliot Asimof's 1963 book of the same name, the film visually captures the cultural shift from innocent childhood to troubled adolescence in post–World War I America. In that setting, Sayles reinforces the noxious environment of the city that facilitated the fix and perpetuated the dominant hard power structure of MLB. Stephen C. Wood and J. David Pincus assert that the Black Sox scandal "continues to define the dark side of the national pastime."[17] One can view much of MLB's subsequent soft power activities as attempts to atone for that original sin and others, such as racial segregation and performance-enhancing drugs.

Cultural anthropology offers insight into the complicating and contradicting evolution of baseball lore. Anthropologist James Clifford observes "the predicament of culture," reflecting observers' self-fashioning of culture. The net result, he contends, is the transformation of the nineteenth-century linear evolutionary model into a pluralist "ethnographic subjectivity." Since cultural difference ceased to be stable, he notes, "self-other relations are matters of power and rhetoric rather than of essence."[18] According to Warren Susman, "A culture is in fact defined by its tensions, which provide both the necessary tensile strength to keep the culture stable and operative, and the dynamic force that may ultimately bring about change or complete structural collapse."[19] Clifford concludes that the resulting confrontation and conflict have been both destructive and inventive, producing a replacement of the present stasis with a new aftermath. The Black Sox scandal and responsive aftermath, variously interpreted over the years, illustrate Clifford's and Susman's theses. MLB tightened its governance to prevent such a recurrence by hiring a hard power commissioner, Kenesaw Mountain Landis.

While directed at fellow ethnographers and anthropologists, Clifford's thesis is also applicable to general baseball history as a significant part of a uniquely American culture. He concludes that modern culture is a continuing social construct, shaped and reshaped over time by the dynamic interaction of varying—sometimes opposing—elements. As "a collective fiction," culture becomes, for Clifford, "the ground for individual identity and freedom."[20] Cooperstown and Dyersville are conflicting social constructs. Baseball's history includes such reshaping and continues as an influence on and a reflection of Americana. Throughout that history, MLB has reinforced its mythological tendency to reconstruct or obscure actual events, as the Barthesian thesis generally observes.

BASEBALL IN TIME AND SPACE

In its dynamically interactive rural-urban construction of cultural symbols, baseball uniquely incorporates both time and space. As contrasted with other major team sports, time and space are theoretically limitless in baseball. The flexibility of time and space inherent in the game reinforces the mythical quality that enables it to engage the fan. In Eric Rolfe Greenberg's novel, *The Celebrant*, the protagonist's father-in-law tells future Hall of Fame pitcher Christy Mathewson that baseball is "totally artificial, creating its own time, existing within its own space," and Mathewson concurs while asserting that it is "a game of intricate simplicity," reflecting its contradictory nature.[21] There is no clock, only untimed innings to measure the game. It is somewhat fitting that a game that eschews the clock also has origins that cannot be pinpointed.

Despite its city origins, baseball in the early twentieth century recalled a preindustrial, unhurried world. It appealed to urbanites beset by fast-paced control of their modern lives and desirous of a romanticized past that these individuals may not have actually experienced. As several authors observe, baseball provided urban Americans with a pastoral "imagined community," as generally defined by Benedict Anderson.[22] Fans could escape to their field of dreams while still in the city and share a pastoral experience among themselves and with the players.

Warren Goldstein argues that baseball's time progression is both linear and cyclical—linear during the game and cyclical during its seasons.[23] The game proceeds in an orderly manner, with each team batting until three outs are recorded and the process repeated through nine innings. The season follows the agricultural cycle—from planting (spring training) through a growing summer (regular season) to harvest (playoffs) and a southern migration (Latin American leagues) or dormancy (Hot Stove League discussions and trades) in winter, punctuated by three significant festivals (Opening Day, All-Star Game, World Series).[24] Like growing crops, a baseball game is discontinuous and arguably too slow, but the rhythm of the game encourages intermittent fan interaction (cultivation) with each other and the game. Such interaction reinforces the community aspect (soil development) of baseball. Some delays in the cycle may be spontaneous (a foul ball or rain), while others may be strategic (a pitcher-catcher conference or crop rotation). And, like farming, baseball demands patience. MLB and particularly Minor League Baseball (MiLB) seek to capitalize on this timelessness by offering alternative entertainment before, during, and after the game as a way to reinforce family and community values and enrich the soil (ballpark) for future revenue growth.

The playing space also mimics a farm by re-creating a pasture in the middle of a city. It is outdoors and has special dirt and a green field that is a nonstandard shape except for the infield diamond. Even the ball has a form of fertilizer: New Jersey swamp mud to condition its surface. The player/farmer needs to adjust to the specific parameters of the particular field. Like a farm but unlike any other major sport venue, the entire area, including foul territory, is usable. About half of the balls hit in a game are foul, and many become fan/visitor property, like fallen apples on the edge of an orchard. Although fences and grandstands were added when the game modernized in constricting urban space, the ball can go beyond them to paying or outside spectators as well. Cooperstown's simulated nineteenth-century town field is fenced, while the Dyersville rural diamond's outfield blends seamlessly into adjacent cornfields. Modern parks continue to compromise pastoral space but try to preserve the illusion of open fields.

The recent history of Major League ballparks also reinforces the game's link with its agrarian myth. When the two Major Leagues organizationally joined in the early 1900s, the owners took advantage of new construction technology—in particular, steel-reinforced concrete—to build fireproof venues, called "parks" or "fields" to reflect the game's pastoral heritage in urban settings. That building phase, which produced new homes for fourteen of the sixteen MLB teams, started with Shibe Park in Philadelphia in 1909 and culminated with Yankee Stadium, "the House That Ruth Built" and the first to be called a stadium, in 1923.[25] Fenway Park in Boston and Wrigley Field in Chicago, remaining tributes to that early blend of the pastoral with the city, have staunchly withstood replacement while incorporating modern amenities.

As professional football grew in popularity with the advent of television, host cities, forced by team leverage into public financing, sought to economize by developing dual-purpose stadiums to accommodate both sports in the 1960s. While operationally efficient, the venues lacked specific characteristics for either sport. Since football's requirements were more rigid and used artificial turf to reduce bad-weather influence, baseball lost some of the connection with the natural setting and open flexibility that had reinforced its rural identity. In the early 1990s, however, the media-enhanced prosperity of both football and baseball facilitated the construction of venues tailored specifically for each sport. While football continued with large-scale symmetrical designs, baseball teams built smaller retro-looking parks, starting in 1992 with Baltimore's Camden Yards, which recaptures the pastoral irregularity and intimacy of older playing fields within a city while accommodating entertainment centers, food and merchandise outlets, and luxury boxes that enhance team income opportunities and fan pleasure. Emerging history indicates, however, that the positive influence of new baseball stadiums on fan attendance is short-lived. What most influences attendance beyond the first few years is whether the stadium houses a winner. Nevertheless, newer MLB parks continue to reinforce nostalgia, adding technology and luxury to facilitate a broader entertainment experience and mitigate the negative impact of a noncontending team.

Citing Cincinnati's Great American Ball Park, opened in 2003, as the low point in retro design, Christopher Hawthorne sees an emerging modification in baseball stadiums, such as in San Diego's PETCO Park, to retain but not highlight traditional elements within a contemporary framework.[26] As local government forces team owners to pay a greater share of the construction costs, owners are co-opting corporations by selling them stadium naming rights, like Great American and PETCO, and designated sponsorships. The mythical setting is framed in a contrived reality built by capital.

Since Camden Yards, more than half of MLB teams have moved into new parks, while the others have upgraded existing venues or are in planning or development stages for new facilities, thereby repeating the early 1900s building boom at much higher costs. In 2009, New York fans witnessed the opening of new parks for both the Mets and the Yankees and anticipated a new stadium for the football Giants and Jets in 2010. While public financing as well as corporate licensing have played a role, the teams are setting records in ticket pricing.

The best seats at the $800 million Citi Field, named for financial conglomerate Citigroup, which is paying $20 million per year for naming rights, cost Mets fans $495, up from $276 at Shea Stadium in 2008. The new park seats 42,500, down from 57,333 at Shea, contributing to the escalation. In strategic contrast to Shea's sterile cavern, the Mets established an intimate layout to recall Ebbets Field, the neighborhood home of the Brooklyn Dodgers. The objective was to "unite the close-up feel of baseball in the 1950s with the luxuries the fans expect from new parks in the modern era." To dramatize this soft power nostalgic connection with the Bums, Citi Field's entrance is the Robinson Rotunda, a tribute to Dodger great Jackie Robinson and a larger modern reminder of the entrance rotunda that existed at Ebbets Field.[27]

The new Yankee Stadium, costing almost twice as much as the smaller Citi Field, seats 53,328 fans, about 4,000 less than the prior version. While rejecting corporate sponsorship to maintain the stadium's iconic name, team officials have raised its top seat price from $1,000 to $2,500 for 147 exclusive seats. If all tickets are sold, the 2,285 seats priced at $350 and up would generate annual revenue of $135 million, including $30 million from the top 147 seats, thereby allowing for more affordable seats for the Yankees' large fan base. Yankee chief operating officer Lonn Trost asserts that the new stadium is like a "five star hotel with a ballpark attached." Though it lacks a hotel (present in Toronto's Rogers Centre), the new Yankee Stadium does have numerous amenities that give it a luxury feel.[28]

The construction of the new stadium has enabled MLB to find another way to market its pastoral myth: Yankee Sod, a bluegrass blend that is used at the park, and Yankee Grass Seed, which produces the blend. DeLea Sod Farms, which has supplied turf to the team since the 1960s, is selling both the sod and seed in the New York City area. Pending customer reception, MLB is withholding licensing to other team sod suppliers. If this new product area is successful, it could conceivably be extended to Cubs Ivy as well as numerous other products used in sports venues.[29]

Although MLB prices, supported by its longer season, remain relative bargains when compared with professional football, basketball, and hockey, they financially challenge the "average" fan. MLB and its teams compensate by offering free broadcasts and telecasts as well as extensive paid packages on cable, satellite, and the Internet in an effort to perpetuate the myth of spectatorship outside the ballpark. In reality, however, rising admission and food prices make going in person increasingly less affordable for the "average" fan and thereby jeopardize that significant experiential reinforcement that comes from physically attending the pastoral game at the MLB level. The new packs and pricing schemes target the corporate customer more than the individual fan.

MLB attendance in 2008 was about 1 percent less than the prior (record) year. The higher New York prices and smaller stadiums may reinforce a downward attendance trend, particularly in difficult economic times, thereby challenging MLB's critical balance of myth and reality. Increasingly, MiLB, with its continuing attendance growth and more affordable prices, is providing more of the pastoral experience for baseball fans in many more venues, offering small parks and a relaxed atmosphere. MLB still must face the recession-fueled economic challenges that affect MLB in the current economy.

Given baseball's closely interwoven myth and reality, however, it is still doubtful that further research will alter public opinion of baseball's American identity. Representative of that identity is Little League (LL), started in small-town Williamsport, Pennsylvania, in 1938. With organized play now expanded to 2.7 million five- to eighteen-year-old boys and girls in more than one hundred countries, LL globally portrays baseball as family values, highlighted in the annual LL World Series in Williamsport.[30] LL's global reach also facilitates MLB's international strategy. At home, however, baseball is losing a battle with soccer for the youth market. Abroad, soccer and other sports are already entrenched among the young, thereby limiting global expansion.

Calling baseball "a cultural mirror," Gerald W. Scully observes that its development has been "haphazard, fortuitous, and, from the perspective of hindsight, often illogical, inefficient, or even peevish."[31] James Quirk and Rodney Fort assert that baseball shares with America a sense of confusion.[32] Nevertheless, baseball has been a "remarkably stable game," observes Paul J. Zingg, reflecting on its continuing adherence to its early, albeit mythologized, development, which has overridden its actual history.[33] Barthesian observations of mythology apply to MLB: "It establishes a blissful clarity."[34]

Basketball, football, and hockey, the three other major American professional team sports, lack this mythic connection with our pastoral history despite some small-town regional amateur hotbeds—Texas and Florida for football; Indiana, Kentucky, and North Carolina for basketball; and certain New England and Upper Midwest areas for hockey. Those pro teams appear less capable of exploiting their amateur local roots. As Joel Zoss and John Bowman conclude, "Myth is truer than history in baseball,"[35] and MLB reconstructs history through its reinforced mythology.

A MODERN SPORT?

In *From Ritual to Record*, Allen Guttmann logically describes the evolution and characteristics of modern sport and offers a cogent explanation of how and why baseball became America's national sport. He develops a paradigm initially derived from a concept of play, which he defines as "any nonutilitarian physical or mental activity pursued for its own sake."[36] He sees play as a realm of freedom enhanced by the advent of industrialization and urbanization, both of which structured life according to time-governed work. A complementary consequence, however, was the emergence of leisure time, which regularly permitted play to emerge in various forms. Michael Mandelbaum notes that the word *sport* is related to *disport*—that is, "to divert or entertain oneself."[37]

In Guttmann's paradigm, play can be either spontaneous or organized. He classifies organized play as games, which sacrifice some of play's freedom to achieve order. He then differentiates games into those that are competitive and those that are not. Competitive games become playful contests, as contrasted with those that are not playful, such as wars or legal proceedings. Finally, he subdivides organized, competitive forms of play into those that are intellectual, such as chess, and those that are physical, such as baseball. He labels this final category "sports": organized, competitive, physical play.

Having logically derived this concept of sports from play, games, and contests, he then distinguishes modern sports as having seven characteristics not present in primitive or medieval sports:

1. secularism, as contrasted with primitive sports, which were usually associated with religion and/or ritual;
2. equality of opportunity to compete and equality in the conditions of competition, although inequalities exist in practice;
3. specialization of roles, enhanced by stress on achievement;

4. rationalization through universal rules;
5. bureaucratic organization to administer rules;
6. quantification to measure achievement;
7. records as goals quantified.

Although he designates baseball a modern sport, he indirectly hedges that categorization by calling baseball a "quantified pastoral."[38] In that sense, one can consider baseball a transitional sport rather than a completely modern one. Far more than other sports, it retains a ritualistic, almost religious, quality of primitive sport while complying with Guttmann's six other elements of modern sport. Baseball has generally been meritocratic, with some notable historical deviations, such as its former racial segregation practices. It has developed specialized roles, such as a closer, with emphasis on achievement. It has promulgated and reinforced universal rules through a comprehensive organizational structure, MLB. It has almost obsessively quantified achievement through statistical techniques, such as Bill James's sabermetrics, associated with the Society of American Baseball Research and its more than seven thousand members, and has maintained and revered ever-increasing sets of records. Fueled by the society, fantasy leagues, and sports reporting, baseball enhances its imagined community.

While underscoring Guttmann's thesis, Riess observes that "the evolution of the city, more than any other factor, influenced the development of organized sport and recreational athletic pastimes in America." In the city, sport was rationalized, specialized, organized, commercialized, and professionalized. Because of the number and frequency of its games, MLB requires larger markets than other professional sports to build and maintain attendance and thus is arguably the most urbanized. For example, Green Bay (National Football League) and Oklahoma City (National Basketball Association) could not support MLB teams.

Within this urban development context, Riess contends that sport became a substitute for the lost frontier and small-town life as catalysts that built character, raised morality, and improved health.[39] Michael N. Danielson observes that professional sport continues to sell itself as a game rather than as a business.[40] MLB uses its mythology to sell itself. Frederick L. Paxson calls sport a "safety valve" that provided aptitudes of community from a frontier that is yielding to the needs of city life.[41] John R. Betts sees it in a more complicated role, as both a product of and antidote for industrialization.[42] Pope calls it "social glue" for class, region, ethnicity, and politics, while Eric M. Leifer uses the phrase "a sort of culmination of the civilizing process."[43] Michael Burke, president of the Yankees during the CBS ownership period in the 1960s and early 1970s, asserts, "A baseball club is part of the chemistry of the city. A game isn't just an athletic contest. It's a picnic, a kind of town meeting."⁴⁴ The newer ballparks reinforce that observation.

According to Riess, baseball builds on Jacksonian ideology. Supporters of the game have claimed that it provided catharsis for boring work, imitated idols, served as a panacea for youth problems ("playing catch" is still revered as an admirable duty of fatherhood), leveled social classes, improved public health, acculturated immigrants, and enhanced progressive education.⁴⁵ Goldstein observes, however, that baseball was never far removed from the world of work, as indicated by work and baseball languages being used to describe each other, usually with the common metaphor of team: "step up to the plate," "sacrifice," "strike out," "hit a home run," "get on base," "score," "win," "shut out." While baseball is play for fans, it is work for players, who play for keeps.⁴⁶

Despite baseball's ideological foundation, however, Riess concludes, "The arcadian, integrative, and democratic attributes of professional baseball were largely myths."⁴⁷ The game was more urban than rural and more an escape from than a panacea for urban and family ills. Baseball's value in assimilating immigrants, he contends, was overrated and essentially unsubstantiated. Its mass appeal was soon manipulated by capitalist owners as the game professionalized. These observations suggest that baseball's relationship to emerging American society is complicating as well as reinforcing and that its mythology simplifies the complications of reality, as Barthes notes.

While sports development in the United States is comparable to that elsewhere, the country has historically considered itself exceptional, Guttmann points out, and baseball is an example of that consideration.⁴⁸ As Spalding's creation campaign and the resulting Cooperstown myth suggest, early-twentieth-century American leaders had a desire to identify a uniquely native sport. Baseball's compulsive connection to the pastoral, with its links to the nostalgic, rural, seasonally warm outdoors, coupled with obsession on extensive and intensive rules and quantification, gave it a paradoxical combination of the primitive and the modern that took precedence over the more indigenous sport of basketball during the Progressive Era.

Later, in the second half of the twentieth century, Leifer contends, "Major League Baseball backed into the modern era" and suffered in popularity as television-friendly football and basketball flourished.⁴⁹ Since the mid-1960s, football has been the most popular U.S. sport according to the annual Harris survey, with professional football chosen by 30 percent and college football by 12 percent, compared to 15 percent of Americans who chose baseball in 2008. The National Football League also claims revenue that is almost one billion dollars higher than that of MLB as well as the most tie-in video games sold and the most fantasy players. Basketball is the most popular participant sport, according to a recent Sporting Goods Manufacturers Association survey. MLB attendance still exceeds that of professional football and basketball because of the greater number of games.[50]

Guttmann concludes that a more recent reason for baseball's decline is that America no longer needs or values a transition or bridge between old and new.[51] Leifer observes that baseball now seems less able to attract a national audience or to solidify local fan support, particularly among youth. "Baseball seems to be in the most precarious position of all sports, anchored more by its traditional popularity than its ability to produce a small group of rival superteams for national publics or a pattern of winning home games that draw local publics."[52] One can argue, therefore, that America could benefit from the influence of baseball, with its traditional values emphasis, as it interacts with increasingly aggressive global competition.

A SECULAR RELIGION

"Is this heaven?" is the recurring question asked by the resurrected ballplayers in *Field of Dreams*. "No, this Iowa," is the recurring reply.[53] Baseball's continuing devotion to and reinforcement of its pastoral mythology provides a marked difference, in degree if not in kind, from Guttmann's other "modern" sports. This observation also calls into question connections among sports in general, baseball in particular, and religion, all of which underwent significant change in the late-nineteenth-century United States.

Jay Coakley calls all sports "quasi religious," observing a symbiotic relationship between American sports and Christian religions since the mid–nineteenth century. In that sense, he at least partially contradicts Guttmann's first principle of modern sport. Coakley sees the disciplined rational lifestyle of sports linked to the Protestant ethic, much as Max Weber connected that ethic with capitalism. Coakley further contends that organized religion used sports as recruiting tools and sports used religion as a moral control.[54] He divides sports into two models: power and performance versus pleasure and participation. While the latter, which corresponds with Guttmann's games, is quite compatible with religion, the former has potential conflicts: attacking versus turning the other cheek; pushing the body beyond normal limits versus nurturing the body; focusing on personal success versus dedication to serving others. While Coakley argues that baseball generally conforms to the power and performance model, it does lag behind football, basketball, and hockey in the degree of physicality of these conflicts with religious practices. For example, while Zoss and Bowman observe that baseball is ritualized combat, Jacques Barzun considers it "a kind of collective chess" that is "the most active, agile, varied, articulate, and brainy of all group games."[55]

A number of other scholars also consider sport in general and baseball in particular as a replacement for or even as a form of religion. Baseball mythology has a quasi-religious element. In linking baseball's emergence to American cultural history, Robert F. Burk observes that it was "a secularized offspring of the congregational fellowship of their ancestors." Baseball had "one primary cultural midwife—the Puritans of New England."[56] In chronicling late-nineteenth-century American history, Ted Vincent writes, "Sports in America seemed to increase in popularity in inverse ratio to the decline in the power and influence of organized religion."[57] Skolnik notes that baseball provides security comparable to that of religion. "Baseball's fundamentals are not unlike the rituals of religion. Both provide assurance and stability, serve as a discipline that reduces the need to think and, because they produce a sense of well-being and accomplishment, they are their own reward."[58]

Noting that both sport and religion stand outside the working world and address spiritual needs, Mandelbaum offers three satisfactions that previously came only from religion: a welcome diversion from daily routines; a model for coherence and clarity; and heroic examples to admire and emulate.[59] The need for diversion became more acute as the country modernized and the unknown outcome of sports drama captured individual interests. Organized sport offered a definitive, transparent alternative that made sense to the spectator or participant. In comparison with another emerging diversion, the cinema, sports heroes appeared more authentic than movie stars because actions were not scripted and outcomes predetermined.

Baseball's religious overtones extended to the development of youth through hero worship that placed emphasis on character building, fair play ("sportsmanship"), and clean living, notes Richard C. Crepeau.[60] While Major League players did not always provide positive role models for such development, baseball's mythology prevailed in positioning the sport as part of the "muscular Christianity" movement that emphasized nurture of body and soul in the late nineteenth and early twentieth centuries. Baseball's nostalgic pastoral facilitated both one's remaining a boy and one's becoming a man. Its team orientation also stressed moral values of obedience, sacrifice, and discipline that enabled men to acclimate themselves to the new capitalist order.[61]

In industrializing, urbanizing America, Sunday was the laborer's holiday and thus the only opportunity for extended leisure. During the Progressive Era, Sunday became a contested time, as religious leaders, supported by controlling upper-class and political forces, sought to preserve as much time as possible for church-related activities as a means of maintaining moral conformity. "The issue of Sunday baseball exemplified the problems that advocates of a pluralistic, secular modern society faced at the end of the nineteenth century."[62] While playing games was generally applauded as a relief from tensions of scheduled routine work, organized sports—particularly spectator sports such as professional baseball—became prey for blue laws, which restricted the commercial opportunities of purveyors to the working class. Baseball emerged as alternative to religion and perhaps even an alternative religion itself.

Secular activities won out in the early twentieth century as religious power receded in urban America. In Riess's words, "The development of Sunday baseball typified the route that social change followed as the United States modernized." That route started in the West and Midwest, then migrated to the East and then to the South. For the geographically constricted National League, the route was Midwest to East. Following the league's 1891 merger with the more liberal American Association, teams had the option of holding Sunday games, the first of which occurred in Chicago on May 14, 1893. In New York, however, the first Sunday MLB game did not take place until April 17, 1904, and then only as a test case in Brooklyn. New York's general prohibition prevailed until 1919, when the state legislature gave cities local option to hold Sunday games. The last MLB city to host a Sunday game was Pittsburgh in 1934, following Pennsylvania local-option legislation; Atlanta hosted its first Sunday professional ball game the same year.

Riess further contends that baseball helped the working class internalize the American value system. "Baseball, America's secular religion, would eventually succeed where the voluntary, nondenominational pietistic organizations had failed."[63] Calling it a "great exemplification" of civil religion, Christopher H. Evans and William R. Herzog II reinforce baseball's mythical allure by contending that baseball "embodied the soul of a nation," illuminated "significant patterns of faith and meaning in American culture," and served as an important expression of one's "search for the American dream." They see a quasi-religious quest for purity and simplicity in the pastoral orientation and the healthful, masculine focus that underscored late-nineteenth-century America. Spalding considered his players "missionaries" on his 1874 and 1888–89 international tours to promote baseball for commercial purposes in other countries.

But Evans and Herzog also note negative parallels to organized religion abuses. Racial and gender discrimination often superseded the game's meritocratic emphasis on fairness and team excellence. Capitalist owners exploited the mythology of individual and group fulfillment while purporting to serve the masses. "Baseball loses its redemptive quality when it emphasizes extreme individualism." Like organized religion, these observers conclude, baseball "occupies a unique crossroads between historical realities and popular myth."[64] MLB's continuing challenge has been to manage effectively its business realities while marketing its mythological illusions.

A. Bartlett Giamatti, a classics scholar who became president of Yale University and subsequently commissioner of MLB, asserts that sport in general (and baseball in particular) ultimately subverts religion by failing to care for its consequences. Rather, he contends that playing sport is akin to making art, an autotelic activity that seeks to fulfill itself only for its own sake. He likens sports to Aristotelian leisure rather than to a remnant of primitive religion, a means of self-transformation through self-knowledge. Calling it "re-creation," he contends that all play aspires to "the condition of paradise." Such aspiration nevertheless seems quasi-religious. While Giamatti cites the artistic and ceremonial aspects of sport, he points out that it also became conventional and commercial, thanks to the influence of cities. The sports venue itself, he observes, is a small city, with the subversive qualities of its urban surroundings.[65] He does not mention that organized religion often subverts primitive religion. Likewise, organized sport, including baseball, subverts primitive sport, or play, as Guttmann defines it.

Religious scholar Hyman S. Baras whimsically cites a number of biblical references that support an ancient legacy of baseball:

And Moses lifted up his hand and smote with his rod (*Numbers* 20:11) the . . . hide (*Leviticus* 20:4) a long blast . . . (*Joshua* 6:5) [outside] the camp (*Judges* 7:17) [for] an 'omer (*Exodus* 16:36) And the men of Israel and Judah arose, and shouted (1 *Samuel* 17:52).[66]

In this rendition, Moses performs as Casey was unable to do in the popular poem "Casey at the Bat."

As a quasi-religion, baseball employed the soft power of cultural persuasion to promote the sport and to use hard power tactics to exploit players and fans in the Progressive Era. Both use and abuse continue today as organized religion has become more polarized as a societal influence. But by also linking baseball's place to the nation, sometimes intertwined with its quasi-religious position, the sport has broadened its soft power resource.

A PATRIOT GAME

Baseball emerged in the late nineteenth century as America's national pastime, an urban sport with mythological rural roots and quasi-religious characteristics. Its development intertwined with that of the nation itself. Anderson defines a nation as "an imagined political community—and imagined as both inherently limited and sovereign."[67] It is imagined because all members do not know each other, limited because it has finite boundaries, sovereign because it is free, and a community because it has a deep, horizontal comradeship. Using this definition, one can observe that nineteenth-century baseball reproduced the qualities of a nation, thereby reinforcing its position both as America's pastime and as a community itself.

In describing the interdependent parallels of identity and memory, Pope contends that baseball became a part of the national memory shared by people who do not know each other yet think they have commonalities. "The invented mythology of baseball was ultimately convincing because it was tied to nations."[68] Mandelbaum observes that as the national game, baseball crossed race, class, geographic, ethnic, age, and religious boundaries. It is, therefore, appropriate that MLB calls its two leagues American and National, thereby reinforcing the sport's connection with the United States.

As a quasi-nation, baseball allied itself with national rituals and patriotic events. Because of seasonality, football identified with Thanksgiving, but baseball's primary holiday connection was with the Fourth of July, "the national Sabbath," which affirms popular sovereignty and unity with trappings that blur the distinction of the sacred and the secular in a quasi-religious mode to celebrate national community at midseason between pastoral baseball's planting (spring training) and harvest (playoffs). As the holiday became more leisure oriented in the industrializing, urbanizing United States following the 1876 centennial, baseball contributed to and commercially exploited that shift.[69]

Complementing baseball's quasi-religious nationalism is its association with American military and political history. Although the other major team sports—football, basketball, and hockey—are physically more combative, baseball has continuously parlayed its national image into a patriotic connection with the military. Often, however, it has been a self-serving patriotism that on the production side sought to protect players from serving in the military while waving the flag to increase fan support on the consumer side.

Mythically created by Doubleday when he was a West Point cadet, the sport expanded geographically from its northeastern base during the Civil War as soldiers on both sides played to relieve the stress of real combat. That activity also facilitated the extension of the game beyond gentlemen to all social classes. An unprecedented crowd of forty thousand soldiers saw a Union game on Christmas Day 1862 in Hilton Head, South Carolina. Thomas Dyja's 1997 novel, *Play for a Kingdom*, focuses on Union-Confederate baseball competition during the war. Dyja's soldiers not only seek stress relief through the games but also transpose their field of battle to the diamond.

Military and naval troops introduced baseball to Puerto Rico, Cuba, and the Philippines during the Spanish-American War, which lasted only about the length of a baseball season. Dr. Arlie Pond won thirty-four games as a pitcher for the then National League Baltimore Orioles in 1896–97 before enlisting in an army medical unit that went first to Cuba and then to the Philippines. Remaining in the military, he devoted most of the rest of his life to combating disease in the Philippines.

Canadian baseball players in the British army taught many British and Australian soldiers baseball during World War I in England. The Canadian forces overseas baseball championship in 1917 involved 101 teams. A U.S. Army-Navy troop benefit game drew forty thousand spectators on July 4, 1918, in London. In May of that year, provost marshal General Enoch Crowder issued a "work or fight" order to provoke nonessential workers—including baseball players—to join the U.S. war effort. Relatively few players joined until MLB shut down its season early in September, but by November, 247 major leaguers were in the military. U.S. troops introduced the game to France. Sunday games in public parks, such as the Bois de Boulogne, became common in 1918.[70]

While Europeans did not adopt the game during American troops' short tenure abroad, their presence positioned baseball internationally as the game of democracy. The "Star-Spangled Banner" was institutionalized at most MLB games at home to assert patriotic support for the American Expeditionary Forces abroad, although the song was not designated the national anthem by Congress until 1931 and not universally adopted by all MLB teams at all their games until the Vietnam War.[71] In the July 26, 1919, issue of *Dial* magazine, Marcus R. Cohen argued for international baseball competition to promote healthy national rivalries as a soft power alternative to war's hard power military and economic weapons.[72] Viewed as a force for democracy, baseball became part of the Americanism movement between the world wars, reinforced by the melting pot of white ethnic players, but the military had negligible influence during peacetime.

In the early days of World War II, Franklin D. Roosevelt sent a "Green Light" letter urging Commissioner Kenesaw Mountain Landis to continue a full Major League Baseball schedule as a morale booster on the home front. John P. Rossi observes, "Baseball meant normalcy, something the American public longed for during World War II."[73] The 1942 film *The Pride of the Yankees* depicted its subject, future Hall of Famer Lou Gehrig, as an inspirational hero who, although never a soldier, lived a moral life and died bravely. A year earlier, Gary Cooper, who portrayed Gehrig, had the title role in *Sergeant York*, a biopic of a World War I hero. The opening passage of the Gehrig film, narrated by Damon Runyon, explicitly linked the ballplayer's courage with that of an American soldier, and Cooper's presence reinforced that connection. Such patriotic associations were common in World War II–era films.[74]

An estimated fifty-four hundred of the fifty-eight hundred MLB and MiLB players on 1941 rosters served in the World War II military, and more than fifty died. The length and breadth of the war facilitated baseball playing in virtually every part of both the European/African and Pacific theaters. Japan, which had an established professional league, began drafting its players into the army in 1938. While still operating, the league changed its team names, uniforms, and baseball terms from an American-influenced to a national militaristic mode. League officials replaced *besubôru*, the Americanized term for baseball, with *yakyû*. When postwar play resumed in 1946, American occupation forces facilitated the transition as American influence returned to the reconstituted pro leagues, reflecting baseball's soft power negation of the prior hard military power impact.

In the United States during the war, many players continued playing at domestic training bases, signaling the military's tendency to offer them special treatment, which continued thereafter. The navy baseball talent was concentrated in Norfolk, Virginia; the Great Lakes; and other training centers, while the army stockpiled players in Hawaii and selected onshore forts. Commanding officers occasionally transferred player-soldiers among stations to satisfy units' needs to stock certain positions. Meanwhile, MLB pursued its market-oriented support efforts by raising funds at games and providing baseball equipment for troops. A July 7, 1942, game between American League all-stars and American League service all-stars drew 62,094 fans to Cleveland's Municipal Stadium and grossed more than $140,000, most of which went to purchase baseball equipment for servicemen. A May 24, 1943, army-navy baseball game in Washington raised $2,000,000 in war bonds.[75]

Although no large-scale call-up occurred, the Korean conflict also included mixed baseball messages. MLB sponsored off-season player visits to the front, but there were too few enlistments or draftees from player ranks to alter the game. The army got most of the affected players. Hall of Famer Lefty O'Doul brought an all-star team for a military base exhibition tour after the 1951 season. Commissioner Happy Chandler publicly intimated that MLB might have to shut down the sport during the war. That position, added to his earlier controversial support of Jackie Robinson's entry, led to his dismissal by team owners. Befitting its military penchant, MLB briefly attempted to draft retiring general Douglas MacArthur as Chandler's replacement.[76]

MLB continued its contradictory military stance during the Vietnam War. The *Sporting News* offered its annual *Official Baseball Guide* free to servicemen, and MLB owners took out one hundred thousand subscriptions to the weekly newspaper for those serving in Vietnam. Commissioner William Eckert, a former army general, received a Pentagon citation for MLB's contribution to morale in Vietnam.[77] President Richard Nixon wore a baseball cap on his 1969 world tour and, supported by Eckert's replacement, Bowie Kuhn, used baseball references to reinforce his connection with the "silent majority."

While continuing the sponsorship of off-season tours of overseas bases and hospitals, MLB officials nevertheless did not encourage player participation in the military. MLB management apparently directed players and perhaps influenced government to place players in the National Guard or reserves, usually with special assignments, such as public relations or recruiting roles.[78] My Army Reserve unit in Los Angeles in the late 1960s included a half dozen Dodger and Angel players who did not participate in conventional work assignments normally befitting their ranks or military occupational specialties.

Michigan Democrat Lucien Nedzi, a member of the House Armed Services Committee, complained about favorable treatment of professional athletes, prompting the Department of Defense to reveal in the spring of 1967 that 360 professional athletes, including 145 baseball players, were in the guard or reserves. Of those, 311 had joined after becoming pro athletes. Facing mounting criticism, Secretary of Defense Robert McNamara issued a February 1, 1967, order that guard and reserve vacancies henceforth would be filled on a first come, first served basis.

In *Ball Four*, his controversial account of his 1969 Seattle Pilots season, pitcher Jim Bouton criticizes the hypocrisy he perceived in the baseball establishment's flag waving. As with other national venues at the time, the baseball diamond became a contested arena between traditional values and counterculture, observes David Zang in his review of 1960s sports.[79] MLB did not tie as emotionally to the Korean and Vietnam conflicts, however, perhaps foretelling the subsequent fall in baseball's popularity as well as reflecting its increased duplicity in promoting patriotism. In the 1970s, James Michener noted a historically increasing, politically driven overemphasis on sports nationalism. In asserting that the Watergate White House needed more Abraham Lincoln and less Vince Lombardi ("Winning is the only thing"), Michener observed that politicians have misused sports as propaganda for particular parties, as a buttress for military goals, and as a vehicle for shallow patriotism.[80] Politicians and MLB openly used each other for mutual benefit.

With federal and local political support, MLB actively attempted to reassert its patriotic connection following the 9/11 disaster. For the remainder of the 2001 season and playoffs, MLB required that "God Bless America" rather than the traditional "Take Me Out to the Ball Game" be sung at all games during the seventh-inning stretch. President and former MLB team owner George W. Bush threw out the first ball at the first Yankee home game of the World Series. HBO captured baseball's soothing effect on the country at that time in a 2004 documentary, *Nine Innings from Ground Zero*.

The lone public dissent lodged by an MLB player came in 2004, when "God Bless America" continued to be sung in some parks. Carlos Delgado, a Puerto Rican then with the Toronto Blue Jays, contended that the song was being used to justify American military intervention in Iraq rather than to honor 9/11 victims. Delgado has also protested the U.S. Navy abuse of the environment and people of the Puerto Rican island of Vieques while it was a weapons testing area. He continues to provide financial support for that area, which has an abnormally high cancer rate and 50 percent unemployment since the navy pullout.[81]

In retrospect, World War II was perhaps the turning point in America's preference for particular team sports. As men returned from America's most pervasive war, they embraced football, "the war game." In *The Meaning of Sports*, which looks at baseball's, football's, and basketball's comparative historical attraction for U.S. fans, Mandelbaum metaphorically describes the war game: "Playing with warlike, albeit nonlethal brutality, football employs an infantry (offensive line), cavalry (running backs), and artillery (quarterback), to avoid a defensive 'blitz.'"[82] As U.S. military history shifted to global assertion during and after World War II (the U.S. role in World War I had been more defensive), baseball became less relevant in what Dwight D. Eisenhower called the "military-industrial complex." America's growing popular culture emphasis on violence also contrasts with baseball's modest physical contact activity.

Comedian George Carlin contrasts the differing objectives of football and baseball:

> In football the object is for the quarterback, also known as the field general, to be on target with his aerial assault, riddling the defense by hitting the receivers with deadly accuracy in spite of the blitz, even if he has to use shotgun. With short bullet passes and long bombs, he marches his troops into enemy territory, balancing this aerial assault with a sustained ground attack that punches holes in the forward wall of the enemy's defensive line. In baseball the object is to go home! And to be safe—I hope I'll be safe at home.[83]

Football's greater popularity suggests U.S. citizens' preference for surrogate war rather than surrogate peace.

Over the July 4, 2008, weekend, MLB celebrated a soft power initiative that positively complements the geopolitical hard power act of war. With teams wearing combat-fatigue-patterned uniforms, they publicized a project spearheaded by Fred Wilpon, head of the New York Mets, to help returning veterans. Supported by MLB, Major League Baseball Advanced Media (MLBAM), and the McCormick Foundation, Welcome Back Veterans seeks to raise one hundred million dollars to help provide psychological counseling and one hundred thousand job opportunities for returning veterans of the Iraq and Afghanistan wars.[84]

To publicize baseball's continuing claim to being the national pastime, the Hall of Fame and Museum organized a more than six-year tour for its Baseball as America exhibition, which started in New York City on March 16, 2002, traveled to fifteen cities, and was seen by 2.5 million people. Organized into seven themes—Weaving Myths, Our National Spirit, Ideals and Injustices, Rooting for the Team, Enterprise Opportunity, Invention and Ingenuity, and Sharing a Common Culture—the exhibition featured five hundred artifacts from the museum archives, among them the Doubleday Ball discovered twenty-seven years after the Mills Commission report establishing the Doubleday myth, the Honus Wagner T206 baseball card that is the world's most valuable, shoes that belonged to Shoeless Joe Jackson, FDR's "Green Light" letter to Landis, and the Wonder Boy bat used by Robert Redford in *The Natural*.[85]

A CULTURAL FORCE

Describing baseball as "a safe vehicle for nationalism," David McGimpsey nevertheless asserts that there is nothing special about baseball that makes it uniquely suited to cultural representation.[86] But owners, players, fans, scholars, journalists, and literary, musical, and visual artists have made such representations throughout the sport's history. Albert Theodore Powers observes, "Baseball's influence on society, culture, and literature is far more pervasive than that of any other sport."[87] A particularly symbiotic partnership has developed between baseball and another notably American popular culture vehicle, film. Both are soft power resources that can reinforce each other's cultural influence.

The Natural (1984), based on Bernard Malamud's 1952 morality novel of the same name, illustrates not only baseball's tension between myth and reality but also its reflection of a changing society. When Malamud published the book, the United States was in the midst of the McCarthy era, a perversion of the historical populism that has been a continuing element in the country throughout baseball's segment of its history. In the climactic end of the novel's battle of good and evil in a symbolic quest for the mythical Holy Grail, protagonist Roy Hobbs, who had twice succumbed to evil influences, strikes out (like Casey at the Bat) in his comeback, and his New York Knights lose their quest for the championship.

In the movie version, released during the Reagan era's return to nostalgic populism, director Barry Levinson and screenwriters Roger Towne and Phil Dusenberry collaborated to reassert the importance of a second chance and the resiliency of the individual. Hobbs homers to win the pennant/grail and retires to play catch with his son in a baseball heaven, the country farm of his first love/wife. The film reinforces four populist themes: the pastoral framework, with land as heaven and city as hell; the celebration of family, with emphasis on father-son relationships; the principle of goodness in people, with resolution of a clash of opposites; and the strong earth-mother heroine, with provision of pastorally grounded human values.[88]

It is also coincidentally appropriate that Reagan started as a radio baseball broadcaster and starred in Hollywood's *The Winning Team* (released in 1952, the same year as Malamud's novel) as Grover Cleveland Alexander, a farmer who became a Hall of Fame pitcher. Further, Reagan's subsequent political career was one of an old man making a second-chance comeback, much like Hobbs after his mysterious sixteen-year absence from baseball.

Baseball's relationship with the media also reinforces its mythology/reality tension as well as the media's changing role in U.S. history. In the early days, MLB teams had a collusive relationship with baseball newspaper writers, who promoted the team and the city at home and on the road. Progressive Era baseball journalists were primarily responsible for establishing baseball's conservative ideology as a salve for the wounds of industrialized society. Marshall G.

Most and Robert Rudd note that a primary function of sport in modern states is to express and to cultivate dominant cultural values—that is, to bind together participants and fans in a shared cultural vision. Baseball journalists helped to establish MLB's imagined community and to sell newspapers. Because of baseball, the sports section became the most popular part of the daily newspaper. Anderson uses newspaper vernacular to shape his concept of the imagined political community.

With the support of the sports media, baseball lingo permeated U.S. English and reinforced baseball's role in the national community. Expressions such as "striking out," "scoring," "stepping up to the plate," "taking one for the team," "pitching in/out," and "stealing" joined "home run," "foul ball," "shutout," and "free pass" as common language elements that originated or were popularized in baseball. As noted earlier, many of these terms are used in the workplace, thereby mollifying the negative connotations of work by injecting terms from a leisure activity.

The *Sporting News*, founded in 1886 as a baseball weekly, became the "house organ for Organized Baseball's establishment." Unwritten rules at the paper apparently minimized coverage of such negative issues as organized gambling, player personal exploits, and segregation. G. Edward White concludes, "Baseball journalists became significant figures in perpetuating one of the myths about professional baseball that is embodied in the phrase 'national pastime.'"[89]

John Thorn contends that journalists have been more effective than novelists at capturing the cultural essence of baseball. Baseball journalism, featuring writers such as Ring Lardner, Grantland Rice, Jerome Holtzman, and Leonard Koppett, has been "the game's literary glory." Arguing that extended baseball fiction "usually ends up as a corkboard, push-pinned with colorful but exceedingly lightweight ideas," he asserts, "A baseball writer does best when he stays grounded in the game, wedded to his details as a poet might be." Thorn deems it critical that novelists, like journalists, recognize "baseball's fundamental unreality."

His best examples of baseball fiction are Lardner's *You Know Me Al* (1916), Mark Harris's *The Southpaw* (1953), Goldberg's *The Celebrant* (1983), the opening of Don DeLillo's *Underworld* (1997), and especially Robert Coover's *Universal Baseball Association, Inc., J. Henry Waugh, Prop.* (1968). Coover's hero devises and obsesses over a baseball table game using a fictional league, not unlike current fantasy baseball league fanatics. "In its dark, unreal loneliness, Coover's baseball novel is, for 21st century readers of fiction, the heights, or depths, of realism."[90] Balancing reality and mythology serves the genre well, as it does the game itself. Implicit also in Thorn's commentary is the idea that baseball has survived a proliferation of bad fiction.

Likewise, Terrence Rafferty observes that baseball has persevered despite numerous bad movies. Reviewing the Museum of Modern Art's 2006 film festival, Baseball and American Culture, he observes, "Too many baseball pictures end up looking like fantasy camps for middle-aged actors." While panning "swing-for-the-fences epics" such as *The Natural* (1984) and *Field of Dreams* (1989) as overreaching, he praises *Bull Durham* (1988) as "the best baseball picture of all" because "it's all bunts and hard slides and singles slapped through the holes in the infield."[91] Like novels and journalism, baseball movies are best rendered between the lines.

As radio became operative, it broadened baseball's appeal despite early resistance from team owners, who feared loss of game attendance. Although the first game was broadcast in 1921, New York team games did not reach the airwaves until 1939 because of owner resistance. In 1934, fearing that fans would be diverted from Minor League games, officials tried to get MLB to ban radio broadcasts of its games. Early sportscasters were not baseball men but actors who "re-created" or embellished the brief game reports that came by telegraph from the park. Reagan, for one, started his career as a baseball broadcaster/re-creator in Iowa before moving on to Hollywood. Colorful sportscasters including Red Barber, Mel Allen, Dizzy Dean, and Harry Caray infused their broadcasts with the mystique and pleasure of the game.

Baseball's decline in popularity relative to other team sports can be traced to the suburban migration and the advent of television. The size and irregular dimensions of the field, slowness of pace, pauses in action, frequency of games, and length of schedule all deadened the impact of the game on television. Phil Schaaf concludes, "TV is the reason that football is the most popular sport in America." Indeed, a 1965 Harris Poll reported that Americans preferred football to baseball by a margin of 41 percent to 38 percent, and the gap has since widened.[92] The medium denies fans the release from everyday life that they experience at the park or even over the radio. Benjamin G. Rader contends that it television has "essentially trivialized the experience" of sports by introducing sensations external to a game's core, such as in-game commercials and interviews. It has also made the experience more explicit and left little room for the romantic imaginative experience created by radio announcers. The TV "color commentator" is typically a former player who gives only technical insight. By reducing the myth and magic through extensive and intensive critical coverage, Rader concludes, "Sports will never again be an arena populated by pristine heroes."[93]

D. Stanley Eitzen observes that sport is "inherently contradictory," a characteristic he considers common to all human institutions.[94] He notes that as a social construction, sport

1. is both unifying and divisive;
2. provides solidarity yet demeans through names, logos, and mascots;
3. is rule-bound but open to violation;
4. promotes health but pushes performance beyond good health;
5. stabilizes through social control but maintains discriminatory practices;
6. promotes democratic ideals but is subject to tyrannical leadership;
7. is integral to higher education but detracts from academic pursuit;
8. enhances social mobility but creates unrealistic expectations;
9. benefits cities but costs them dearly.

The history of baseball has reflected all of these contradictions in its juxtaposition of myth and reality. Dizikes sees the contradiction as tension between control and anarchy. When play became sport, he observes, Americans played within and outside the rules.[95] Schaaf concludes that "competition is the true magic of sports entertainment."[96] In summary, "sports reflect, reaffirm, and reinforce the prevailing character of human and institutional relationships within and between societies and the ideological foundations buttressing those relationships."[97] Mythology and reality dynamically intertwine. While reflecting society's ills as well as its strengths, sport is transcendent and satisfies a "human desire to identify with something greater than oneself."[98] John Helyar observes, "Before [baseball] was a business, it was a game."[99] And the game is transcendent. That transcendence, enhanced by mythology, enables MLB to assert both hard and soft power in managing and marketing the game.

SECOND BASE
BASEBALL AS A DOMESTIC MONOPOLY: DEVELOPING POWER

Sport and business have become inextricably linked.
—ALAN BAIRNER

"Play is play, but sport is all business, big business, and it has been for a long time," observes John Dizikes in his history of American sport.[1] Professional sport, including baseball as a significant but declining portion, is now America's tenth-largest industry, with annual revenue approximating $220 billion.[2] Baseball assumed business elements as early as the 1860s. As Roger I. Abrams quips, "Money has been as much a part of the game as peanuts, popcorn, and Cracker Jack."[3] Indeed, ballpark concessions, later broadened from food to merchandise, combined with gate receipts to enhance baseball income in its early business evolution. Broadcast revenues later surpassed stadium-related income as Major League Baseball (MLB) built its national audience and individual teams negotiated variously lucrative local and regional cable television deals. The game, which was labeled America's national pastime in the late nineteenth century, dovetailed with what Albert Theodore Powers calls America's real national pastime: making money.[4]

This chapter traces the business history of MLB as both a positive complement and a negative contradiction to its role as a sport, discussed in the prior chapter. This chapter will deal with both the consumption (marketing) and the production (labor/player) sides of the business. Underlying both is MLB's unique legal status as perhaps the only sanctioned private monopoly in the country, thanks to an irrational 1922 Supreme Court decision and subsequent court and legislative inaction. Monopoly status enabled MLB teams to control their labor until the 1970s through a "reserve clause" and to "own" their local markets continuously through territorial exclusivity.

A critical factor in MLB's success has always been balancing its commercial and cultural elements. In the long run, securing early market dominance and then legal monopoly status hampered MLB's business progression at least as much as it helped it. Yet as previously discussed, its early linkage to American moral values and the continuing emphasis on and exploitation of these values has generally enabled baseball to maintain its significant place in our popular culture. Its mythical mystique at least partially offset its static business practices for most of the twentieth century. Throughout its history, MLB has done a better job of marketing its myth than managing its reality.

MARKETING AND MANAGING

Richard S. Tedlow's study of American marketing provides a historical framework for observing the development of the consumer side of the baseball business. Tedlow observes three generally defined phases of American marketing history: fragmentation, which ended in the 1880s; unification, which continued into the 1950s; and segmentation, which culminated in the 1990s.[5] MLB has increasingly become a marketing organization, particularly after its labor controls were substantially reduced in the last quarter of the twentieth century.

The latter part of Tedlow's fragmentation phase coincided with the beginning of professional baseball and several failed initiatives to create leagues that would bring order and stability to the game. The unification phase embraced the creation of the National League, the establishment of its American League partnership, and the prolonged reinforcement of a surprisingly static two-league MLB organization. The transition to the segmentation phase signaled the geographic relocation and numerical expansion of MLB teams into new markets. This phase also included broadened exploitation of MLB labor sources and product markets as well as the revival and growth of collaborative Minor League markets. Phil Schaaf refers to the progressive segmentation phase as "carpaccio marketing," the slicing of broad consumer categories into increasingly thinner ones.[6] MLB has adopted and developed that approach with growing success since the mid–twentieth century.

The end of that phase witnessed MLB's creation and pursuit of a global strategy, reflecting what was occurring throughout American business. Like

IBM, a multinational corporation pioneer, MLB has increasingly sought to tailor its approach to local cultures through "glocalization" (think global, act local).[7] (For more on MLB's international activity, see the fourth chapter, "Home Plate.") Although reluctant to name it specifically in his 1996 book, Tedlow observes a fourth developing phase, founded in information technology and real time, reinforcing the global village concept. This globalization phase is creating both production (player development) and consumption (marketing) opportunities for MLB.

Tedlow offers six business propositions for understanding the historical development of marketing. Included are MLB-related examples:

1. The strategy of profit through volume is a breakthrough concept, as demonstrated by MLB's expansion from sixteen to thirty teams in the latter half of the twentieth century.
2. The drive and vision of individual businesspeople are essential—for example, Albert G. Spalding, Branch Rickey, Bill Veeck, Walter O'Malley, and George Steinbrenner.
3. Mass production cannot exist without mass marketing, as reflected in MLB's successful ventures into local, national, and international broadcasting and merchandising.
4. First-mover advantages are real, as illustrated by O'Malley's shift of the Dodgers from Brooklyn to Los Angeles in 1958.
5. New entrants have to copy or develop new strategies to turn the market, as shown by the New York Mets' hiring of popular former Yankee skipper Casey Stengel as the team's first manager in 1962.
6. Change is the law of business, and winners manage change, as the Baltimore Orioles did in building a new retro-style park, Camden Yards, in 1992.[8]

This assessment of baseball as a business uses these propositions as well as the interactive influence of and impact on what Steven A. Riess calls baseball's four key constituents: fan/spectator, owner, player, and government.[9]

Baseball owners' self-interests have mirrored those of other sectors of American business, observes economist John Fizel.[10] The late 1800s saw rapid American business expansion, and the formative baseball business was a part of that movement. Mark Twain called baseball "the very symbol, the outward and visible expression of the drive and push and rush and struggle of the raging, tearing, booming nineteenth century."[11] The period approaching the turn of the century included general business-related shifts from a rural agricultural to an urban industrial economy with a time-controlled wage system. There emerged a concurrent emphasis on consumption resulting from more defined leisure time and predictable wages associated with urban work. At both the participant and spectator levels, baseball benefited from these socioeconomic changes.

Another American literary icon, Walt Whitman, saw baseball as anticapitalistic because it offered respite from monetary pursuits. It overtly conformed to and reinforced a Victorian moral code that recalled traditional agrarian values.[12] Urban-related sins such as gambling, drinking, and rowdy behavior that accompanied the early professional game belied such adherence to the moral code. MLB nevertheless preached the moral gospel as part of its rural mythology and continues to do so despite the concurrent risk of individual noncompliance. The juxtaposition of progressive, aggressive commercialism and emphasis on moralistic traditionalist themes, as contrasted in Twain's and Whitman's observations, remains an element in MLB's often contradictory business conduct.

The Cincinnati Red Stockings, formed in 1869, are generally considered the first professional baseball team. Establishing a pattern that would continue throughout baseball's business history, the team paid its players relatively well—about seven times the average national wage. That relationship, Abrams observes, continued until the advent of free agency and concurrent market influence in 1976, when MLB salaries (then averaging eight times the national wage) began their dramatic escalation to their current levels (more than fifty times the national average) in an economy that values celebrity.[13] Introduction of free agency substantially removed the labor side of MLB from monopoly constraints and enabled Adam Smith's "invisible hand" of the marketplace to determine salary levels for free agents. Irrational competitive bidding, particularly among well-endowed teams, enhanced the resultant rise in salaries.

The touring Red Stockings, who went undefeated (one tie) in their first year, signaled the advent of owner- rather than player-run professional baseball teams. Nevertheless, the team's difficulties in retaining players and scheduling games illustrated the business need for a league organization to control production (players) and consumption (scheduling). The National Association of Base Ball Players, which had formed in 1858 to assert player dominance of the game, addressed the emerging conflict of professional and amateur status and subdivided in 1870 into two organizations. Both of these player-led groups collapsed by 1875, shortly before William Hulbert, a Chicago coal baron and Chicago White Stockings owner, led the creation of the National League of Professional Base Ball Clubs (NL) on February 2, 1876, the date considered the birth of MLB.

The shift of professional baseball leadership from player to owner proved permanent despite several player-organized challenges starting in 1871 and continuing for the remainder of the century. Most notable was the Players League, started by John Montgomery Ward, a lawyer and player who established the National Brotherhood of Professional Baseball Players in 1885. Beginning play in 1890, the Players League competed effectively with the NL for one season but could not sustain itself financially and folded the following December.

These organizational failures were comparable to those of other worker-led business ventures during the period as U.S. business resolved its management-labor dynamics. As in general business, professional baseball segregated management/ownership from the workers/players and imposed manager/owner control. This approach conformed to what business historian Alfred D. Chandler Jr. describes as the "visible hand of management," which influenced and in some situations replaced Smith's invisible hand in guiding business in the United States during the late nineteenth century. Despite the general shift from owner to professional management, MLB teams continued with owner-dominated management well into the twentieth century, when the professional general manager emerged.[14]

Billy Evans, a twenty-nine-year veteran American League umpire, became MLB's first titled general manager, with Cleveland in 1927. Branch Rickey, who set the gold standard in the function, had previously performed in that capacity with the St. Louis Cardinals but did not receive the designation until 1929.[15] Owners had either served as their own general managers or used hard power tactics to dominate their management staff. Compounding this practice was owners' tendency to operate independently of MLB leadership in their own markets. The result was not only inconsistent local practices but also difficulty in reaching consensus on national issues. Owner intrusion in on- and off-field management issues has continued sporadically but has diminished as the business has become more complicated.

Slowness to develop professional nonowner general managers hampered MLB's business progress. MLB generally lagged in developing business practices throughout its history since its monopoly status removed the competitive incentive that existed elsewhere. Ironically, MLB later spawned the sport fantasy league business that mirrors the general manager function and now includes thirty million participants, according to the Fantasy Sports Trade Association. Begun in 1980 with the Rotisserie League in New York City, fantasy leagues require participants to act as general managers, drafting and trading players in an effort to win championships.[16]

Industrial engineering scholar Richard J. Puerzer correlates historically evolving management styles with MLB field managers, beginning with industrial engineer Frederick Winslow Taylor's "scientific management," which emerged in the late nineteenth century. Puerzer illustrates his point with early-twentieth-century New York Giants manager John McGraw, a Hall of Famer and the epitome of a hard power, top-down manager. McGraw closely controlled his players on and off the field and produced ten pennants and three world championships in his thirty-one years at the helm. In contrast, contemporary Hall of Famer

Connie Mack was a precursor of the soft power human relations management model that prevailed at midcentury. Encouraging independent thinking from his players and facilitating cooperation and collaboration between players and coaches, Mack used his soft power techniques to develop probably the best labor-management relationship in MLB history during his half-century tenure with the Philadelphia Athletics.

In Douglas McGregor's dichotomy in management theory, described in his influential study, *The Human Side of Enterprise* (1960), McGraw represents autocratic Theory X, while Mack epitomizes democratic Theory Y. Theory X features dominant, directive behavior, whereas Theory Y emphasizes a collaborative, inspirational approach. McGregor sees Theory Y as the emerging, more effective style but acknowledges that both strategies can work, although Theory X tends to be less effective over the long term because of its relative lack of concern for workers.[17] Joseph S. Nye Jr.'s smart power geopolitical theory mirrors McGregor's internal management theory. There is a close but not absolute correlation between Theory X and Nye's hard power and between Theory Y and soft power. McGregor and Nye would probably agree that both X and Y have a place in the smart power model.

In the second half of the century, Puerzer cites Leo Durocher as a superb motivator who used smart power, combining the soft power of friendship and the hard power of fear as tools in the manner of a military field officer but without a consistent managerial philosophy. Durocher's immediate rather than longer-term focus produced varying results, but his approach paved the way for emotional managers such as Billy Martin, Earl Weaver, and Lou Piniella. Puerzer contrasts Durocher with Joe Torre, a leader who has the ability to manage up as well as down the organization to produce results. Recognizing the power shift from the field to the front office in the past quarter century, Torre personifies Chandler's visible hand professional field manager, operating successfully both with ownership that is often far removed from the intricacies of the game and with the hands-on general manager.[18] The evolving general manager is the front office visible hand and an increasing source of smart power, combining effective top-down and bottom-up soft power relations with hard power economic leverage delegated by the owner.

A SYNERGISTIC BUSINESS

An early representative of management's visible hand in baseball was Albert Goodwill Spalding, who later spurred the adoption of the Doubleday creation myth discussed in the preceding chapter. His entrepreneurial vigor exemplified Tedlow's second proposition: drive and vision of individual businessmen. Spalding's biographer, Peter Levine, describes him as "a flamboyant personality possessed of an insatiable ego" and likens him to both promoter P. T. Barnum and evangelist Henry Ward Beecher. Spalding became "the key figure in the establishment of the white world of professional baseball as a viable commercial enterprise and as an acceptable pastime for Victorian America." In a career that spanned American business's shift from the individual entrepreneur to the corporate capitalist, he saw baseball's potential as dependent on promoting its social purpose. He operated "at the cutting edge of business development at the turn of the century."[19]

He was recruited at age seventeen from rural Rockford, Illinois, to play for the "amateur" Chicago Excelsiors baseball team, which offered him a job as a grocery clerk at forty dollars a week (about ten times normal pay). Spalding thus "came face to face with the business end of the game." The grocery business that supported the team failed after Spalding had appeared in only one game, so he returned to Rockford and its Forest City team, which became a regional power over the next three years and defeated Harry Wright's Cincinnati Red Stockings in 1870.[20]

The next year, Spalding joined Wright, who moved to the professional Boston Red Stockings and helped establish them as America's best team. The British-born manager became Spalding's mentor and chose him to lead a generally unsuccessful promotional tour of Wright's homeland, a trip that further reinforced Spalding's business focus and sparked his international interest. Hulbert, the Chicago White Stockings owner who was forming the National League, later lured Spalding and three other Boston players to Chicago for the NL's 1876 inaugural season. The egotistical Spalding subsequently claimed to be a cofounder of the NL, although his role was probably simply that of an aide to Hulbert.

Spalding, a pitcher, not only led Chicago to the first NL pennant with a league-leading forty-seven wins but also became a "pitchman," as Roberta Newman observes.[21] Like Wright and his brother earlier in New York, Spalding and his brother opened a sporting goods emporium in Chicago as his first initiative into what would become a sports business empire. The following year, with his playing career ended by injury, he became team secretary; he assumed the presidency when Hulbert died in 1882. Spalding concurrently expanded his collateral business activity in 1876 to include the annual publications of the NL-sanctioned *Official League Book* and an unsanctioned *Spalding's Official Baseball Guide*. He quietly rescinded the *Guide*'s official label sanction six years later, after it had become established.

In 1879, he started manufacturing sporting goods to feed his retail business and other distributors.[22] The Wrights did the same, but Spalding later bought their company, then called Wright & Ditson. The Spalding brand, which capitalized on Albert's celebrity status, ushered in "the age of product endorsements by celebrity athletes," which still exists. Spalding paid the National League a dollar a dozen for the right to promote his baseballs, which became the league's official ball. As "the father of the official sports tie-in," he developed and manipulated the concepts of "official" and "authorized" to gain (or imply) league endorsement protection and to add perceived value and to his products and raise their prices. Those concepts continue as fundamental elements of MLB (and other sports) licensing and sponsorships.

In his dual role as team owner and collateral businessman, he "established baseball as a stable commercial enterprise," what he called a "systematic business" following Taylor's new scientific management principles. Spalding's synergistic business approach has been employed over the years by many team owners who had business interests, ranging from brewing to broadcasting, that complemented baseball.[23] Related-party transactions currently enable some teams to shelter income and gain significant competitive financial advantages within their corporate structures.

The first auxiliary industry was the baseball card, introduced with Black Jack gum in 1870 to appeal to youth. Soon thereafter, some tobacco companies got into the act by issuing cards with cigarette packages, capitalizing on the father-son bond that baseball provided and beginning the process of marketing tobacco to youth. The tobacco industry received an unanticipated boost from the government breakup of the American Tobacco Company monopoly in the early twentieth century. As competition among tobacco companies increased, they regularly used baseball cards as sales incentives.

Bull Durham, the leading tobacco brand at the time, became a baseball brand as well when the Durham Bulls team was established in 1902. Although the team folded soon thereafter, the name has sporadically reappeared, was popularized in a movie bearing its name, and exists today as the AAA farm team of the Tampa Bay Rays. Baseball lore states, perhaps apocryphally, that the term *bull pen*, designating the pitchers' warm-up area, came from the original Bulls field, which had an American Tobacco Company billboard with its trademark bull adjacent to the warm-up area.[24] The baseball card and the team branding were early examples of Tedlow's third proposition, which requires mass marketing to complement mass production.

The purveyors took advantage of the popularity of players in the early stages of what Michael J. Wolf now calls "the entertainment economy," where "celebrity is the only universal currency."[25] As baseball evolved from a sport to a business, MLB sought to enhance the commercial value of its entertainment elements, and players were and still are its most valuable element. Cards provided multidimensional vehicles for profitably popularizing the sport, serving simultaneously as "commercial artifacts, forms of visual media, advertising mechanisms, popular art, and objects of exchange." Other sports and entertainment outlets subsequently adopted cards as a consumer product.

The connection with tobacco waned after several decades, to be replaced again by gum. In the post–World War II consumer economy, new gum promoters, including Topps in 1951, reintroduced cards as premiums. Topps achieved virtual monopoly status by buying out Bowman, its chief competitor, in 1956. It flourished as leagues expanded, teams relocated, players were traded, and free agency emerged. The changing of teams and player movement added incentive for consumers to purchase new player cards. Fleer, a rival gum manufacturer, won a restraint-of-trade suit against Topps in 1980, and the market, which by then included other sports, opened up. The card now stands alone, without gum, as a collectible consumer product. Upper Deck, formed in 1988, has emerged as the leading sports card manufacturer.

Enhanced by the growing general popularity of collectibles and organized appraisal and trading facilities, the broader sports card market exploded from the trade-restrained $50 million in 1980 to $1.5 billion by 1992.[26] In 2002, Topps created an online trading facility that featured weekly IPOs (initial player offerings), aping stock market IPOs (initial public offerings) in an effort to stimulate an already oversupplied market. Both Topps and Upper Deck now offer "virtual cards" that can trigger video use and interaction with others.[27]

The general baseball collectibles market, spawned by cards, produces about $1 billion in annual sales, but market efficiencies and expanding product lines have driven down prices for recent specific card issues. Conversely, vintage objects have appreciated, befitting MLB's adherence to a traditional past. This emphasis is reflected in the prices of vintage baseball cards compared with those from other sports. A Honus Wagner card from the 1890s has sold for $2.3 million. The highest price paid for a football card, an 1874 John Dunlop of Harvard, was just over $10,000 in 2007. In 2004, the bat Babe Ruth used to hit the first home run in Yankee Stadium sold for $1.2 million. Baseball has used its tradition to enhance the game's commercial aspects.[28]

Celebrating its cultural as well as commercial appeal and reflecting baseball's historical juxtaposition, New York's Metropolitan Museum of Art established a permanent baseball card exhibit in 1993. The Met collection began fifty years earlier with a gift of thirty thousand baseball cards among three hundred thousand consumer advertising items and is now the largest in the world.²⁹ This display reinforces baseball's blending of the historical and commercial in a fluid cultural environment.

MLB teams have capitalized on the collectibles phenomenon as part of their marketing strategy to bring fans to the ballparks. In the 1930s, teams offered a few valuable prizes to lucky ticket holders. By the 1950s, the approach shifted to offering less expensive prizes to more—sometimes all—fans. Renegade owner-promoter Bill Veeck introduced Bat Day, when any youngster who came to the park with a paying adult received a youth-model bat. Some fifty thousand people attended the first Detroit Tigers Bat Day in 1965. Such a lure more than paid for itself with increased adult attendance and concession sales. When fans had to be turned away—usually with a rain check for the prize at a future game—teams began limiting the offer to the first several thousand fans, thereby reducing costs but preserving the lure. Teams subsequently persuaded corporations to pay for the giveaways, which carried corporate logos, and began offering non-baseball-related prizes.³⁰ Many products that began as giveaways have become regular team merchandise items without the corporate sponsor label.

Baseball cards helped to initiate the business of licensing for MLB. While appropriately avoiding producing baseball-related products such as equipment, MLB has increasingly become involved in selling its endorsement to manufacturers through "authorized" or "official" licensures. As one who straddled both sides, Spalding foresaw the mutual benefit of such partnerships. The arrangements reinforce Tedlow's first three business propositions: profit through volume, drive and vision of individual businessmen, and mass marketing. The evolving expansion and complications of licensing underscore the remaining three propositions: first-mover advantages, new entrant challenges, and importance of change.

OWNER HARD POWER DOMINANCE

Critical to the continuation of the owner-controlled business model on the production (labor) side was the NL's creation of what became known as the reserve clause on September 28, 1879. This provision, which was included in every player contract, enabled team owners unilaterally to retain a player automatically in perpetuity, thereby precluding the player from seeking employment from another team without consent from the original team's owner. Through this hard power dominance, owners had the indisputable right to set players' salaries and to trade them to other teams. The only player recourse was not to play in the league. As the NL solidified its dominance as the Major League, playing elsewhere involved a substantial pay cut as well as a blacklisting that would likely preclude players' return. Such control facilitated the profitable growth of the NL and its later partner, the American League (AL), because player salaries were the largest cost item on the income statement.

Of the various new owner-initiated competitive leagues in the late nineteenth century, only the American Association, established in 1881, achieved any success, and it did so by appealing to a lower-class audience. The moralistic Hulbert believed that baseball should appeal to the genteel classes and eschewed both beer and Sunday games and charged fifty cents per ticket to assure higher-class patronage. In contrast, the Association, whose teams were owned by beer barons, charged only a quarter for admission, included beer among its concessions, and played games on Sunday, a strategy consistent with Tedlow's fifth proposition of new entrant strategies.[31]

Ultimately a realistic businessman, Hulbert saw the need to accommodate competitive ideas and reached a mutuality pact with the American Association before his 1882 death. The evolving results were the Association's recognition as a Major League in 1883, a National Agreement establishing common practices in 1885, and eventually an 1891 merger that produced a new National Agreement among clubs for the NL, which now included twelve teams (the original eight plus four of the former American Association teams). This progression reinforced Tedlow's first proposition of profit through volume and solidified the NL as baseball's only Major League for the next decade.

One outcome of the merger agreement was a general salary reduction for players during what was a difficult economic period for the owners and the country. "That the owners gained immediate financial benefit from their assertion of wide-ranging controls upon their players' livelihoods and incomes is incontrovertible," concludes historian Robert F. Burk. National League fields became "diamond-shaped versions of shop floors."[32] Unlike industrial businesses, however, baseball owners could not easily replace their uniquely skilled players with machines or scabs, so the reserve clause was crucial to team profitability. Further, with such player control, NL owners felt no need to expand their recruiting to African Americans; as part of their self-appointed rule of the entire professional game, they instead simply extended sanction to the League of Colored Base Ball Clubs to operate separately.

Another consequence of the merger was stronger territorial exclusivity for each club. Through the National Agreement, each team had assurance that it would not face market competition from another National League team in a broadly defined geographic market surrounding its home. Combined with the reserve clause, territorial exclusivity established the NL and later MLB as a monopoly cartel. As an ongoing cartel, MLB has artificially limited the number of franchises, thereby enhancing the opportunity for individual team profitability in a given market.

In 2001, Commissioner Allan H. "Bud" Selig, acting on behalf of his team owner bosses and citing aggregate MLB financial losses, proposed reducing the number of MLB teams from thirty to twenty-eight, with Montreal and Minnesota the likely casualties. Without territorial exclusivity, economist Andrew Zimbalist estimates that the current U.S. market could support forty teams, some of which would encroach on current team territories, without adverse financial impact.[33] After meeting substantial public resistance to the proposal, particularly from within Minnesota, MLB maintained its team level and bought the Montreal franchise and moved it to Washington, D.C., for the 2005 season. That move, however, required intensive but secret negotiations with the Baltimore Orioles, who claimed that such a move violated their territorial rights. MLB and the Orioles reached a compromise, one aspect of which facilitated the creation of a regional sports network mutually owned by the two teams. The buy/sell maneuver of the franchise also resulted in significant windfall profit for MLB and the owners of the other teams when the Washington team was resold to local owners for considerably more than its Montreal purchase price.

The combination of control and release present in the monopolistic league-team relationship is a critical success factor in consumer culture, according to Jackson Lears, because it facilitates local market sensitivity while preserving the uniform integrity of the brand. That dynamic tension of "think global, act local" continues as a fundamental element in MLB's business strategy as it expands abroad. MLB's flaw is that its lack of consistent owner control makes it vulnerable to the ripple effects of often inconsistent individual team actions in the local markets. Its success in the Washington deal depended significantly on soft power collaboration.

In his history of American advertising, Lears also identifies another key element that from the beginning formed a fundamental part of MLB's marketing strategy: the appropriation of the past.[34] Baseball early on addressed the potential conflict of progress and nostalgia, with the objective, not always achieved, of preserving and emphasizing traditional agrarian values while demonstrating modern enhancements in the product/game. MLB has not always balanced these elements well, significantly lagging in modern improvements until recent years and obsessively clinging to outmoded traditions.

Underscoring Tedlow's sixth proposition that winners manage change, Thomas K. McCraw concludes in his history of twentieth-century American business, "Almost nothing is permanent in business, and the market punishes those who don't adapt."[35] Like Henry Ford in the automobile business, MLB secured many advantages of a first mover (Tedlow's fourth proposition) in the sports entertainment market but calcified and ultimately failed to adapt sufficiently to market changes (the sixth proposition) to maintain the dominant position it reached in the late nineteenth century.

One of the areas where MLB has lagged other professional sports has been in use of technology to enhance the game's fan appeal. While other sports have long used instant replay (official review of video to resolve play decisions), MLB resisted until August 28–29, 2008, although television regularly showed replays and announcers constantly second-guessed umpires' decisions. Selig explained this resistance by asserting that "the human element in baseball is very important."[36] Baseball purists prefer to continue the tradition of manager-umpire rhubarbs over disputed plays. To date, MLB has limited instant replay solely to the determination of home runs—fair or foul, over the fence or not—thereby enabling most games to occur without the need for replays. Adding instant replay required intensive negotiation between MLB and the Major League Baseball Players Association (MLBPA) and especially the umpires' union, which continues to resist the technology. Speculation ensued that this move was a further step along the path of umpire monitoring started several years earlier.

Behind the scenes, MLB had previously implemented QuesTec, a video monitoring system designed to help judge the accuracy of umpires' ball-strike calls. Umpires resisted that intrusion, but MLB officials insisted that it is a tool to help umpires improve. The use of QuesTec and MLB's addition of background investigations of umpires have resulted in an increasingly hostile relationship between MLB and the umpires' union, exemplified by the union's refusal to allow its umpires to work the initial World Baseball Classic and periodic threats to strike. Such technologies provide MLB with continuing challenges to balance the traditional and the progressive in a smart power collaborative strategy.

MLB LEADERSHIP

MLB solidified its dominant sports market position with the merger of the NL and AL in 1903. Byron Bancroft (Ban) Johnson had secured control of the minor Western League in the early 1890s and boldly changed its regionally confined name to the American League in 1899. In 1901, he reconstituted an eight-team organization including 111 former National Leaguers. After the upstart

AL outdrew the NL the following season, the leagues entered into a National Agreement that established MLB in essentially the same form that exists today.

Concurrently, John McGraw, the future Hall of Fame manager, jumped from the AL Baltimore Orioles to the NL New York Giants for the 1903 season. The AL retaliated by relocating the Baltimore team to New York as the Highlanders (later the Yankees) to take advantage of that lucrative though already competitive market. The NL had the Giants and Brooklyn Dodgers in the area. The move gave the new league more credibility and ultimately the strongest franchise in professional sports. It was the last franchise shift in MLB for fifty years. Given MLB's established dominance, it is not coincidental that during that half century, only two minor, short-lived competitive threats—the Federal League (FL) in 1914 and the Mexican League in 1946—emerged to challenge MLB. Without ongoing competitive pressure, the monopolistic MLB ignored both marketing and production opportunities that could have broadened and strengthened its position in the broader sports entertainment business. For example, MLB would likely be relatively stronger among professional sports today had it expanded geographically and integrated sooner.

Structural design of the newly merged AL-NL organization created dissent among owners. Owner Andrew Freedman of the Giants wanted to create a broad, owner-controlled trust but was opposed and defeated by Spalding in a power play that caused Freedman to sell his team. Following Spalding's approach, the new National Agreement between the leagues provided for a three-man governing National Commission—the two league presidents and a mutually acceptable chairman—to supervise organized baseball. While a trust would have provided for more balanced control among owners, the commission opened the door for dominant influence by certain owners, such as Charles Comiskey of the Chicago White Sox. Such selected owner dominance would again resurface after Judge Kenesaw Mountain Landis's dictatorship ended with his death in 1944.

Reflecting owner control, neither the Minor Leagues nor the players had representation or influence on the commission. With the merged structure in place, MLB further strengthened its already dominant relationship with the Minors and secured cheaper talent through its unified approach. Among its first acts was to establish fixed prices for drafting Minor League players, thereby asserting MLB's controlling hard power over its primary labor source and rendering unnecessary any need to overcome racial bias to recruit African American players. The ethnic composition during MLB's first decade remained relatively constant, with British, German, and Irish descendants comprising more than

90 percent of the players. Ethnic representation subsequently expanded, but the chromatic racial door remained shut until 1947.

Antilabor rulings as well as private owner collusion to limit salaries characterized the National Commission's seventeen-year history. The inevitable result was a two-tier wage system that held most player salaries flat for a decade while permitting higher amounts for a few selected stars. That pattern generally continued, with the bottom tier adding minority players after integration, until arbitration and free agency replaced the controlling reserve clause in the mid-1970s. A basic union seniority system then emerged that kept newer players at the bottom until they were eligible for arbitration and then free agency. The star salary premium has always existed but has increased significantly to reflect the disproportionate growth in celebrity value.

Owner heavy-handedness provoked establishment of a union, the Fraternity of Professional Baseball Players of America, in 1912. Under the leadership of David Fultz, the union quickly secured a majority of each team roster as members. It began peppering the commission with complaints—a total of 11,859 in 1913—but only 139 decisions resulted, most of them against the players. The commission initially did not recognize the Fraternity as a plaintiff in good standing, and the owners continued their abusive labor practices, so the Fraternity occasionally resorted to court action.[37]

The Fraternity's fate soon became intertwined with what would prove to be the last directly competitive domestic threat to MLB.[38] The FL emerged as a Minor League in 1913 with a midwestern power base. It was organized as a trust, like Freedman's failed MLB scheme, and used such soft power approaches as long-term player contracts and guaranteed salary increases as counteroffers to the MLB reserve clause system. The eight-team FL included competitors to NL teams in Brooklyn and Pittsburgh and to teams from both the AL and NL in St. Louis and Chicago.

Fultz and the Fraternity played the insurgent and established leagues against each other and received some concessions from MLB, which tried to prevent players from jumping to the FL. Most players recognized that the new league had little chance for success but used the situation as leverage to improve their salaries. During the two years of the FL-MLB war, only 18 MLB players broke extant contracts, and 63 others ignored club reserve clauses to become part of the new 264-player league. The average MLB salary jumped from about three thousand dollars to about five thousand dollars between 1913 and 1915. The high Minor Leagues, which lost 140 players to the FL, were significant victims of the war. Caught in the cross fire, many Minor League teams sold top prospects at bargain prices to MLB teams both to secure funds for continuing operations and to curry favor with MLB. The Minor League Baltimore Orioles sold Babe Ruth to the Boston Red Sox for twenty-five hundred dollars. The Minors realized that they needed to strengthen their ties with MLB to survive, and MLB teams took advantage of this leverage.

As in most consumer businesses, the customer determined the outcome of the league competition, and MLB won handily. Hurt at the gate in the first year, 1914, MLB still showed a composite profit, while the FL lost money. In 1915, MLB attendance rebounded, while the new league reportedly lost $2.5 million. In a collateral move, the FL sought an injunction in the U.S. District Court of Northern Illinois in January 1915 to prevent MLB's enforcement of the reserve clause and blacklisting of players. The FL chose that venue in the hope that Judge Landis, with his track record as a big-business trustbuster, would be sympathetic. Instead, Landis, an avowed traditional baseball fan, chastised the insurgent league for jeopardizing the hallowed game and indefinitely delayed making a decision. With no legal relief and losses mounting, the new league executed a treaty with MLB on December 22, 1915, that paid off selected FL team owners and amalgamated two of its teams with MLB teams. Ignored in the settlement, the Baltimore FL team owners brought another antitrust suit against MLB.

The settlement proved the death knell for the Fraternity, which had lost leverage with MLB despite increasing its membership to 1,215 Major and Minor Leaguers by the end of 1916. After pressing demands and threatening a strike, the union still could not get a hearing with the commission and relented in early 1917, lingering only in form for another year. Fultz served as a World War I aviator in France, where he was joined by several hundred other Major Leaguers by the end of the war, and never reentered baseball.

Following war-shortened seasons in 1918 and 1919, MLB began to ride the postwar economic boom, but baseball's progress was thwarted by the Black Sox scandal, a public climax of a gambling problem that had accompanied professional baseball virtually from its inception. The incident exposed the flaws in MLB's three-man commission leadership system, and public confidence needed to be restored in the wake of the scandal. To do so, the owners took the unprecedented and previously inconceivable step of going outside their closely knit cartel for a leader. After a series of interowner squabbles and maneuvers, MLB created a single commissioner job and gave it to Landis in appreciation of his favorable nonresponse during the FL war. Burk observes that Landis's FL inaction indicated his unwillingness "even to conceive of baseball as an industry, one as capable as any other of exploitive, monopolistic practices. Instead, he had insisted upon viewing the sport as a 'national institution' somehow divorced from the economic realities of his time."[39]

THE COMMISSIONER AND THE BABE

Landis's background presaged his performance as commissioner. A Progressive midwestern lawyer, he benefited from family political connections to secure federal bench appointments. As judge of the Northern District of Illinois, he presided over three cases that helped to define his ongoing behavior as commissioner. Perhaps most famous was his imposition of a $29.4 million judgment against Standard Oil. Although it was later overturned, the ruling demonstrated Landis's disregard for corporate power. The trial of 113 members of the Industrial Workers of the World, the largest number of defendants ever tried in a single U.S. criminal case, reflected his penchant for publicity.[40] Finally, his "strategic inaction" in delaying a decision on the FL lawsuit against MLB reflected his unequivocal love of the game and enabled parties to reach a settlement that preserved MLB's cartel status. Zimbalist observes that Landis's "chief characteristic on the bench was caprice, blended with strong antipathy to any view left of Teddy Roosevelt, and abiding emotionalism, a flair for the media and the dramatic, and a foul tongue."

Landis initially defined the role of commissioner as he shifted from the role of federal judge. He took advantage of owner panic resulting from the Black Sox scandal and internal conflict swirling around Ban Johnson, head of the AL and commissioner wannabe. Using that situational hard power leverage, Landis essentially dictated the terms of his contract and secured "a grant of unprecedented power over the game."[41] His early actions—a legally correct ruling against the aggressive Branch Rickey on player Phil Todt's contract and summary banishment from baseball of eight Black Sox players despite their court acquittal—solidified his position. As former Pennsylvania governor Dick Thornburgh notes in his foreword to David Pietruska's biography of Landis, the decisive Black Sox action "saved baseball from joining boxing as a perpetually discredited enterprise."[42] Landis had "an inflexible hatred of gambling," as evidenced by decisions he had made from the bench as well as by his institution of bans on another fourteen players by 1927.[43] Landis's genuine love of and respect for the game helped to mitigate his autocratic self-promoting tendencies.

Larry Moffi temperately describes Landis the commissioner as a "czar with a conscience."[44] An outspoken fan of baseball and its players, Landis became an icon who effectively controlled MLB owners. According to historian Benjamin Rader, Landis was publicly "benevolent toward players and surly toward owners" yet "treated the questionable actions of the owners far more gingerly than he did those of the players."[45] He apparently used some soft power tactics behind the scenes. Despite his aversion to gambling, he overruled his adversary, Johnson, when he sought to ban future Hall of Famers Ty Cobb and Tris Speaker for gambling activities that preceded Landis's commissionership and used the incident to force Johnson's retirement.

Landis retained the reactive behavior of a judge in too many of his leadership situations—"Do it and I'll rule on it." And at times, echoing his strategy in the FL case, he chose to avoid ruling. Without proactive leadership, MLB "remained substantially static during the Judge's tenure."[46] At the end of Landis's twenty-three years at baseball's helm, the same sixteen teams existed in the same cities, there were no consequential rule modifications, there were minimal changes in the ballparks, and the sport remained segregated. Having been dominated by this virtually omnipotent leader, MLB owners subsequently hired commissioners that they perceived as yes-men who were directed generally by the owners, particularly the more powerful ones, such as Walter O'Malley of the Dodgers.

As Powers observes, two diametrically opposed men dominated MLB after World War I. "The face of the game off the field, characterized by the craggy, austere visage of Judge Landis, was authoritarian and dictatorial. On the field, the robust and joyous countenance of the swashbuckling Babe Ruth embodied America in this most optimistic decade. That these two forces of nature ultimately would collide was inevitable." Landis represented baseball as a mythical sport, with its moral tradition, while Ruth symbolized baseball as a consumer business, with its amoral marketing. The Roaring Twenties, with both Prohibition and speakeasies, provided an appropriate environment for their contradictory behavior.

The juvenile delinquent son of a Baltimore tavern owner, Ruth had both the genes and the background for a freestyle life, and his baseball talents enabled him to pursue it. As a pitcher, he led the Boston Red Sox to a world championship in 1918, a feat the team did not replicate until 2004. The long drought led fans (and others) to believe that his 1920 sale to the Yankees to facilitate Red Sox owner Harry Frazee's financing of Broadway musicals, including *No, No Nanette* several years later, left Boston with the Curse of the Bambino.

The Babe's arrival in New York coincided with the emergence not only of a fast-living decade but also of a livelier ball that enhanced his performance as a home run hitter. Playing first in the Polo Grounds and then in the new Yankee Stadium, both of which had short right-field fences, enhanced his home run feats. In the wake of World War I and the Black Sox scandal, MLB produced a more tightly woven ball to create more offense and fan interest, and the Sultan of Swat became the sport's poster boy in 1920 by greatly extending his own MLB season homer record of twenty-nine, set the preceding year, to fifty-four, more than any other American League *team* produced that year. "Ruth was not only baseball's greatest and most exciting player, he became the most celebrated and venerated man in America."[47]

Ruth's boyish charm and voracious appetite for booze, cigars, food, gambling, and women gave him celebrity status far beyond the foul lines. He thrived both personally and financially on the attention available in New York City, America's entertainment and media epicenter. In his study of fame, Leo Braudy observes, "The test of performance in sports, as in show business, had become not merely doing your best so much as whether you could take immense focus on you while you were doing."[48] Ruth aced that test and became America's first significant star commodity, enhancing the soft power of attraction by being both naughty and nice.

In so doing, he established a model for celebrity currency in the growing entertainment economy. From his first media endorsement—describing for the United Press how to hit a homer, for which he earned five dollars—he went on to hawk a myriad of products, including candy, cereal, cigarettes, soap, and even Babe Ruth All America Athletic Underwear. He was not the first baseball star to endorse products. Spalding had promoted the first official baseball by branding it with his name. Future Hall of Fame shortstop Honus Wagner endorsed a Hillerich & Bradsby Louisville Slugger bat in 1905, thereby establishing the endorsement practice of player-signed equipment. Wagner also used his celebrity currency to promote nonbaseball goods ranging from Coca-Cola to gunpowder. Ruth, however, brought celebrity leverage to an unprecedented level, "perfect[ing] modern player endorsement marketing."[49] Kristen Jones, a curator at the National Baseball Hall of Fame and Museum, observes, "Through advertising, baseball is not only the national pastime, but has become a national product."[50] Sports celebrity marketing has since become a major element in the entertainment economy.

Reflecting celebrity's impact on the business of baseball, Ruth also became a well-paid revenue generator for the Yankees. He produced an estimated additional two million dollars for the club during the 1920s, and his annual salary rose from twenty thousand dollars to eighty thousand dollars by the end of the decade. Nevertheless, despite salary increases for selected stars, player compensation continued to decline as a percentage of total expenses. In the early days of the NL, player salaries amounted to three-quarters of expenses; by 1929, that figure had dropped to 38 percent as revenues increased and owners leveraged the reserve clause to control labor costs. Ruth's increased salary, therefore, remained a bargain relative to the revenue he generated.[51] Today, in the era of free agency, player salaries account for slightly more than half of expenses, while player development constitutes another 10 percent.[52]

Ruth's celebrity attraction, combined with the Yankees on-field success, enabled the team to construct Yankee Stadium, known as the House That Ruth Built. Costing the owners $2.5 million, about 2 percent of the 2009 stadium, it opened on April 18, 1923, and Ruth appropriately hit a home run that day. Including a short right-field porch only 296 feet from home plate for the left-hand-hitting Ruth, the stadium helped him to continue his home run dominance, which included twelve league homer titles in fourteen years.

Before establishing his personal national brand with product endorsements and many unmemorable short and feature films as well as vaudeville appearances, Ruth led groups of Major Leaguers on off-season barnstorming circuits. After the 1919 and 1920 seasons, these junkets matched his MLB salary. These activities, combined with his growing amoral public persona, provoked a confrontation with Landis, who thought barnstorming was an affront to the hallowed game. When Ruth disobeyed Landis's order to stop barnstorming after the 1921 season, Landis suspended the player for the first forty games of the 1922 season.[53] The issue of barnstorming, with its light-hearted commercialism, illustrates the juxtaposition of Landis, the traditional moralist who seemingly had little appreciation for business, and Ruth, the carefree amoralist who wanted to make money and have fun.

MEDIA AND MARKETING

The 1920s also spawned the broadcast media, which subsequently formed a synergistic partnership with baseball and other sports. From its early days, MLB had enjoyed a positive relationship with print media. Stimulated by baseball's popularity and long season, the sports section became the most widely read part of the newspaper. In baseball's early days, sportswriters unabashedly promoted the game and developed close, positive clubhouse connections to fill their pages. If, in Tedlow's marketing history phases, a newspaper was a fragmented marketing medium, radio began the unifying process, television both enhanced unification and established segmentation though local and cable channels, and the Internet globalized them.

The first baseball radio broadcast occurred in 1921, and the first World Series was broadcast locally in 1922 and nationally in 1923, but not until 1939 did all MLB teams broadcast games.[54] About that time, fledgling television stations were already experimenting with baseball. The first television commercial occurred during a 1941 Brooklyn Dodgers–Philadelphia Phillies telecast, an indication of baseball's commercial value.[55] Typical of their conservative, monopoly-conditioned behavior, many owners feared that broadcasts would keep fans from attending games, thereby reducing revenues. They failed to foresee that team revenue growth would come increasingly from nongate sources. Today, while broadcast revenue source percentages vary considerably among teams because of the differences in local television contracts, the growing aggregate media impact has resulted in the ballpark now supplying only about half of the average MLB team income.[56]

In 2005, ESPN, the cable sports network that has become sport's leading media brand, announced an eight-year deal that, when added to the network's radio and highlights deals, would pay MLB an average of $337 million annually, a 71 percent jump over its prior arrangement. Additionally, Sirius XM Satellite Radio now pays MLB almost $60 million a year to carry games beyond traditional radio ranges and has money available in escrow to cover contract costs through 2010 as the company goes through bankruptcy proceedings. MLB also shows games on its captive Internet site, MLB.com, which is owned by all thirty teams and includes enhanced video and user-selected replays. In 2008, Major League Baseball Advanced Media (MLBAM) and ESPN expanded and extended a digital agreement until 2013. This arrangement, which licenses ESPN for digital transmission and some syndication, complements earlier agreements for ESPN TV coverage of Sunday and Wednesday games and exclusive U.S. radio broadcast of those games. These national contracts account for more than 10 percent of aggregate team annual revenues.[57]

To increase broadcast revenue, MLB launched the MLB Network, a 24/7 baseball channel, on January 1, 2009. The National Basketball Association, National Football League, and National Hockey League already had such channels. Recognizing that fans are allied with local outlets, Fox, ESPN, or TBS for games, Tony Petitti, president of MLB Network and former CBS Sports executive, stated, "We want to be the next choice." MLB began with an endowment of fifty million subscribers by selling one-third ownership in the channel to DirectTV, Comcast, Time Warner, and Cox, thereby ensuring wide distribution.[58] Telecasts of the January Hall of Fame election announcement and selected World Baseball Classic and spring training games not already committed to other networks enabled MLB Network to meet initial revenue projections. It broadcast twenty-six regular season games as the exclusive national provider on Thursday nights.

MLB and other sports face a growing online piracy threat, not unlike the film and music recording industries. David Price, head of piracy intelligence at Envisional, which helped prepare a report for the Organization for Economic Cooperation and Development, notes that unlike music or film recording, sporting events are live, so the opportunity to gaining later revenue from recording sales is minimal. MLB, which employs three piracy monitors, documented 5,000 incidents during 2,430 games in 2008, up from 3,000 incidents the prior year. MLB has stated that it will not sue pirating fans but will rely on moral suasion through cease-and-desist letters and discussion with foreign governments.[59]

Local broadcast revenues, which are not shared, vary considerably by market. Some teams, like the Yankees, have their own cable networks; most teams contract with local or regional networks. Those teams that have affiliated businesses use inter- or intracompany accounting to optimize composite profit by masking what true market level revenues might be attributable to the team. With revenue sharing mandated between large and small market teams, it is likely that media revenues are understated on large-revenue-team income statements.

At the MLB level, the MLB Properties division handles the aggregate broadcasting deals as well as sponsorships and merchandising, with those revenues going into a central fund that is shared equally among the teams. The average team currently derives about 25 percent of its total revenue from the central fund. Key MLB sponsorships have included a longtime partnership with MasterCard as well as more recent deals with General Mills, General Motors, DHL, and Home Depot. For one hundred million dollars, Bank of America became the "official bank of Major League Baseball" for five years.

While MLB consolidates and shares those revenues equally among the teams, individual teams still have separate opportunities beyond local broadcasting deals. A notable, relatively recent, and lucrative phenomenon has been stadium naming rights. In some sense, they represent the ultimate extension of the advertising signage that has covered the outfield walls since the early days of the game. Most MLB parks now carry corporate sponsors' names. Some, like Yankee Stadium and Fenway Park, have kept their original names to maintain tradition while charging higher prices to compensate for forsaken naming revenue. An early preserved but not original name is Wrigley Field, which became the first corporate-named park in 1925 when gum producer William Wrigley Jr. bought the Chicago Cubs. On the advice of Albert Lasker, considered the father of the modern ad agency, Wrigley changed the stadium's name from Cubs Park and established a highly visible and enduring endorsement for his products. Only when municipal financing of stadiums ebbed in the 1990s did most teams cut naming rights deals. These names illustrate corporate America's perceptions regarding the attractive marketing value of baseball.[60]

MLBAM handles less traditional business activities, with focus on Internet and related broadband business. In 2005, its principal Web site, MLB.com, signed a five-year, fifty-million-dollar deal with the MLBPA to acquire rights to players' names and likenesses for use in online fantasy games and wireless products. MLBAM also entered into an eight-year, two-hundred-million-dollar exclusive licensing arrangement under which Take-Two Interactive Systems would develop video games. The deal still allowed for licensing arrangements with video game console makers, including Sony (PlayStation) and Microsoft (Xbox).

MLB's licensing-related business suffered a setback in its relationship with fantasy leagues. Following formation of MLBAM, MLB decided to run fantasy games on MLB.com and refused to renew a commercial fantasy league's license to run games with MLB players. Contending that MLB statistics are in the public domain, a 2008 St. Louis appeals court ruled that MLB could not require a license. The Supreme Court refused to hear MLB's appeal, thereby negating its control of the statistics.[61] Such a ruling constricts MLB's licensing opportunities and revenues, particularly if the ruling's principles are extended more generally.

MLBAM has a ten-year partnership with the National Association of Professional Baseball Leagues, better known as Minor League Baseball (MiLB), to be its exclusive provider of Internet and other interactive services. Under the arrangement, MLBAM will manage league and team Web sites, become the official Minor League statistician, and handle merchandising, ticket sales, advertising, and sponsorships. To facilitate ticket handling, MLBAM bought Tickets.com for sixty-six million dollars. This deal solidifies MLB's previous dominance of the Minor Leagues but places the relationship on a more mutually beneficial soft power basis than had previously been the case.[62]

In addition to servicing MiLB, MLBAM provides Internet-related services for the National Football League and National Hockey League, thereby indicating its superior technological capability among professional sports organizations and suggesting its strategic potential in a growing global business, discussed further in chapter 4 ("Home Plate"). As baseball's on-field revenues face the challenges of competition and recession, MLBAM provides opportunity for off-field revenue growth.

To build fan support, MLB has undertaken some innovative advertising approaches. Acknowledging football as the more popular sport, it targeted the 2004 Super Bowl audience by buying a $1 million, thirty-second spot during the *Survivor* episode that immediately followed the Super Bowl. MLB's ad featured three popular baseball players discussing the Budweiser and Pepsi commercials that had aired during the Super Bowl (at $2.3 million for each thirty-second spot). Encouraged by that result, MLB spent $2.5 million for a thirty-second spot during the 2006 Super Bowl itself to advertise the following month's initial World Baseball Classic.[63]

For its 2005 season-opening campaign, MLB deviated from a typical adulatory star player approach and featured fans in team-themed costumes lightheartedly reinforcing the campaign theme "I live for this."[64] This approach not only curried favor with fans but also reduced possibility of a backlash against promoted players who subsequently engaged in misconduct. All of these deals, relationships, and activities suggest that MLB is becoming more progressive and innovative. It is abiding by Tedlow's sixth proposition: managing change.

THE LAW, LABOR, AND THE UNION

In the 1920s, the business of baseball received a much greater boost from the Supreme Court than it did from its commissioner or even the Bambino. On May 22, 1922, the court issued its ruling on the Baltimore FL antitrust suit. In a majority opinion that read more like a paean to the national pastime, Judge Oliver Wendell Holmes, a former amateur player, maintained curiously that baseball games were local events, not interstate commerce. Although the players traveled across state lines, the games were "purely state affairs."[65] Therefore, baseball was not subject to antitrust regulation of interstate commerce. By enabling MLB to maintain both its territorial monopolies and player control, the ruling essentially precluded any direct business competition or labor challenge for decades.

The Supreme Court had two state court decisions as precedents: *Philadelphia Ball Club, Ltd. v. Lajoie* (1902) and *American League Baseball Club of Chicago v. Chase* (1914). In both rulings, the courts had determined that baseball was not commerce. The Supreme Court later reinforced its federal ruling in *Toolson v. New York Yankees, Inc.* (1953) by denying that restraint of trade had existed in the team's treatment of a player, the culmination of what legal scholar Lief Carter describes as "a series of decisions that hardly seems stable, that violates reliance expectations to the extent that there are any, and that does not treat equals equally."[66]

In the interim, Congress had taken no action regarding MLB's unique monopoly status. Conversely, the Court ruled in *Radovich v. National Football League* (1957) that professional football was subject to antitrust laws but restated that Congress should deal with baseball's status. "It appears that the Congress and the Supreme Court were playing a game of cat and mouse," observes Zimbalist.[67] Apparently, each body determined that it would be politically incorrect to tamper with the national pastime.

Congress eliminated "the most potent weapon in the struggle to repeal the Federal Baseball exemption"[68] when it passed the Sports Broadcasting Act of 1961, which allowed all professional sports teams to negotiate TV contracts collectively as leagues, thereby putting other professional sports leagues on an equal footing with MLB. It also gave those leagues quasi-exemption status by allowing them to negotiate with collective clout rather than as individual teams.

In dismissing *Flood v. Kuhn* (1972), the Court again upheld the federal ruling through the "positive inaction" doctrine. Focused on the reserve clause, the decision denied St. Louis Cardinals outfielder Curt Flood's right to refuse a trade. Again, the majority decision, written by Harry Blackmun, was a baseball ode citing poetry and specifically naming eighty-eight individual baseball luminaries, while Thurgood Marshall's minority opinion asserted that the clause "virtually enslaved" Flood and other players. "*Flood* stands as a notable example of judicial powerlessness in the face of a self-created dilemma, an object lesson in conservative principles run amok, and a textbook example of the limits of the reform power of public institutions," argues Abrams.[69] That decision steeled the recently strengthened player union's resolve to remove the clause through bargaining.

While the MLBPA had been formed in 1953, it operated like a compliant company union until it named Marvin Miller, a lawyer and former United Steelworkers executive, as its first full-time executive director in 1966. Over the next decade, Miller used his professional acumen and experience to help the MLBPA develop into one of the strongest unions in the country.

In one of his early moves to build confidence with the players, Miller addressed MLB's first auxiliary business, baseball trading cards. Topps, which had a virtual monopoly at the time, was paying players only $125 each a year with no royalties. Miller renegotiated with Topps and later other vendors on behalf of the players so that by 1968 there was a royalty-based contract in place that produced several million dollars for the players and provided for incremental increases with expanded sales.[70] By picking Topps as a first target, Miller used a low-risk approach to establish credibility with and unity among members. Building slowly but strategically, Miller educated his members and created future opportunities in the First Basic Agreement with the owners, concluded in 1968. That agreement raised minimum salaries, allowed players to hire agents, provided for grievance arbitration, and authorized a joint study of the reserve clause. It also established a hard power economic negotiation process.

The union demonstrated unity in the first regular season strike—the first strike in professional sports history—which lasted only nine days in 1972. In the Third Basic Agreement, the union secured impartial arbitration of contract disputes, paving the way for the historic 1975 arbitration decision that permitted pitchers Andy Messersmith and Dave McNally to become free agents. The 1976 Fourth Basic Agreement officially removed the reserve clause from all contracts by the following year. While MLB clubs continued their monopoly exclusivity in designated territories, they lost their leverage over players. They also lost all of the ensuing bitter labor conflicts with the MLBPA over the next two decades. In their historical essay, William W. Wright and Mick Cochrane observe, "The recent history is a humiliating losing streak: the owners are the Washington Senators of labor wars." For much of its history, the Washington team was "first in war, first in peace, and last in the American League."[71]

At the helm for the owners during this time was Bowie Kuhn, a former NL counsel who became commissioner on February 4, 1969. Miller observes that Kuhn was "plagued by the ghost of . . . Landis." Kuhn's fifteen-year tenure, third-longest behind Landis and Selig, illustrates the fallacy of overreliance on hard power, although, unlike Landis, Kuhn was usually just fronting for the owners in wielding that power. Miller concludes that the Dodgers' O'Malley was "baseball's real czar."[72] It is therefore notable that the Hall of Fame admitted both Kuhn and O'Malley in 2008 and again shunned Miller.

Ironically, Kuhn decided not to pursue a hard power opportunity when Messersmith and McNally filed their joint free agency grievance. While such action could have been adjudicated solely by Kuhn as a complaint instead of an arbitration grievance, Kuhn declined to do so, rationalizing that denying the players' pursuit of free agency would have provoked a strike.[73] In retrospect, since the arbitrator ruled for the players, thereby paving the way for removal of the reserve clause, Kuhn perhaps squandered an opportunity to preserve this critical hard power resource, which had been historically supported in court cases.

The most significant strike of Kuhn's tenure occurred in 1981 and resulted in the cancellation of more than seven hundred games and likely prompting the owners' decision not to renew his contract. The trigger issue was what compensation a team could receive for losing a free agent. This matter had been festering since the Collective Bargaining Agreement (CBA, formerly called Basic Agreement) negotiated at the eleventh hour a year earlier had passed it on to a study group. Miller claims that Kuhn told him just before the 1980 negotiations that the owners needed a "victory."

Miller describes the 1981 strike as "the most principled strike" he ever participated in and the MLBPA's "finest hour."[74] Calling Miller "a prisoner of his own ego above all things," Kuhn considers the strike "an inexcusable miscalculation by Miller of the clubs and me." A critical factor in the MLBPA's dominance of the owners in bargaining was Miller's soft power effect on the press and the public, which strengthened the union's bargaining position and outflanked Kuhn and the owners, who chose not to curry public favor. Kuhn acknowledges Miller as a "superior communicator" whose "ability to cultivate the press was perhaps his greatest talent."[75] Observing that Kuhn had "role confusion" because he thought he represented the players, Miller sardonically concludes that Kuhn was "the most important contributor to the successes of the Players Association."[76]

In calling Miller "the most effective union organizer since John L. Lewis," blue-collar author Studs Terkel observes that Miller "brought an end to the age of innocence" by changing the business of baseball.[77] Kuhn and Miller dueled in five work stoppages, and while their successors faced off in another three between 1972 and 1995, no strikes have taken place since, reflecting the mutual prosperity owners and players have enjoyed and their greater, though still guarded, willingness to collaborate in soft power negotiations.

The sixth stoppage, in August 1985, pitted Peter Ueberroth, Kuhn's wunderkind successor, against Donald Fehr, Miller's successor, and lasted only two days before Ueberroth dictated a settlement without owner approval. Ueberroth, who had reinvigorated the commissionership with a strong marketing focus, incurred owner wrath by not including requested salary-containment items in the settlement. Without them, the owners entered into a multiyear collusion to limit player salaries that ultimately cost the owners $280 million in damages and further calcified the hard power adversarial relationship between players and owners that continued for another decade.[78]

The climactic 1994–95 strike, which lasted 232 days, shortened each of the two seasons. Moreover, the climactic and revered World Series had continued through international wars but could not endure a labor feud, and the 1994 postseason was canceled. "The player strike of 1994–95 signaled the end of baseball's reign as America's national pastime," asserts Jerold J. Duquette.[79] Owners had delayed for seventeen months opening negotiations on a new CBA and exercised a hard power push to include a salary cap, which the MLBPA strongly resisted. As a result of 1994 changes in the commissioner's role and divided opinions among owners, confusion ensued about what acting commissioner Selig could and could not do in the bargaining process.

Since the playoffs generate about three-quarters of MLB's national television revenues as well as disproportionately higher gate-related income, the strike had a significant negative impact on MLB and club profits. The strike began on August 12, by which time players had received most of their pay for the year, timing that strengthened the blow to the owners. While the owners had built up a war chest, the players' union had also prepared for the event by amassing a $175 million strike fund from licensing revenues from baseball cards and other products over the preceding four years. Therefore, each player with four years' experience had about $150,000 to ride out the strike.

Acknowledging baseball's position as the national pastime, President Bill Clinton even intervened, appointing Bill Usery, former Steelworkers head and a prominent negotiator, to mediate. Usery shifted the primary bargaining issue from a salary cap to revenue sharing but could not secure an agreement. The president then proposed binding arbitration, but the owners refused. The old CBA was reinstated on March 31, 1995, so that the season could start, and a new CBA was not concluded until after the 1996 season.

Sports economist Paul D. Staudohaur uses a model with four isolated elements to analyze that strike: the allocation of revenues through collective bargaining between the union and the owners, the exploration of mutual gain through cooperation, the behavioral atmosphere at the bargaining table, and the accommodation to the differing interests of the negotiators' constituencies. The first element, he observes, is difficult because there are relatively few participants—about 750 players and 30 owners—so each has a lot at stake. The second and third elements are compounded by a history of distrust. The fourth reflects the disparate constituencies—large-, medium-, and small-market owners; rookie, veteran, journeyman, and superstar players. Therefore, Staudohaur concludes, the strike was a logical outcome.[80]

Such a conclusion should indicate that more strikes will occur unless MLB and MLBPA establish ongoing soft power collaboration in their bilateral monopoly. But since then, no strikes have taken place. In the wake of the 1972 strike, the longest prior truce had been 4.5 years (1985–90). Contributing to the peace was the 1996 CBA. It included substantial reforms that enabled MLB to move toward more collaborative governance: revenue sharing, a luxury tax, an Industry Growth Fund to spur global promotion, and an agreement to seek a partial lifting of the antitrust exemption (which culminated in the 1998 Curt Flood Act).

A principal figure in that climactic strike and in the subsequent peace is Allan H. "Bud" Selig, who became interim commissioner in 1992 while still serving as managing partner of the Milwaukee Brewers. Despite this blatant conflict of interest, Selig continued in that capacity until 1998, when he put his Brewer holdings in a blind trust, picked his daughter to run the Brewers, and became permanent commissioner. He did not divest himself of ownership until 2005.[81] George Vecsey of the *New York Times* has aptly labeled Selig's predecessor, Fay Vincent, "the last commissioner," because Selig is clearly the owner representative, not an independent leader of MLB.[82] His selection overtly acknowledged that MLB is an owner-controlled entity with the commissioner as chief executive officer. Like the CEO of a typical business organization, Selig seeks to optimize MLB's performance, including profit pursuit, brand enhancement, customer and employee satisfaction, and government compliance. Influencing the "best interests of baseball" approach, however, is an obvious recognition of the owners, who, in fact if not on paper, control his destiny. Despite this hard power owner relationship, Selig has generally relied more on his soft power skills with the owners and other constituents throughout his tenure.

Zimbalist concludes that Selig "was the right person to shepherd this transition" of baseball to a competitive business.[83] Citing his skills in conciliation, particularly among owners, Kuhn calls Selig, "baseball's Henry Clay."[84] Moffi states that MLB is a "limited partnership" owned by all teams with a five-person board of directors and two "independent members," MLB president Bob DuPuy and former Expos owner John McHale. As CEO, however, Selig must deal with the fact that the partners have an inherent tendency to put their individual interests ahead of the MLB enterprise.[85]

Selig has had his share of successes and failures during his tenure, now expected to last until 2013 as a result of contract renewal. While these developments do not simply reflect soft or hard power emphasis, the successes have tended to be more a function of soft power and the failures more a function of hard power. Two years after making him permanent commissioner, the owners enhanced his power by amending the MLB constitution to eliminate the AL and NL presidents, put the leagues directly under Selig for most governance purposes, and include revenue-sharing procedures, within CBA constraints, as part of reinstated "best interests" authority, which the owners had removed in 1994. Reacting at that time to unilateral actions by Kuhn in 1976, Ueberroth in 1985, and Vincent in 1990, owners had then denied the commissioner the authority to act unilaterally to resolve collective bargaining disputes.[86] Later, after Selig had demonstrated that he was acting in the owners' best interests, they reinstated the authority that had been removed in 1994.

During the current peace, the MLB and MLBPA have narrowly averted one strike, agreed on realignment, reached progressive resolutions (with prodding from the U.S. Congress and the Mitchell report) on the drug issue, and collaborated on creation of the World Baseball Classic. They quickly and amicably negotiated a new CBA.[87] Selig's fan-oriented changes—three divisions with a wild card playoff entry, interleague play, and league realignment—have generally met with success. Vince Gennaro calls the wild card Selig's "single biggest stroke of genius" because it enhances September competition for playoff berths and resultant fan interest.[88] Conversely, his future-oriented Blue Ribbon Panel, which in a hard power action did not include a player representative, was ineffective and generally disregarded. And his failed unilateral attempt to impose team contraction, which prompted legal retaliation in Minnesota and a general player grievance, was a public relations disaster.

Economists Tony Lima, Leo Kahane, and Nan L. Maxwell call the MLB-MLBPA relationship a "bilateral monopoly" because each acts as a single unit in negotiations. In using game theory, they extend the "prisoner's dilemma" economic game to a profit- (or wage-) maximizing model to reflect the actual baseball situation. The prisoner's dilemma game has three possible outcomes in its crime scenario: one of two partners (MLB or MLBPA) confesses, so one is punished and the other is not; both confess, and each gets light punishment; or neither confesses and neither is punished. In this model, the optimal outcome is achieved by soft power cooperation (neither confessing). In baseball, however, the requisite mutual trust has not been present to facilitate cooperative behavior, but Lima, Kahane, and Maxwell optimistically observe that cooperation usually ensues if the game is played long enough.[89] Recent MLB-MLBPA behavior confirms that observation.

The economic model and analysis identify cooperation as the critical factor for mutual MLB-MLBPA satisfaction and therefore underscore the value of soft power collaboration. The 2006 CBA resulted from such cooperation. The steroid issue in particular highlighted the continuing need for cooperation and probably facilitated the quick, collaborative resolution of the CBA. The World Baseball Classic, which benefits both parties, demonstrates that cooperation can occur if mutually beneficial objectives are set and pursued.

A MANAGEMENT-UNION TEST

Player use of steroids is one issue that has challenged MLB and MLBPA to cooperate. The issue affects both parties, potentially devaluing MLB's celebrity currency and thereby creating an imbalance in its managing the mythology and reality of the sport. While use of performance-enhancing drugs has been a contested issue in sports, particularly the Olympics, for the past half century, MLB had generally avoided public scrutiny, probably because of its mythical status and decreased emphasis on physicality relative to other sports. Concurrently, however, use of legal and illegal drugs had become a significant societal issue. Alcohol has been part of MLB history from the beginning. In the 1970s, some MLB players were publicly exposed for using cocaine and stimulants. Since then, legal drugs such as cortisone became common as "performance enablers" in injury rehabilitation, while healthy athletes covertly tried other chemicals as "performance enhancers." The line between the two became increasingly blurred.

During the 1998 season, Mark McGwire of the St. Louis Cardinals and Sammy Sosa of the Chicago Cubs waged a dramatic yet friendly competitive assault on the single-season record of sixty-one home runs set in 1961, when Yankee outfielder Roger Maris broke Ruth's 1927 mark of sixty. McGwire won the well-publicized contest and set a new record of seventy homers, only to be surpassed three years later by Barry Bonds, who hit seventy-three. The 1998 homer race substantially helped to restore MLB's popularity, which had plummeted in the wake of the 1994–95 strike. With smaller ballparks, a tighter strike zone, and no scrutiny of drugs, MLB provided an environment as well as stimulus for increased home run production.

During the race, however, a journalist reported seeing a bottle of androstenedione, a legal supplement that mimics a steroid, in McGwire's locker. He admitted to using andro, which was banned by the Olympics and the National Football League, as well as creatine, a power supplement that Sosa also admitted using.[90] MLB and MLBPA, aided by perennially supportive sportswriters, used their soft power to suppress the story and preserve the public relations value of the competition between the quiet all-American McGwire and the likable Dominican Sosa. With the ingrained arrogance of a bilateral hard power monopoly, however, neither organization chose to address the underlying problem immediately despite its prevalence and the initiatives taken by other sports. MLB's emphasis on the home run as a marketing attraction had stimulated supplement usage in what had traditionally not been viewed as a power sport.

Commissioner Selig initiated a comprehensive steroid-testing policy in the Minor Leagues in 2001 and found that 11 percent of players tested positive for anabolic steroids. Presumably influenced by regular testing, that result dropped to less than 2 percent by 2004 and has stayed low. In 2005, MiLB for the first time publicly disclosed names of those who tested positive for performance enhancers to maintain consistency with the then current MLB policy. The Minor League policy bans both drugs of abuse, such as amphetamines, marijuana, and cocaine, and performance-enhancers, such as steroids and its precursors. The 2001 policy, however, did not apply to the Minor Leaguers who were on the forty-man Major League rosters because they were MLBPA members.[91]

MLBPA continued to resist Major League action until the conclusion of the 2002 CBA, which included a modest drug policy (added at the last minute) that also covered Minor Leaguers on MLB. Although MLB and the MLBPA avoided a work stoppage, the testing program did not satisfy the press, anti-drug activists, or the public, which had become more attuned to the issue and its negative impact on the nation's youth. MLB-MLBPA's minimalist strategy worked until September 3, 2003, when Internal Revenue Service agents raided the Bay Area Laboratory Company (BALCO), a Burlingame, California, facility that acknowledged Bonds and fellow superstars Jason Giambi and Gary Sheffield as customers. While Sheffield denied steroid use, Giambi admitted to a grand jury that he used steroids, and Bonds acknowledged unknowingly using the designer steroid cream THG, supplied by BALCO. In September 2005, BALCO founder Victor Conte was sentenced to eight months in prison for illegal drug distribution. Bonds was subsequently indicted for perjury, released by the Giants after the 2007 season, and not signed by any other team. His Hall of Fame election prospects have clearly diminished.

In April 2004, the Senate Commerce Committee summoned MLB-MLBPA representatives to a hearing and threatened legislative action if the sport did not enact a new, harsher drug policy. MLB and MLBPA responded with an unprecedented reopening of the CBA and adoption of a somewhat stricter drug policy, announced on January 13, 2005. Still dissatisfied, the House Government Reform Committee called various players and management representatives to a March 17, 2005, hearing, at which McGwire, who had retired before 2002 season and awaited eligibility for the Hall of Fame, repeatedly refused to respond to questions about steroid use, thereby implicating himself. Baltimore Oriole first baseman Rafael Palmiero also testified and strongly denied any steroid use, but he tested positive shortly thereafter.

The Senate Commerce Committee held another hearing on September 28, 2005, again to chastise baseball's representatives. Members of Congress directed particular criticism at Donald Fehr of the MLBPA, since Selig had repeatedly voiced desire to enact stronger antidrug controls.[92] Republican Senators John McCain of Arizona and Jim Bunning of Kentucky, the latter a former Major Leaguer and member of the Baseball Hall of Fame, introduced a uniform drug-testing bill that would apply to all professional sports. This continuing congressional pressure provoked MLB and MLBPA to reach agreement on a second, tougher policy within two months.

On November 15, 2005, management and the union jointly announced that the drug policy would be strengthened so that a first offense would result in a fifty-day suspension; a second positive test would result in a player's suspension for one hundred days; a third offense would bring a lifetime ban, though the player could appeal for reinstatement after two years. The new policy added testing for amphetamines, with mandatory testing resulting from the first positive test, a twenty-five-game suspension the punishment for a second offense, an eighty-game suspension resulting from a third offense, and discipline up to a lifetime ban for the fourth offense. "Amphetamines have become as much a part of the clubhouse scene as card games and hot seat," quipped ESPN's Jerry Crasnick at the time.[93]

In a further effort to move from damage control to a proactive policy that would satisfy public constituents, Selig asked former Senate majority leader George J. Mitchell to head a task force investigating use of steroids and other performance-enhancing substances. Mitchell submitted his report with twenty recommendations on December 13, 2007.[94] Describing MLB as "a social institution with social responsibilities" and the report as "a call to action [on which] I will act,"[95] Selig quickly implemented unilateral recommendations designed to extend and tighten testing, including the establishment of a department of investigations as a permanent branch of the commissioner's office.[96] Again, MLB and MLBPA opened the current CBA, which runs through the 2011 season, and agreed on other recommendations dealing with the regulation of the testing program.

While the creation and implementation of the report provided overt positive response to critical constituents, notably Congress, it also improved MLB's control of the drug problem. Further promoting a proactive image, MLB joined three other sports organizations—the U.S. Olympic Committee, the U.S. Anti-Doping Agency, and the National Football League—in fund-raising to support research into the detection and consequences of doping.[97] The new MLB-MLBPA drug agreement might foretell a more balanced, collaborative relationship between the owners and the union, but there are also indications that the MLBPA might retaliate in other areas because of the public perception that it was the greater offender.

At the same time, MLB has enjoyed strong attendance (and MiLB has enjoyed even better patronage) and exciting pennant races. Despite some criticism of baseball's weak drug position, spectator support has remained strong, in contrast with the immediate aftermath of the Black Sox scandal. There appears to be a socially conditioned tolerance for drugs and, more importantly, a fantasy desire to support competitive performance and even specific celebrities, regardless of artificial enhancements. Soft power, albeit misused, seems to prevail as myth trumps reality on the drug issue in the marketplace.

The drug issue also calls into question the commercial exploitation of MLB stars as role models. While, as Wolf declares, celebrity is currency in our entertainment-driven economy, it, like other currencies, risks devaluation through internal and external conditions and events. The reputations of McGwire, Palmiero, Sosa, and Bonds have diminished because of this issue. Bonds's reputation was placed in further jeopardy with the March 2006 publication of *Game of Shadows*, a drug exposé written by two San Francisco reporters.

In early 2009, Alex Rodriguez, MLB's highest-paid player, admitted that he had used steroids during 2001–3 while a member of the Texas Rangers under a ten-year, $250 million contract. Rodriguez blamed the transgression on his youth. While clearly accumulating Hall of Fame player credentials, he has also put his election in possible jeopardy. As these "steroid era" stars become eligible, the Hall of Fame electors will determine whether to grant entrance to such players. Early annual voting on McGwire, the first to become eligible (2007), indicates that he will become the first five-hundred-homer player not to enter the shrine.

With media and advertiser enhancement, baseball players, perhaps even more than other sports figures and entertainers, occupy overly exalted positions that expand their on-field reputations to those of generic role models for every aspect of life. Basketball and football players arguably generate more negative press with their off-field actions, but those sports, with their greater emphasis on physicality, seem not to have the mythical moral aura that surrounds baseball. Therefore, those players arguably have less far to fall than do baseball players.

As a business, MLB could serve itself and its market more effectively by focusing its players more on meritorious on-field behavior and channeling the leveraging of its celebrity currency into less vulnerable off-field leadership roles. The reality is that MLB players, like other professional athletes, are simply well-paid gladiators who compete to please audiences and secure revenue for owners. As competition intensifies, athletes seek new means to enhance performance and win, a situation in which the risk of illegal and/or perceived immoral acts increases.[98] Continuing emphasis on the sport's moral mythology to enhance business opportunities opens MLB to recurring criticism when the gladiators are scrutinized and found imperfect beyond the playing field. Further, one has to question how effective broad application of the myth will be in an international market that includes countries with varying cultural norms. MLB needs to be compliant with local interpretation and modification of its myth.

THIRD BASE

BASEBALL AS A NEOCOLONIALIST: ABUSING POWER

While the racial environment in sport may be improving,
it seems like it is worsening in society at large.
—RICHARD LAPCHICK

As MLB evolved from a sport and matured into a business, it increasingly sought what all businesses seek in the face of competition: cheap resources in the form of players. In baseball, however, the player is the labor as well as the raw material, while the processors are managers, coaches, and trainers. As a combined labor/material resource, a player group is subject to neocolonial appropriation in baseball as in other "manufacturing" processes. MLB's history reflects its internal and external neocolonial initiatives among European immigrant, Native American, rural white, black, and Latino players. MLB's neocolonial pursuits result from nineteenth-century cultural influences that contributed to baseball's development as a white, urban, middle-class sport and as a Progressive Era business.

MLB's strategy and tactics mirror America's social and business development of the times and reflect an increasing emphasis on exploiting the sport as a profitable business. To accomplish its procurement objectives, MLB employed economic hard power coercion more than soft power attractions, resulting in the buildup of a resistance that eventually resulted in the loss of control of labor costs. Integration of the sport was fundamentally a business decision to secure cheap player talent. While removing the color barrier in 1947 was profitable,

MLB nevertheless enhanced opportunities for racial minorities in the sports and broader entertainment businesses.

Although the game started as an amateur, Anglo-oriented, middle-class urban sport, it also quickly attracted working-class European immigrants and their sons, who helped form an inexpensive source for players as the game turned professional in the latter part of the nineteenth century. Much of the team ownership emerged from that immigrant group, which achieved middle-class status in the melting pot era. As the twentieth century arrived, MLB selectively recruited financially disadvantaged Native American and white Cuban players but eschewed African Americans because of the prevailing biases of segregated black-white American society.

MLB's exploitation of Native Americans, however, was not so much in securing cheap player talent as in insensitively translating their culture into demeaning mascots, logos, and team nicknames. Two of the sixteen teams that comprised the American and National Leagues from 1903 to 1952 had Indian nicknames and the concomitant logos and mascots. Those two teams maintained their Indian identity as MLB shifted locations and expanded. No new teams, however, have used an Indian connection, perhaps to reflect cultural sensitivity or at least to demonstrate political correctness. As Philip J. Deloria observed in a book of the same name, "playing Indian" was very popular in early 1900s America, reflecting a romantic desire to preserve the frontier mythology.[1] White American males appropriated and essentialized Indian rituals and dress in various fraternal groups. This appropriation complemented MLB's pastoral mythology.

The Boston NL team changed its nickname from Beaneaters to Braves in 1913 and the Cleveland AL team switched from Lajoies to Indians two years later. Boston's name derived from its new owner, James Gaffney, who used the nickname of his Tammany Hall fraternal society and political machine. Cleveland sportswriters chose "Indians" as a generally popular replacement for its nickname, which had honored the since departed player-manager and future Hall of Famer Napoleon Lajoie. To defend against subsequent Native American protests, the club falsely claimed that it chose the nickname to honor Louis Sockalexis, a Penobscot Indian who briefly played outfield for the team in the late nineteenth century. In fact, local sportswriters recommended the popular school/college nickname to the team without referring to Sockakexis.[2]

Major League teams' pursuit of cheap players in selected areas (colonies) of the country from the 1920s through the 1950s resembled a domestic version of nineteenth-century European colonialism. In the late 1920s, the St. Louis Cardinals, located at MLB's western boundary, ventured south and west into rural America to recruit poor white farm boys. Other teams later followed the initiative throughout the country and thus created what MLB appropriately called the farm system that controlled the Minor Leagues. In post–World War II America, which was rethinking its segregationist position against African Americans because of their wartime contributions, MLB teams recruited players from the racially separate Negro Leagues. As those domestic white rural and African American "colony" sources matured, teams then sought teenagers from Caribbean countries, which had enthusiastically embraced baseball since its introduction there in the late nineteenth century by U.S. military personnel and sugar capitalists. In each of those pursuits, MLB teams leveraged economic hard power to acquire talent, thereby reducing labor costs and increasing profits.

In 1961, Ghanaian president Kwame Nkrumah defined *neocolonialism* as the last act of imperialism, continuing the colonial tradition by capitalism-based economic means rather than by territory-based political or military means. The exploiter creates an empire with economic rather than political colonies by using capital to appropriate resources.[3] As general manager of the St. Louis Cardinals, Branch Rickey began the baseball neocolonial practice at home by securing white rural players; then, as general manager of the Brooklyn Dodgers, Rickey switched to African American players from Negro League domestic colonies through hard power economic leverage. That approach continued in an even more exploitative manner, also promoted by Rickey as head of the Pittsburgh Pirates, when MLB teams expanded player recruiting to the Caribbean.

Shortly before Rickey signed Jackie Robinson as the first African American Major Leaguer in seventy years, Gunnar Myrdal concluded in *An American Dilemma* (1944) that exploitative capitalism contributed to the U.S. black-white racial discrepancy. That observation about exploitative capitalism held true in MLB's farm system covering white rural America, in its raids on the Negro Leagues, and in its subsequent capitalist-racist incursion into Latin America.[4]

In affirming the commonality between the African American and Native American internal colonies and the Caribbean countries, E. San Juan Jr. quotes Robert Blauner: "The communities of color in America share essential conditions with third world nations abroad: economic underdevelopment, a heritage of colonialism and neocolonialism, and a lack of real political economy and power."[5] Gayatri Chakravorty Spivak observes this global commonality as well: "The general ideology of global development is racial paternalism . . . its general economics capital-intensive investment; its broad politics the silencing of resistance and of the subaltern as the rhetoric of their protest is constantly appropriated."[6] MLB teams conformed to those neocolonial patterns in their exploitative quest for cheap talent at home and abroad.

Baseball has a long history of racism. Etienne Balibar observes that racist organizations tend to call themselves nationalist, as does MLB, the "national pastime." While lacking the all-encompassing relationship of a country with its citizens, MLB, with its exemption from U.S. antitrust laws, its self-contained government, and its unilateral contractual relationship with its players reproduces in a neo-Marxist sense the form of a nation-state. As discussed in the first chapter, MLB has continuously allied itself with American nationalism.

Balibar sees the notions of nationalism and racism developing at home and abroad in a "cycle of historical reciprocity. . . . Racism is constantly emerging out of nationalism, not only towards the exterior but towards the interior." Balibar uses the terms *external racism* to describe international xenophobia and *internal racism* to denote domestic prejudice. The United States has demonstrated this reciprocal process in its history through its imperialist leadership abroad and its implementation of segregation at home. On a much smaller scale, MLB, in its pursuit of cheap labor, likewise has colonized the Caribbean while maintaining domestic racial biases in hiring and compensation for much of its history. It has practiced both external and internal racism.

Balibar further describes the community produced by a nation-state as a "fictive ethnicity," since he concludes that no nation has a true ethnic basis. This fictitious ethnicity can be produced through either common race or common language. MLB has used the latter as colonizer by employing its own game-related jargon to ally non-English-speaking players with their English-speaking counterparts. Conversely, in resistant mode, Latino players from various countries have used their native Spanish to create and preserve a subcommunity within MLB. Observing the challenges in taking either route, Balibar projects the nation-state and its participants internationally:

> Every "people," which is the product of a national process of ethnicization, is forced today to find its own means of going beyond exclusivism or identitarian ideology in the world of transnational communications and global relations of force. Or rather: every individual is compelled to find in the transformation of the imaginary of "his" or "her" people the means to leave it, in order to communicate with the individuals of other peoples with which he or she shares the same interests and, to some extent, the same future.[7]

Edward Said observes that all cultures are involved with one another; therefore, all are hybrids. But he also acknowledges that all American discourses deal with power.[8] MLB has leveraged its soft power attraction and peculiar language to embrace foreign players but has also exerted its neocolonial hard power to dominate relationships with Latino recruits. Conversely, Latinos have used their nationalism and language as expressions of resistance to that dominance.

Nkrumah also asserted that neocolonialism works to the detriment of the exploiter as well as the exploited because of victims' inherent resistant reaction to the oppressor.[9] Just as MLB suffered modestly from Minor League contraction, particularly in the segregated South after the Robinson signing, it later incurred more significant negative consequences—a strong player union, final-offer salary arbitration, and player free agency—from players' organized resistance to MLB's imperialist abuse of monopsonistic power.

In *Games and Empires*, Allen Guttmann contends that the major causes of ludic diffusion (geographic spread of games) are the relative political, economic, and cultural power of the nations involved. Rejecting the term *cultural imperialism* as a descriptor for this diffusion, Guttmann argues that *cultural hegemony* is more accurate because it allows for active selection and selective retention by the dominated people. He disagrees with the argument that adoption of a dominant culture's sport is loss of authenticity because that argument is based on the false premise that cultures are static. He asserts that the result is often an indigenous subversion of externally imposed ludic forms coupled with a nationalistic desire to beat the dominator at its own game. In so doing, he reinforces both the resistant tendency that Nkrumah observed about neocolonization and the (ab)uses of hard and soft power described by Joseph S. Nye Jr.[10]

In *Beyond a Boundary*, a 1963 cultural study of Caribbean cricket, C. L. R. James observes that liberation from class and race occurs only during transcendent moments of play, only within the boundaries of the game, and only for the gamers: "The brotherhood of the game is only of the game." In colonial situations, he notes, a young native man's only capital is his body because he lacks alternative opportunities. James asserts, "How society can nurture the dream without cynically exploiting it may be the true sports challenge of the century."[11] So it was for MLB, which until the last quarter of the twentieth century attracted athletes with the soft power dream of playing in the Majors and then treated players as owned property to be exploited for profit. The attraction continues, but exploitation has reduced considerably in the past few decades as the Major League Baseball Players Association (MLBPA) and player agents have gained power and leveraged it on behalf of the players and as owners, fueled by prosperity, have competitively bid up signing bonuses and salaries.

THE MORAL CAPITALIST

Rickey, MLB's leading neocolonialist, was "a man of ultimate paradoxes, a capitalist/moralist/competitor/do- gooder/visionary/reactionary all rolled into one."[12] As an MLB executive from the 1920s to the 1950s, he operated in a protected business environment, a legal monopoly that gave owners and executives virtually complete control over their players, "enabled by the overwhelming power of the perpetual reserve system."[13] Such an environment facilitated MLB's neocolonial practices, which Rickey exploited.

Befitting other neocolonialists and reflecting his strong personality, Rickey always offered strong moral justification for his actions. He piously maintained that he was giving his lower-class recruits a lifetime opportunity: "I offered millhands, plowboys, high school kids a better way of life."[14] When preparing to trade surplus players, he effusively offered "sweeping praise and unequivocal raves" about them while rationalizing that they would have greater opportunities with other clubs.[15]

An avid Methodist from the Midwest, Rickey claimed to adhere to the capitalist teachings of John Wesley, the founder of Methodism, in his essay, "The Uses of Money," with three rules: gain all you can, save all you can, and give all you can. The first rule encouraged pursuit of success but tempered it with the admonition not to hurt others in the process. The second warned against superfluous spending on self and indiscriminate giving to family. The third reinforced man's position as a steward rather than proprietor of possessions and urged him to share wealth according to God's word.[16]

While Rickey publicly claimed to follow these rules, he often simply behaved like an amoral capitalist by unduly withholding money from players or excessively spending it on his own behalf. His prevailing nickname, the Mahatma, came from Mohandas K. Gandhi via sportswriter Tom Meaney, who cited historian John Gunther's description of the Indian leader "as an incredible combination of Jesus Christ, Tammany Hall, and your father." The nickname acknowledged Gandhi's best and worst qualities, including an overbearing pomposity and insufferable certainty.[17] It provided amoral dimensions to earlier Rickey moral monikers, the Preacher and the Deacon. Holding court with sportswriters in his Dodger office, called the Cave of the Winds, Rickey "was never one to keep his advice to himself."[18] Indicative of his prolific persona is the collection of 131 containers of his writings in the Library of Congress.[19] Commissioner Kenesaw Mountain Landis, a perennial Rickey adversary, implicitly acknowledged his moralist-capitalist paradox by calling him "that sanctimonious so and so."[20]

Rickey strongly exemplified Richard S. Tedlow's second and fourth business propositions (drive and vision of a leader and first-mover advantages) in his development and exploitation of what became known as the farm system. An inveterate risk taker, he operated according to the maxim "Never surrender opportunity for security."[21] Following the concept of philosopher William James, Rickey, the moral capitalist, practiced "the moral equivalent of war" to achieve war's positive spiritual results in the competitive business of baseball through adherence to military traits of discipline, order, devotion, fitness, and exertion.[22]

He had a keen eye for baseball potential in a prospect. "Nobody could ever match his talent for putting a dollar sign on a muscle," observed Harold Parrot, Rickey's traveling secretary with the Dodgers. To develop these recruits while with the St. Louis Cardinals, Rickey created the first formal working agreement with a Minor League team. The agreement provided that the Cardinals would recruit players and supply them to that team, which would develop the players and subsequently return them to the Major League club. When the 1921 National Agreement among MLB clubs again permitted them to buy Minor League teams, Rickey quickly extended the working agreement concept into what he called the "production and duplication" system, a term that lacked the panache of farm system, the eventual label.

Renowned for his tightfisted treatment of players and called El Cheapo by a New York sportscaster in his Dodger days, Rickey did not skimp on his personal business expenses, which included a car and driver and airplane and pilot, and developed compensation schemes that enabled him to be the highest-paid MLB executive. Typical of this maneuvering was a 10 percent commission on the sale of players. Since his wholesale recruiting and disciplined development system produced a surplus of players, Rickey substantially increased his personal earnings along with the team's profit by selling off excess talent. In 1928, for example, he added thirty thousand dollars in player sale commissions to his already high sixty-five-thousand-dollar salary.[23]

Through his innovative farm system, Rickey developed what sociologist Duncan J. Watts calls an economic "cumulative advantage" or "rich get richer" effect during his stints with the Cardinals and Dodgers. Watts observes that if one object or idea happens to be more popular or successful than another at just the right time and place, it will tend to become even more popular or successful, generating significant long-term differences between it and its competition.[24] Rickey again capitalized on this innovation with the Dodgers because he increased recruiting and development during World War II while other clubs, including the Cardinals, were cutting back on their recruiting and farm networks.

INTERNAL COLONIES

MLB's cultural hegemony began with internal colonies—European immigrants and their sons, Native Americans, rural white Americans, and African Americans. Bret J. Billet and Lance J. Formwalt observe that "baseball originated in the United States during perhaps the most blatant period of overt (i.e., traditional) racism," the late 1830s and early 1840s.[25] First considered a gentlemen's game, it was soon adopted by white ethnic minority working-class men whose aggressive play helped to distinguish baseball from its English roots. According to Peter C. Bjarkman, "For each of these ethnic groups, the national pastime quickly became a broad avenue into the promised land of a fleeting American dream."[26] Thus, baseball's soft power of attraction began.

During the Civil War, Union Army units played integrated baseball games, Confederate units played segregated games, and the two antagonists occasionally played against each other, with resulting geographic expansion from baseball's northeastern origins. As Reconstruction waned, baseball echoed the sentiments of Jim Crow racial backlash. By the end of the 1880s, professional baseball, by then controlled by white capitalist team owners, had become established as a bourgeois white man's sport exploiting white ethnic ballplayers, just as industrial capitalists exploited white ethnic laborers. Blacks also played, but in all-black leagues in less attractive venues. The game's original ethnic diversity did not beget racial diversity or equality.

"In a sad irony," notes Robert F. Burk, "the representatives of machine-based, more ethnically diverse clubs in both the Northeast and Midwest, having forced grudging respect through their blunt exercise of political power, now used their clout to adopt a policy of racial exclusion from the association's player force to suit their own social prejudices." MLB owners demonstrated what George Lipsitz calls "a possessive investment in whiteness," an exclusionary practice of white supremacy.[27] While some African Americans previously had played integrated professional baseball, the organizing owners of the National League reached tacit agreement to exclude blacks. With unilateral control of costs, an ample supply of white players, and growing urban consumer markets, owners exercised hegemony over the game.

Befitting broader societal norms, racism was a prevailing attitude of the players as well as the owners. Although the ethnic mix increased through immigration during the latter part of the nineteenth century, the U.S. melting pot was white, and so was the national pastime. When owners recruited Landis to clean up MLB following the 1919 Black Sox scandal, they received strong reinforcement of their implicit racist practices. An ardent segregationist, Landis used his considerable power to assure that the game would remain white during his twenty-three-year reign. As in other socioeconomic venues, class and racial/ethnic exploitation were linked to an imperialist assertion of hard power.

While heading the St. Louis Cardinals in the 1920s and 1930s, Rickey built exclusive working relationships with certain Minor League teams (colonies), which he populated with white players (raw materials) signed inexpensively by his scouts. The Minors developed the players (processed resources) for use by the Cardinals in selling MLB (the finished product) to fans. Because the Cardinals were at the time MLB's westernmost team, this recruiting strategy, reinforced by the advent of radio broadcasts of games, also broadened the team's fan base throughout the farm belt. The Cardinals increased both production (players) and consumption (fans) in the process, as other teams later did in their expanded markets.

In earlier years, each Minor League team had scouted and signed players in its local area, developed them through its league competition, and sold the top players to the highest Major League bidder. As other teams implemented the Cardinals' farm system approach, MLB imposed a neocolonial dominance over the Minor Leagues, and although relations are now more collaborative as a result of soft power strategies that are mutually beneficial, MLB still exerts critical controls over the Minors. Rickey's "exploitative process," which he later used in the Caribbean, included "the use of non-binding agreements, which he called 'desk contracts,'" reports Samuel O. Regalado. This name applied because the scout kept the signed player contract in his desk and usually did not give the recruit a copy. In rural America and especially in the Caribbean, some recruits could not have read the contracts anyway. Scouts consequently could often keep players from referring to contractual provisions or even deny that contracts existed. Rickey's scouts signed numerous prospects on a conditional basis for a modest (or sometimes no) bonus, thereby taking them off the market yet incurring minimal financial risk in the event of subsequent poor performance.

Rickey referred to his approach as the "quality out of quantity" principle. While only relatively few of the recruited players would become Major Leaguers, this low-cost wholesale signing strategy substantially increased the probability that the better Major Leaguers would come from his pool. His initial scouting criterion was player speed, a nearly natural skill that he used as a proxy for athletic ability in an untrained talent pool. Having tested it successfully in the farmlands, he then applied it to African American and later Latin American players.[28]

Unofficial but closely controlled segregation remained intact in professional baseball until after World War II as part of MLB's unwritten but rigid racist policy. A few players of color, however, usually Native Americans and Cubans, played in the Majors during that period. Although often ridiculed, the Native Americans were a notable exception to the color rule, perhaps because there were few initially, such as Athletics Hall of Fame pitcher Albert "Chief" Bender, and they all but disappeared by 1920. Both the early and the later players, such as Pepper "Wild Horse of the Osage" Martin in the 1930s and Allie "Superchief" Reynolds in the 1940s and 1950s, usually had mixed blood and were light-skinned. As with much of U.S. society, organized baseball's racial attitude was dominantly chromatic: light skin was acceptable, dark skin was not.

THE COLOR BARRIER

Rob Ruck reaches the same conclusion for Latinos: "The crucial factor in controlling the entry of Cubans and other Latin Americans to the major leagues was skin color."[29] The first Latin professional player in the United States was Esteban Enrique "Steve" Bellán, a light-skinned Cuban who played for the Troy Haymakers and New York Mutuals of the National Association from 1871 to 1873. The first Latino to play in the current Major Leagues was Louis R. Castro, another light-skinned Cuban, who briefly appeared with the Philadelphia Athletics in the American League in 1902.[30] Hall of Famer Ted Williams was half Mexican, but his eligibility was never questioned throughout a Major League career that spanned four decades (1939–60) because he was light-skinned and had an Anglo surname and perhaps because he was among the best pure hitters in MLB history.[31] Unsubstantiated rumors had earlier circulated that Babe Ruth was black and perhaps were dismissed for similar reasons.

Since the black-white prejudice was stronger, light-skinned African American players often attempted to pass as Latinos to gain entry to the white leagues and even to market themselves more attractively as independent barnstormers. One of the most popular barnstorming teams of the first half of the twentieth century was the Cuban Giants, which had considerably more African American than Cuban players. The black players would often chatter in gibberish on the field to feign Spanish and maintain their ruse.

Relegated to their own teams and leagues, African American (and African Caribbean) players developed a strong market following not only through their barnstorming tours but also through the formalized Negro Leagues in the 1930s and 1940s. When playing against white Major League barnstormers during the off-season, the African American teams more than held their own through the efforts of such stars as Satchel Paige, Josh Gibson, James "Cool Papa" Bell and other notables, many of whom were elected to the MLB Hall of Fame beginning in 1971, when former Negro Leaguers achieved eligibility. Even though most of these teams were black-owned, they usually had to rent playing space from white Major and Minor League stadium owners, who extracted a substantial share of the gate, thereby maintaining white capitalist hard power leverage over the black game as well.

Toward the end of World War II, changing governmental attitudes toward African Americans, who had served their country admirably in the conflict, pressured baseball owners to sign black players. When Landis died in 1944, an opportunity arose to reconsider integration, but the owners shared Landis's bias and continued to resist. While overtly responding to New York state and local government pressure by setting up a committee to study the issue, the dominant owners maintained their collusive segregationist position by slowing the committee process and never producing a report. Club owners voted fifteen to one (Rickey dissenting for the Dodgers) to maintain segregation in 1946.

At the same time, the prospect of rising labor costs affected baseball as it did the rest of the postwar economy. With some government support, returning servicemen, including players, demanded their old jobs back at higher pay. Since the Majors had continued to operate during the war, albeit with lower fan revenues and profits, it had an oversupply of players, which hampered efforts to achieve quick profits. To comply with government job-guarantee provisions, MLB developed a skill test trial that resulted in jobs for only three hundred of one thousand returning Major and Minor League players. Nevertheless, payroll costs still rose about 60 percent from 1945 to 1946, spurred not only by higher-priced veterans replacing wartime players but also by a Mexican baseball league recruiting effort that gave returning veterans negotiating leverage. Pent-up demand spiked attendance, however, providing owners with higher revenues to prevail against the Mexican raid. Profits doubled despite salary increases.[32]

This episode exemplifies what Immanuel Wallerstein calls "the essential contradiction of capitalism."[33] He observes the tension between capitalists' desire to maximize profits and membership in a class that cannot make money unless members of society share in the benefits. Players as well as owners benefited, but the seeds of labor unrest in the "proletarian" players group had been sown, reinforced by extensive national union activity supporting returning veterans in other industries. Although a concerted effort to unionize players failed, it forced management to respond to some demands, including institution of a pension plan and creation of player representatives, who became the organizational basis two decades later for what has become one of the strongest U.S. unions.

Sensing that the time for MLB integration was approaching because of changing wartime sentiment, Rickey said, "The very first thing I did when I came to Brooklyn in late 1942 was to investigate the approval of ownership for a Negro player." He said that he had earlier concluded that such could not have occurred in St. Louis because of its "stony soil"—a southern segregation-based environment.[34] As usual, he was quick to provide a rationale that would both justify his actions and provide appealing copy for the writers. The moralist Rickey claimed to have been motivated by an incident that occurred in 1903, when he coached the Ohio Wesleyan ball team, which included Charles Thomas, a black first baseman. When the team was in South Bend, Indiana, to play Notre Dame, a hotel manager denied Thomas a room. Having earlier overcome a University of Kentucky refusal to play against Thomas, Rickey argued with the manager but was permitted only to house Thomas in his room. A dejected Thomas responded by rubbing his skin, trying to wipe off the black color. Rickey claimed to have had a "recurrent vision" of Thomas's reaction.[35]

Having persuaded a Dodger trustee to proceed, Rickey devised a six-step plan to find and sign a black player:

1. gain backing of Dodger directors and stockholders;
2. pick an African American who would be the right man on the field;
3. pick an African American who would be the right man off the field;
4. get a good reaction from the press and the public;
5. secure backing from African American leaders;
6. facilitate acceptance by teammates.[36]

By forming a Brooklyn Brown Dodger team in the new black United States League in 1945, Rickey gave himself public license to scout black players as well as to criticize the established Negro American and National Leagues.[37]

On August 28, 1945, Rickey signed Jackie Robinson, a college-educated, World War II veteran army officer and current Negro League player, to a professional player contract.[38] Two months before Robinson's Brooklyn debut, Rickey met with local black leaders as part of his plan and pleaded for calm rather than overtly celebratory support for the player, using the slogan, "Don't spoil Jackie's chances." On April 15, 1947, Robinson became the first publicly known African American to play in the Major Leagues since the 1880s. His distinguished ten-year career resulted in his election to baseball's Hall of Fame in 1962, his first year of eligibility.

His on- and off-field conduct both stimulated and facilitated racial integration, albeit gradual and uneven, throughout baseball, other sports, and society in general despite continued white resistance. The signing "equated the Dodgers with American pluralist democracy," according to Peter Rutkoff, making Robinson "a standard by which Americans reflect on the issues of race and class, of equity and fairness that have informed and deviled this society from its inception."[39]

Although boxing had been integrated for most of the century and African Americans had already entered professional football and basketball, Rickey's signing of Robinson became not only a major cultural breakthrough for baseball and other sports but also a very visible impetus for racial integration throughout the United States. It preceded *Brown v. Board of Education* by nine years and the most important civil rights act of the twentieth century by almost two decades. Anthony R. Pratranis and Marlene E. Turner analyze the Robinson integration within the context of affirmative action, which they define as "the proactive removal of discriminatory barriers and the promotion of institutions leading to integration of in- and out-groups." Identifying nine principles associated with Robinson's integration, they call it "the first, largely successful, affirmative action program in human history."[40] Jules Tygiel calls it "a blueprint for liberal dreams of racial equality in post World War II America."[41] But MLB and the rest of society were slow to follow that blueprint.

Despite the success of Robinson, a dark-skinned African American, baseball's chromatic attitude persisted. "Skin color remained the key element in hiring decisions until long after World War II," concludes James D. Cockroft.[42] The final MLB team to integrate its roster was the Boston Red Sox in 1959, but many teams seemed to operate on a tacit quota system that restricted the number of black roster players through the 1960s. Because of continuing owner/commissioner racial bias, Robinson was unable to secure a job in MLB after his retirement as a player. From his new position as a corporate executive, he criticized MLB for its continuing racial discrimination: "Baseball, like some other sports, poses as a sacred institution dedicated to the public good, but it is actually a big, selfish business with a ruthlessness that many big businesses would never think of displaying."[43] In his final public appearance at the 1972 World Series, he again chastised MLB for not hiring and developing black on- and off-field management.

Today, however, baseball is the most racially diverse sport in the country, with African Americans, Latinos, and Asians combining to constitute approximately half of the combined Major and Minor League rosters. Early development of that diverse profile, however, stemmed from MLB's profit-oriented neocolonial strategies, not from a perceived duty to provide societal leadership in integration and assimilation. MLB continues to promote the significance of that hard power action through soft power attractions. On the fiftieth anniversary of Robinson's entry, MLB officially retired his uniform number, 42, so that it could no longer be used by any player. (Active players were permitted to use that number for the remainder of their careers.) In 2004, MLB decreed that April 15, the date of his debut, would be celebrated at games each year as Jackie Robinson Day.[44] Each year, some players, coaches, and managers wear 42 on that day in Robinson's honor. The entrance to the Mets' new stadium, Citi Field, features the Robinson Rotunda, in tribute to Jackie and to the Brooklyn Dodgers' Ebbets Field, which also had an entrance rotunda.

In 1999, MLB honored Hall of Famer Hank Aaron on the twenty-fifth anniversary of his breaking Ruth's career home run record by establishing an award to be presented annually to the best offensive player in each league, on par with the annual Most Valuable Player and Cy Young awards. As a generalized recognition of African American integration each year since 2007, two MLB teams have played a spring exhibition game to benefit the Martin Luther King Museum in Memphis.

African American player participation in MLB peaked at 27 percent of rosters in 1975, but its current 8 percent level substantially lags those in professional basketball and football, in which blacks constitute a majority of players.[45] The 2005 World Series roster of the NL champion Houston Astros contained no African Americans, the first time a team's World Series roster had lacked an African American since the 1953 New York Yankees. While blacks have modestly penetrated the glass ceiling of on- and off-field management, *Black Enterprise* counts only five MLB-affiliated persons in its 2005 list of the fifty most powerful African Americans in sports.[46]

While applauded for his morally courageous move to integrate MLB, Rickey was foremost a shrewd capitalist, as Burk observes: "Having identified blacks as the untapped source of first-rate, inexpensive playing talent, he had concluded that they could secure pennants and profits for his long-struggling franchise while also killing off the gate rivalry posed by the Negro Leagues." Rickey had an attendance bonus in his contract.[47] Developed as a resistance-retaliation response to segregation, the Negro Leagues had put their own stamp on the game through emphasis on entertainment complemented by barnstorming tours, including playing against teams of white Major Leaguers in the off-season, and featuring innovations such as night baseball that MLB later adopted. These initiatives reinforced Tedlow's fifth proposition: new entrants develop new strategies. However, the Negro Leagues could not compete financially or emotionally with the white Majors for black talent. Black baseball fans switched their allegiance to MLB as its teams added black players, thereby eroding the market for the Negro Leagues, which folded during the 1950s. Racial integration first benefited the Dodgers and later other teams on both the production and consumption sides, as had the farm system earlier.

Rickey's racial recruiting strategy was one of the many baseball practices that can be linked to hard power neocolonial capitalism. He did not compensate the Negro League teams when he signed Robinson, Roy Campanella, and Don Newcombe, whereas Bill Veeck, the Cleveland Indians owner who signed the first American League black, Larry Doby, and other executives provided such compensation.[48] By signing Robinson, Rickey began a process that appropriated cheap labor (from the U.S. internal colony of African Americans), destroyed the counterpart industry (the Negro Leagues), and sold the finished product (team games) back to them as consumers (black fans). Rickey's strategy approximates a twentieth-century modification of the imperialist/colonial "triangular trade" that had brought African slaves to the Americas two centuries earlier. In his minority opinion related to the Supreme Court's *Flood v. Kuhn* (1972) decision, Justice Thurgood Marshall criticized MLB's maintenance of "virtual slavery" in its treatment of African Americans.[49]

HARD POWER DISCRIMINATION

Even after MLB's color barrier was surmounted, racial prejudice remained present in signing bonuses and salaries. By 1961, sixteen years after Robinson signed (for a $3,500 bonus), seventy-two MLB players had been signed for bonuses of $20,000 or more, but only three of those players were not white. Robinson, who led the Dodgers to six pennants in ten years, had a top salary of only $42,000, less than half what his white peers were earning.[50] Bruce K. Johnson's study of Major League salaries in the 1980s suggests that a player's salary depended on the racial composition of the team. Developing a "coworker discrimination model" that reflects George Lipsitz's thesis of the "possessive investment in whiteness," Johnson concludes that white players required a salary premium to team up with minorities.[51]

In Balibar's terms, this is another form of "internal racism." This dynamic is also consistent with David Roediger's observation that white workers attempt to differentiate themselves from black workers to demonstrate superiority.[52] It also suggests that racism in baseball has not simply been a Marxian class issue driven by the owners. MLB players reflected the black-white prejudice of the times despite the integration of the game. Called a mirror of society by many observers, baseball displayed general societal attitudes toward race.

Owners took financial advantage of minorities' limited bargaining power before the emergence of the union. For minorities, baseball nevertheless represented a quantum leap in socioeconomic status from poverty or near-poverty levels. "Ethnic minorities have sought through sports, which requires only particular athletic skills, what they could not attain elsewhere because of education and language difficulties," observes Gerald W. Scully.[53] This leveraged situation reinforced the conventional neocolonial capitalist rationalization, cited by C. L. R. James and others, that both the dominant Self and the subordinate Other benefit, thereby refuting the contention of exploitation.

Racism extended beyond the literal paycheck at that time. Scully and later Phillip M. Hoose document racial stereotyping by player position in baseball.[54] African Americans became outfielders and later first basemen, while Latinos became middle infielders and later catchers. Only recently did many members of either group become pitchers. For example, by 1965, African Americans comprised half of Major League outfielders but only 16 percent of infielders and 9 percent of pitchers. In a study correlating positional segregation with performance between 1961 and 1990, Eric Eide and Daraius Irani conclude that "the overall quality of major league baseball may be improved by reducing positional segregation."[55] There are indications of more balanced integration in recent years, particularly among pitchers.

The implicit financial hierarchy of positions not only relegated minorities to lower salaries but also reduced or delayed their post-playing-career opportunities to become managers, who typically had been infielders (other than first basemen) and catchers. Coaches came from the same group plus pitchers. By 1962, seventeen years after Robinson's signing, the big leagues had no minority managers and only one minority coach.[56] The first African American Major League manager was Hall of Fame outfielder Frank Robinson (no relation to Jackie Robinson), who took over the Cleveland Indians in 1975, thirty years after Jackie Robinson's signing and three years after his death. The 2005 World Series champion Chicago White Sox had a black general manager (Ken Williams) and a Venezuelan field manager (Ozzie Guillén).

The opening of the Majors to African Americans had a negative reactionary effect on the Minors because of their disproportionately larger concentration in the southern United States, which had no Major League teams at the time. That area of the country aggressively resisted any societal integration during the late 1940s and 1950s, so many Minor League teams refused to take African American players or to allow visiting teams to field black players. In 1957, for example, a Louisiana sports segregation law, passed the prior year, enabled the all-white Shreveport Sports of the Texas League to keep opposing teams from fielding any black players at games in Shreveport. As perhaps just retribution, the team finished last and folded after the season.[57]

Elsewhere, Major League teams withdrew support, and Minor League teams and leagues disbanded. By the end of 1964, an estimated 320 communities had lost teams since the Minors' heyday of the 1940s. Although other factors, including prior overexpansion, the emergence of alternative entertainment outlets, the development of college baseball programs, and the addition of MLB teams in some of these markets, contributed to that reduction, integration of the Majors was also significant. This southern segregation position indirectly reflected the resistance that is an inherent binary in neocolonial oppression. Integration also indirectly contributed to the relocation and expansion of Major League teams. Noting that integration created new problems that reflected continuing intolerance in northern cities such as Philadelphia, Christopher Threston concludes, "There's no doubt that the racial chasm between black and white forced removal of the Athletics and the relocation of the Phillies to a less threatening part of the city."[58] Boston and St. Louis, other cities known for racial polarization, also relocated teams in the early 1950s. While Philadelphia, Boston, and St. Louis each retained one team, it is likely that bigoted white fan response was a factor in the departure of the second team.

CARIBBEAN EXPLOITATION

As a harbinger of the forthcoming Caribbean "invasion," Clark Griffith, the longtime owner of the Washington Senators, began using Rickey's "quality out of quantity" scouting and contract approach to sign players in Cuba during the 1930s. "Caribbean baseball's headwaters were in Cuba," stemming from its early exposure to the game through U.S. sailors in the mid–nineteenth century. In yet another challenge to the claim that baseball originated in the United States, however, Bjarkman asserts that the sport has its primary roots in Latin America as a derivative of *batos*, played by the Sihoney Indians of Cuba, and a game played by Puerto Rico's Caguana Indians before Columbus's arrival, although no evidence links those activities with the development of the modern game.[59] Baseball in the Caribbean originated with Nemesio Guillo, who returned from Alabama's Spring Hill College to Cuba in 1864 with a bat and a ball.[60] Nevertheless, the U.S. military introduction, indicative of a colonial initiative, started formal implementation of the game in Cuba, from whence it spread throughout the Caribbean.

As a young Cincinnati Reds executive in 1911, Griffith had signed two light-skinned Cuban players, Armando Marsans and Rafael Almeida, to play in the Majors. After moving to the Senators and facing depression-related financial pressure to lower costs, he reflected on that early experience and dispatched an aide, Joe Cambria, to Cuba as a permanent scout in 1934. Over the next twenty-five years, "Papa Joe," who became popular enough in the country to have a cigar named after him and imperialistic enough to be called an "ivory hunter" by Washington columnist Bob Considine, signed four hundred players to unilateral desk contracts, using a "sign them then scout them" approach. This hard power strategy proved particularly helpful to the Senators during World War II, when many U.S.-born Major League players served in the military. The historically poor Senators finished second in the American League in 1943 and 1945.[61]

The white U.S. public differentiated between Cubans and African Americans, but not necessarily in a totally positive way. "To be Latin was to be a curiosity, a person somehow less repugnant to the racist mind yet stripped of all legitimacy as a man and player," note Marcos Bréton and José Luis Villegas.[62] When Rickey began his search for an African American to integrate baseball, a leading prospect on his list was Silvio Garcia, a legendary Afro-Cuban infielder. Rickey apparently concluded that the language and cultural barriers would have further complicated the task, but he may also have been influenced by Garcia's advanced age and/or tendency to drink excessively and emote angrily. Nevertheless, the wartime infusion of Cubans not only helped prepare for Robinson's debut but also stimulated broader interest in Latin America as a player resource. Robinson, in turn, further facilitated Latino player entry.

After he left the Dodgers in 1951 to become head of the Pittsburgh Pirates, Rickey adopted and improved on Griffith's Caribbean strategy. Rickey had been impressed with Puerto Rican outfielder Roberto Clemente, a future Hall of Famer who was then a Dodger prospect, and secured him for Pittsburgh. Betting that there was more Caribbean talent to be recruited, Rickey designated a valued assistant, Howard Haak, as Pittsburgh's scout in the area. Unlike Cambria, who never left Cuba, Haak traveled extensively throughout the Caribbean, principally in Puerto Rico, Panama, and the Dominican Republic, for almost fifty years. Haak "truly open[ed] up Latin America to the big leagues," concludes Bjarkman. "An unreconstructed Rickey man," Haak ran Latin American tryout camps at which he would sift "through six hundred players in one day by using a sixty-yard dash as a strainer."[63] Following the "quality out of quantity" principle, he signed hundreds of players to desk contracts.

The Caribbean became the source of choice for the beginning globalization of the game. According to Bjarkman,

> The Latin baseball invasion is unlike all earlier ones in substance and impact. Here for the first time it is truly "foreigners" taking the field as replacement players for the indigenous Iowa or Arkansas farmboys and California and Connecticut phenoms. There are no longer the nativized sons of past-generation immigrants, Americanized converts who by inheriting our native game thus shed the last vestiges of ties with their parents' Old World culture. The stakes here have been altered drastically. This is true internationalization at work on the ballfield and no longer simply the homogenizing force of a rampant (and for some, healthy) Americanization.[64]

Caribbean scouting became increasingly important financially to the Major League teams as they competed aggressively, if not stupidly, with each other to sign U.S. amateur prospects during the 1950s and early 1960s, a war that culminated with the Los Angeles Angels' payment of a then-astronomical $205,000 bonus to collegiate star Rick Reichardt in 1964. In an effort to curtail escalating competitive bonus payments, MLB instituted an annual amateur draft the following year. But the draft has been limited to U.S. (including Puerto Rico) and Canadian players, thereby enabling teams to continue signing other Latin American players independently and cheaply. This draft exclusion proved financially beneficial for the imperialist teams because they soon found that they still had to pay significant bonuses to sign drafted U.S. players to prevent them from going (back to) college and reentering the draft a year later.

MLB's most overt example of Balibar's "external racism," or xenophobia, has occurred in Latin America. "The Latin has always been big-league baseball's cheap labor, its migrant worker, the boy who starts as an infant with a cardboard glove, reaches baseball maturity early, and would gladly play for free," declares Hoose in his study of race in sports. In 1984, the average U.S. draftee received a sixty-thousand-dollar bonus as a result of the competitive elements in the MLB amateur draft. Since foreign players (except Canadians) were not (and still are not) allowed to participate in the draft, the average bonus paid to a Latin amateur signed in 1984 was only five hundred dollars.[65] Despite significant subsequent escalations in Latino bonuses, they did not exceed 1984 U.S. levels for nearly a quarter century, although the pace of increase has quickened in recent years.

The average Latino prospect bonus in 2007 was $65,821, double the 2004 Latino average and thirty times what the Oakland A's paid future AL Most

Valuable Player Miguel Tejada when he signed in 1993. In 1999, Willy Mo Pena received a record $2.44 million to sign with the New York Yankees, a record that stood until 2008, when the A's gave sixteen-year-old Dominican pitcher Michel Ynoa $4.25 million, raising owner concerns about further general and top prospect escalation.

During the 1998 international signing period (July-August), MLB clubs inked ninety-seven non-Cuban Latinos to bonuses of at least $100,000, for a total of $42,239,500. The higher bonuses, which have increasingly tempted middlemen to skim or negotiate larger portions of payments, prompted MLB and subsequently FBI investigations and have resulted in the firing or resignation of personnel from several MLB teams. Washington Nationals special assistant José Rijo was fired and general manager Jim Bowden resigned as a consequence of skimming allegations and the revelation that the recipient of the highest bonus they bestowed, sixteen-year-old Esmailyn Gonzalez, who was signed in 2006, was actually Carlos David Alvarez Lugo, who was four years older.[66] This deceptive practice is an extension of the maneuvering done by some local *buscones* (seekers) in the Caribbean for years.

These illicit practices, which include age deception as well as bonus skimming, reactivated discussion of an international draft or inclusion of Caribbean talent in the U.S. amateur draft. While MLB has sporadically discussed an expanded draft since the 1980s, the continuing opportunity to secure Caribbean talent relatively inexpensively has precluded any changes. Further, drafting Caribbean players would require adjusting or eliminating the individual team academy approach. With escalating bonuses, the overall financial leverage has lessened, while low-revenue teams are concerned that they are being priced out of the market.[67]

With historical hard power financial leverage, which has lessened considerably over the years because of increased team competition for Latin talent and increased pursuit from other sports for U.S. talent, it is not surprising that Latin Americans now account for about 40 percent of the combined Major and Minor League player rosters. But the Latin road to the majors has been difficult. In his 1970s study of the largest Latino group of baseball players, those from the Dominican Republic, Allen M. Klein notes that only about 3 percent of Dodger recruits from the Dominican make it to the Majors. He concludes that such a high rate of failure cannot simply be attributed to inferior skills and that Latinos "continue to face subtle cultural and organizational impediments to pursuit of their dreams," including language difficulties, loneliness, quick tempers, visa problems, team changes, and local fan antipathy. Major League organizations have been quick to penalize players for behavioral issues that are culturally based.⁶⁸ With the increasing costs of signing and developing Latinos, however, MLB teams have invested more in cultural acclimation of players through academies and Minor League affiliates to increase the probability of success.

By differentiating between its recruiting of white American and Caribbean players, MLB has explicitly illustrated a class-based approach to race, just as the league did with early African American players' compensation. Edna Bonacich observes, "As capitalism develops, the price of labor-power tends to rise, leading capital to seek cheaper labor-power . . . abroad." In her analytical context, baseball owners followed an imperialist practice of "super-exploitation" of racial minorities that is rooted in Western European colonial capitalism.⁶⁹ A conventional business example of Bonacich's thesis is the production of baseballs in Costa Rica for MLB. Seeking cheap labor, Rawlings Sporting Goods, MLB's licensed contractor, manufactures all its baseballs in that country. The average worker receives about thirty cents for each hand-sewn, 108-stitch ball, but it sells for more than fifty times that amount in the United States. The factory imports the rubber core, cowhide cover, and stitching yarn from the United States but takes advantage of the local, cheap, and painstaking labor as well as a free trade zone (no taxes) from the Costa Rican government.⁷⁰

With the player split-labor approach, MLB owners created a financial surplus that could be used to pay more to the U.S. players, thereby exacerbating the racial bias. Bonacich concludes that such an approach, which could be practiced at home as well as abroad, "helps to stabilize the system by keeping the working class fragmented and disorganized." In its history, MLB first engaged in this process modestly with the few Native American players, then extensively implemented it through the rural farm system desk contracts and subsequently through lower pay for African American players, and finally expanded it abroad. This split-labor market nevertheless creates apprehension among privileged white U.S.-born players that they might ultimately lose their jobs to the lower-paid minority players. U.S. players therefore tend to resist this exploitative approach, but the owners have prevailed at the prospect level because the MLBPA has had no control over players until they reach the Majors.

After Fidel Castro, an avid baseball fan and player, gained control of Cuba in 1959, its political relationship with the United States precluded it from remaining a continuing source of exportable baseball labor talent. It perennially fields a strong Olympic team, which has won a majority of the games' gold medals and is a frequent winner in other international competitions. Some Cuban players have defected and made it to the Majors, recently receiving large bonuses. Ironically, Castro, at the time a young pitcher, tried out at least twice for Cambria, who told the future Cuban leader that he lacked a Major League arm.⁷¹ With the

Cuban market closing, the Major League scouts quickly expanded their activity on other islands. Some Cubans still reach the Majors, but their route is dangerous and circuitous. They typically seek asylum in another country, often during a foreign tournament, then emigrate to the United States. With that significant constraint, the Dominican Republic emerged as the new center of Caribbean baseball and the current principal neocolonial resource for U.S. baseball.

DOMINICAN REPUBLIC

The history of Dominican baseball is tied to the sugar industry, which began on the island in the late nineteenth century when Cuban immigrants brought baseball with them. It quickly became the recreation of choice for the sugar industry workers. Baseball offered an escape from the hard, oppressive jobs in the cane fields or the refineries. Sugar capitalists exploited this soft power attraction and developed teams and leagues to engender worker compliance and popular citizen support. Calling baseball a "filter" through which cultural, societal, and political influences pass, Klein observes, "Caribbean baseball is rooted in colonialism." As with other colonial encounters, the juxtaposition of the superior Self (oppressor) and the inferior Other (oppressed) manifests itself: "The political and economic domination of the game had an ideological consequence: the passing on of the belief that culture in general and baseball in particular was better in the United States than in the Dominican Republic."[72]

Such a predominantly hard power approach distorted the soft power attraction of baseball and later provoked resistance. MLB benefited from the aggregate American hard power base established by its military/political leadership and its sugar capitalists. In *Culture and Imperialism*, Edward Said writes, "The twinning of power and legitimacy, one force obtaining in the world of direct domination, the other in the cultural sphere, is a characteristic of classical imperial hegemony."[73] Colonialism and imperialism, with their racial implications, are interwoven with the hegemonic history of baseball.

Already exploited economically and politically by the United States, the Dominican Republic was ripe for baseball's intrusion. The country's low socioeconomic development, reinforced by American capitalists' efforts to keep labor costs low, made the baseball dream a desirable alternative for local boys. According to Bréton and Villegas, "Latins have always been attractive to major league scouts because they could be signed for less than American players, providing cheap labor like so many other Latin immigrants in other walks of life." MLB could thus use the familiar rejoinder of American neocolonial multinational corporations: baseball presents a positive alternative to indigenous jobs. MLB uses the soft power allure of both a baseball career and an escape to the United States as incentives. In colonial tradition, MLB also leverages the long-standing American political connection with the "colony" to facilitate exploitation of the Dominican players. "The Dominican Republic is in many ways a classic case of underdevelopment," concludes Klein in assessing the country's internal struggles, corruption, and socioeconomic hardships.[74]

Although not a baseball fan (unlike his brother), the country's longtime dictator, Rafael Leonidas Trujillo Molina, placed in charge of the country when the American military left in 1924, saw value in supporting the game for hegemonic reasons at home and abroad. Prior to his 1961 assassination, he lured Negro League stars including Satchel Paige to the island to build popular appeal. When U.S. president Franklin Roosevelt said of Trujillo, "He may have been a bastard, but at least he's our bastard,"[75] he encapsulated the U.S. dominance of the Dominican Republic. A national baseball league was established there in 1951. MLB formalized a working relationship with the league in 1955, crystallizing what would become classic imperialist dominance that continued with the compliant support of Trujillo's successors. The following year, Ozzie Virgil, who had earlier moved to the Bronx, became the first Dominican to play in the U.S. Majors, and Felipe Alou became the first island Dominican signed by a Major League team.

With that formal relationship in place, the scouting frenzy began in earnest, increasing further when Castro secured Cuba in 1959. U.S. scouts, who locally acquired the racist label "black-catchers,"[76] exploited the desk contract tradition, often signing players without bonuses. In those early days, Dominican players had no agents to represent (and protect) them. U.S. scouts engaged in fiercely competitive and deceptive practices to secure talent, and the government permitted the activity to appease its northern neighbor. Given the large number of signees and small number of potential Major League slots, Dominican baseball recruiting mirrored the probability of lotteries, but candidates willingly played because of their abject poverty.

As the market grew, MLB teams co-opted locals in the recruiting and development process. A long-established national hero as a result of his MLB accomplishments, Hall of Famer Juan Marichal has been a *comprador* (buyer) in his role as scout for the Oakland A's. Some three thousand *buscones* now sign young local boys, train them, and then peddle them to MLB teams when they reach the eligibility age of sixteen. In return, the *buscones* receive a high percentage of their protégés' signing bonuses, which have escalated in recent years.[77] In his analysis of Latin American baseball, John Krich calls the Dominican Republic "a pimpocracy."[78]

By the mid-1970s, U.S. Major League players had formed a union, retained agents, and negotiated favorable individual and minimum salaries and working conditions. Through these forms of resistance, neocolonialism was working to the detriment of the exploiter at home. The Marxian concept of bourgeoisie-proletariat "contradiction" had emerged.[79] Domination (MLB) had created a dynamic negation (MLBPA), which achieved balance with domination in 1976 when the union was able to eliminate the reserve clause from player contracts.

In its place came free agency, under which any player with six years of service in the Majors had the opportunity to sign with any team, and "final-offer arbitration," which any player with more than two years of service the option of having an impartial arbiter choose between his and management's salary proposals. As a result of those salary-negotiation changes, the average MLB player salary grew from $52,300 in 1976 to $146,500 in 1980, as owners sought to prevent players from opting for free agency or final-offer arbitration. Management-labor negotiation history has subsequently given labor the edge, as evidenced by the continuing climb in Major League salaries, which now average more than $2,000,000. Owners have contributed to the escalation through often irrational competitive bidding, sometimes goaded by agents. MLB's growing revenue base has also enabled this dramatic salary increase.

The changing owner-player relationship has resulted in increased owner emphasis on neocolonial recruiting of foreign talent, a process formalized through Major League teams' creation of Dominican baseball academies. Klein observes, "The academy is the baseball counterpart of the colonial outpost, the physical embodiment overseas of the parent franchise." Similar to a local subsidiary of a dominant foreign company, the academy secures the raw materials (athletes), refines (trains) them, and ships the products (players) abroad for finishing (minors) and market (fan) consumption. As in neocolonial industrial models, the baseball raw materials are cheap, plentiful, and pliant. Like neocolonial factories, the academies achieve economies of scale at low operating cost in their mass-production process. In 1981, the Philadelphia Phillies estimated that they spent $355,000 to develop an American player and only $25,000 to develop a Latin player.[80] Therefore, the financial leverage generated by baseball imperialists in Caribbean recruiting and development was immense.

The Toronto Blue Jays established the first baseball academy in 1977. After other teams followed, the Dominican academy became "as recognizable a mark of foreign domination as a sugar mill." Supplied with recruits scouted for their potential, the academies offer Dominican teenagers a rigorous thirty-day baseball skills trial; those who pass receive two-year contracts. During the contract period, recruits live at the academy so that teams can protect their investments from outside poaching. The Dominicans develop their baseball talent, improve their nutritional intake, learn some English, and acculturate partially to U.S. practices, all with the objective of migrating to the U.S. Minor Leagues by the end of the contract period and from there to the Majors. Reflecting Rickey's "quality out of quantity" reality, even into the 1990s, about 95 percent of foreign players were released before making it to the Majors, thereby reflecting the split-labor market system model.[81]

This development process recalls the acculturation process of the European colonizers. Ozay Mehmet observes, "Education has been the principal vehicle for transmitting the Eurocentric worldview of distorted images of reality."[82] As "an institution rooted in the increased presence and benevolent paternalism of North American baseball interests in the country," the academy reinforced the superiority of the U.S. way to a captive and compliant audience. Like other U.S. interests in the Third World, MLB promotes "inferiority and subordination in the face of powerful foreigners," concludes Klein. The U.S. government also imposes immigration restrictions on foreign players seeking to play at the Major or Minor League level. This practice correlates with U.S. immigrant labor history: immigrant workers are alternately lured (or forced) and shunned by changing immigration policies that fluctuate with imperialist cheap labor needs. Post-9/11 national security actions have tightened those restrictions, thereby limiting the number of foreign players in the Minor League development process, another example of imperialist protectionism. Despite that restriction, almost 30 percent of the players on Major League forty-man rosters are foreign-born (including 12 percent from the Dominican Republic), a figure that rises to nearly 50 percent for Minor Leaguers.[83] Given the specific immigration restrictions on players, some prospects are coming to this country before signing on with a team. As residents, they then can participate in the U.S. amateur draft.

Those Latin academy players who migrated to the U.S. Minor League affiliates but failed to reach the Majors and were released demonstrate the adverse effects of baseball's imperialist exploitation. "For the losers with Spanish surnames, defeat means they will be punched a one-way ticket home, their visas—the ones ensuring a legal stay in the United States—will be voided immediately, and they will have to face the prospect of returning home a failure," observe Brèton and Villegas. The rejected Dominican players often go to New York City and join its poverty-stricken Dominican community, now numbering a half million, as illegal aliens, but "by staying in the United States, they [have] essentially traded one misery for another."[84]

RESISTANCE

According to Klein, the academies have "fundamentally undermined the long-standing sovereignty of Dominican baseball." The game, which the Dominicans have fervently embraced as their national sport for more than a century, has become infused with a unique, flashy style, locally called *béisbol romántico*. The formalized amateur and professional leagues, imbued with nationalistic pride, have been Americanized, however, to fit the prescribed needs of the neocolonialist employer. Like other neocolonies, the Dominican Republic has an ambivalent, approach/avoidance reaction toward the United States. While the Dominicans give "the appearance of complete accommodation to the United States," notes Klein, "American hegemony is not complete.... Hegemony and resistance coexist in an unstable, dynamic tension."[85]

In citing the general power/resistance binary, Leela Gandhi observes that "the psychological resistance to colonialism begins with the onset of colonialism."[86] As baseball became a source of socioeconomic opportunity for young Dominican boys, it also created a field of resistance where they could assert nationalistic pride. Bréton and Villegas believe that "in the Dominican, baseball symbolized the American occupation," linking it historically with U.S. dominance, including the 1916–24 military occupation.[87] Just as Dominican players tried to defeat U.S. soldiers on the diamond in those days, current Dominicans assert their baseball prowess. As former Major Leaguer Manny Mota claims, the Dominican Republic "doesn't have much, but we know we are the best in the world at one thing"—baseball.[88]

MLB dominates the sport through its academies, its Dominican summer league, its working relationships with Dominican winter league teams, its collusive relationship with local government, and MLB teams' restrictions on Dominican players' winter league participation. Dominican players, fans, and sportswriters, however, continue to insist that the sport be played according to Dominican tradition, style, and rhythm—that is, as *béisbol romántico*. Klein likens this resistance to bricolage, the placing of objects in a new context, as conceived by Claude Lévi-Strauss. It is also a variation on Tedlow's new entrant proposition: new strategies. Klein further asserts that Dominican sportswriters are especially influential in this resistance activity. They lavishly applaud Dominican player accomplishments as well as overall baseball achievement in the United States. At the same time, they sharply criticize the inequalities between Major League teams and their Dominican affiliates and strongly object to the pressure that Major League teams exert on their Dominican players to reduce or eliminate their playing time in the Dominican winter league. These pointed reactions are reminiscent of what Gandhi calls "interpretive autonomy and acumen" in her reading of Indian responses to English texts.[89] As in that geopolitical example, Caribbean acceptance of the imposed norm is only partial.

Arturo Marcano and David J. Fidler contend that MLB, operating as a quasi-nation, is, through scouting practices and the academies, guilty of international human rights and labor standards infractions in the Caribbean. MLB is jeopardizing the rights of children under the United Nations Convention on the Rights of the Child. It is violating the standards of the International Labor Organization in its treatment of young Caribbean athletes. While those rights and standards technically pertain to nations, not private organizations, Marcano and Fidler assert that baseball's practices violate some comparable national laws and that as a responsible international organization, baseball should adhere to those promulgated rights and standards.[90] These assertions are comparable to the complaints of neocolonialism levied against American multinational corporations such as Nike.

Some of the problems have occurred because of rampant misstatement of ages (usually reductions) by the players. A survey conducted by *Baseball America* in the spring of 2002 revealed than more than sixty Caribbean major leaguers had earlier misstated their age, only to be corrected by increased U.S. security checks in the wake of the 9/11 attacks. Players, parents, advisers, and clubs were all potentially culpable, depending on the situation.[91] The combination of increased U.S. government security measures and a stronger local MLB presence has significantly reduced the scope of that problem.

Dominican laws and regulations govern the conduct of scouts and the academies. Marcano and Fidler observe, however, that neocolonial-style collusion prevails, so those laws and regulations tend not even to be implemented, let alone enforced. MLB teams use hard power economic threats of divestment as leverage, as the World Bank and International Monetary Fund do in underdeveloped countries, while rationalizing that the boys are better off in "boot camps" (academies) than in their former lives. Marcano and Fidler further accuse American baseball imperialists of "ethical myopia" in unreasonably promoting the soft power rags-to-riches myth for individual players while failing to contribute hard power economic benefits to the general population. In practicing "systematic and intentional discrimination based on economic status" in the relative handling of U.S. and Caribbean players, Major League teams affirm that it is acceptable to treat poor children worse than affluent youth. And again, the correlation between class and race is strong.

Asserting that MLB teams "behave as if Latino children are commodities," Marcano and Fidler contend that parents receive no respect in the signing and training process. Agents who might act in the best interests of athletes and their families are shunned. General childhood education is sacrificed to facilitate baseball training regimens that are more onerous than work permitted by labor laws for children. MLB, they conclude, should be as accountable for human rights as multinational corporations are.[92]

Agreeing with these observations, Angel Vargas, head of the Venezuelan baseball players association, suggests some remedies:

1. MLB should sanction individual teams for misbehavior and assume an active role in their policing.
2. Local countries should implement better laws and regulations.
3. The MLBPA should stand up for Latin players in cross-border solidarity.
4. MLB's Latin stars should speak out and use their influence on their clubs and countries.[93]

Said offers a cautionary note of optimism in observing the impact of resistance: "At its best, the culture of opposition and resistance suggests a theoretical alternative and a practical method for reconceiving human experience in non-imperialist terms."[94] Soft power collaboration initiatives provide those theoretical and practical alternatives. In his critique of Third World economic development history, Arturo Escobar argues for a hybrid modernity of continuous renovation, multiple group involvement, local heterogeneity, and preservation of the traditional with introduction of the modern. He defends cultural difference as a transformative force, similar to Trinh T. Minh-ha's hyphenated condition. Escobar also argues for a valorization of economic needs and opportunities that are not strictly profit- and market-oriented.[95]

The overall history of oppressive (neo)colonialism and resistant nationalism has generally been negative, if not disastrous, for all involved parties. MLB is clearly the dominant "nation-state" in its Caribbean relationships, so it could learn from history that continued neocolonial imperialism only begets more resistant nationalism. It also could use multinational corporate experience as positive and negative guides for achieving global effectiveness. Although they do not address the baseball situation, Said and Escobar advocate alternatives that involve reinvention, cooperation, and respect for local conditions within an international framework. For the general and specific critics, a successful model would likely include a self-governing federation equitably representing the participating countries, soft power cooperative relationships with the various local governments, processes such as the U.S.-Japanese player movement at the national level, and broad economic participation and support by national leagues in other countries.

END OF NEOCOLONIALISM

Indications of positive maturation, if not a conclusion, of MLB's neocolonial history surfaced during the 1998 season. Baseball was slowly recovering from the adverse effects of the 1994–95 strike, but two 1998 events dramatically restored its popularity and demonstrated its mythical attraction: Cal Ripken Jr.'s surpassing Lou Gehrig's streak of 2,130 consecutive game appearances and, more importantly, Mark McGwire and Sammy Sosa's assailing the single-season home run record, the most revered mark in a game that is replete with records. That number had been etched in baseball lore by Babe Ruth's 60-homer season in 1927 and had stood until another Yankee right fielder, Roger Maris, hit 61 in 1961. St. Louis Cardinal first baseman McGwire, a white thirty-four-year-old Bunyanesque Californian, had positioned himself as a contender the prior year by hitting 58 homers, raising his career total to 387. Chicago Cub right fielder Sosa, a twenty-nine-year-old African Dominican, had hit only 207 in his career and never more than 40 in a season. Suggesting a national and racial bias, a *USA Today* poll conducted during the season indicated that 79 percent of Americans wanted McGwire to break the record, while only 16 percent favored Sosa. *Washington Post* writers Marc Fisher and John Jeter concluded that the contest "illuminates the American dilemma of race."[96]

During their competition, however, both players continuously demonstrated respect, admiration, and obvious friendship toward each other. When McGwire broke the record with a home run against Chicago, Sosa trotted in from the outfield to hug the rival he called "the Man" as he rounded the bases. McGwire established a new season record of 70, while Sosa finished with 66. McGwire reinforced his regard for Sosa a few months later when he contributed one hundred thousand dollars to the foundation Sosa established to help Dominican victims of Hurricane Georges.[97]

Sosa's response to the media's persistent racial focus, which continued even after the season, was, "Come on, man. It's 1998."[98] Sports historian Benjamin Rader sees the 1998 home run competition as good for baseball and the United States. He observes that the contest between the white U.S. native and the black Caribbean-born player "nicely represents the demographic transformation of this country. Sosa represents our society's increasing ethnic diversity, and McGwire represents the well-known tradition."[99] The episode also illustrated a soft power attraction that positively balanced the mythical and the real in MLB, which has continued to promote its player diversity in its imagined community.

Three years later, Barry Bonds, an African American left fielder for the San Francisco Giants, broke McGwire's record by hitting 73 home runs. Sosa hit 64 and McGwire only 29 in the injury-plagued final year of his career; no one seriously challenged Bonds. The quest lacked the hype and fan appeal of 1998, prompting renewal of racial assertions because no white player was involved. Jules Tygiel, who has extensively studied racism in baseball history, concludes that the relative lack of fanfare associated with Bonds's assault on the record was primarily motivated not by race but by a depressed economy and the 9/11 tragedy, which occurred near the end of the season. The lack of a competitive challenge, the short interval (three years) since 1998, and Bonds's lack of rapport with the media also contributed to the relative lack of fan interest.

Meanwhile, MLB was undertaking domestic and international soft power initiatives to mitigate its hard power neocolonial reputation. From a Fan Fest first developed for the All-Star Game celebration, MLB launched a touring Baseball Festival in 1997 and has since sent the promotion to Europe, Asia, Australia, and most extensively Latin America. Designed to explain the game in a fun, interactive outdoor setting, the festival is typically held in conjunction with local games to bridge any cultural gap. Its youth focus encourages participation in games of skill and chance that provide baseball-related prizes.[100] MLB used the 2001 All-Star Game, hosted by the Seattle Mariners, whose Japanese ownership makes them the only MLB team not controlled by a U.S.-based entity, to emphasize the international dimension of the game by highlighting the participating players' national origins and the game's growing worldwide appeal. The ceremonial first pitch baseball toured the world prior to the game. Starting with a March exhibition series between the Houston Astros and Cleveland Indians in Venezuela, the ball traveled to Mexico, Puerto Rico, Japan, South Korea, Taiwan, Australia, England, South Africa, Germany, the Czech Republic, and the Netherlands before completing the 43,894-mile journey to Seattle in July.[101]

To assure ongoing organizational support to the Caribbean, MLB established a branch office, headed by former Pittsburgh Pirates pitcher Rafael Perez, in the Dominican Republic in 2000. The MLB office facilitates cooperation between its clubs and the area's countries and asserts more control over the recruiting and development processes. Specifically, the office supports MLB clubs in logistics, administration, and legal and business issues in the Caribbean; makes sure the clubs comply with MLB rules; and helps promote the game throughout Latin America.[102] This international business initiative suggests that MLB recognizes the need to curtail individual clubs' historical neocolonial tendencies. The office is making progress in fulfilling its missions.

In a further effort to curry favor with the growing Latino market, MLB launched a promotion in the summer of 2005 to select a twelve-player Latino Legends Team and announced the results during the World Series. The team's creation was an overt albeit belated response to the absence of a Latino player on the thirty-man All-Century Team selected in 1999. The promotion did not utilize Latino baseball and marketing experts, however, resulting in some questionable nominees for the ballot and an inadequate voting process. Ballots were available only on the Internet, which Latinos used less than other population segments, and at sponsoring Chevrolet dealerships, not at ballparks or in Latino media or venues.[103] The experience suggests that MLB has more to learn in conducting culturally sensitive activities.

In 2006, the National Baseball Hall of Fame and Museum and the CITGO petroleum company began a five-year salute to Latino baseball, Baseball! Béisbol! The effort included two traveling exhibits, a forum commemorating Hall of Famer Roberto Clemente, and an exchange program to develop relationships with various Latin American national hall of fame curators.[104] A private initiative that honors Latino baseball provided MLB an example of cultural sensitivity. To give more recognition for Latino players, Gabriel "Tito" Avila created the Hispanic Heritage Baseball Museum in 1999 as a traveling exhibition in California's San Francisco Bay area. Aided by private sponsors, including the San Francisco Giants and the Oakland Athletics, the museum entered a permanent home near the Giants' AT&T Park after an exhibition at the World Baseball Classic finals in March 2006.[105]

In the African American internal colony, MLB implemented a Revitalizing Baseball in Inner Cities program, founded by scout John Young in 1989 with funding from the Los Angeles Dodgers and MLB, to provide soft power attraction and development for underprivileged (primarily black) urban youth. The program has since expanded to more than two hundred cities worldwide and added softball leagues for girls. The capstone of the program was the 2006 opening of a ten-million-dollar facility in Compton, California, to house MLB's Urban Youth Academy, which not only teaches on-field skills but also provides guidance and education that could lead to nonplayer jobs in the Major and Minor Leagues and in adjacent areas such as journalism.[106]

The Compton facility, initially derided as showcase tokenism by critics, is the blueprint for planned new academies to be built in Philadelphia; Miami; Washington, D.C.; Houston; and New Orleans. A growing number of Compton graduates are becoming early-round amateur draft selections, but the academy plan has done little to date to encourage preteen involvement in baseball. The older youth program, however, continues to expand. In February 2008, Compton hosted an Urban Invitational competition in which the University of Southern California and the University of California at Los Angeles hosted traditional black colleges Southern and Bethune-Cookman. The event exposed Compton kids to collegiate play and offered specific guidance in college admission and baseball scholarship pursuit. In July 2008, the academy hosted a four-day Breakthrough Series, cosponsored by MLB and USA Baseball, for sixty urban high school baseball prospects from around the country. The event, attended by scouts from all MLB teams, provided instructional clinics and educational seminars.[107] MLB, like other publicly exposed institutions, will likely continue to receive criticism for its race-related shortcomings, but it has demonstrated that it is working to facilitate the unbiased meritocracy for which it stands.

Initiated by a $250,000 grant from MLB in 2000, the Hall of Fame completed a five-year research project on Negro baseball from 1860 to 1960. As a byproduct of this historical research, a special committee elected seventeen new members from the Negro Leagues and prior era to the Hall in 2006, bringing the pre-MLB Negro-baseball-related total to thirty-five. Notable among these electees was Effa Manley, a white co-owner of the Newark Eagles, who became the Hall's first female member.[108]

Incorporation of some minorities in top management positions, albeit decades after Jackie Robinson's criticism, should increase MLB's sensitivity with regard to racial matters. MLB now has two minority executive vice presidents, Jimmie Lee Solomon in baseball operations and Jonathan Mariner as chief financial officer. Bob Watson, a former team general manager and player who was an MLB vice president, has now become leader of USA Baseball. Ulice Payne of the Milwaukee Brewers became the first minority team president in 2002. And MLB currently has four minority general managers: Kenny Williams of the Chicago White Sox, Omar Minaya of the New York Mets, Tony Reagins of the Los Angeles Angels of Anaheim, and Ruben Amaro of the Philadelphia Phillies.[109] Two of these men work for owners, Chicago's Jerry Reinsdorf and New York's Fred Wilpon, who were born in Brooklyn and were children when Robinson was signed. "Brooklyn has always been ahead of its time," quips Solomon, who criticizes the slowness and unevenness of team minority management hiring.

In 2009, minorities held nine of the thirty field manager positions. Since Williams was hired in 2000, only three other minorities—Minaya, who was hired by both the Expos and the Mets, Reagins, and Amaro—have become general managers. MLB teams are gradually adding minority hires in feeder positions, but the slow progress toward MLB's stated objective of minorities in high-level offices is only one reflection of the commissioner's lack of control over team owners.[110] That control problem has permitted some clubs to continue to exercise racial bias.

MLB also has a Latino owner, Arturo Moreno, who purchased the Anaheim Angels from the Walt Disney Company for $184 million in 2003 and renamed them the Los Angeles Angels of Anaheim to broaden their market identity. A fourth-generation Mexican American, Moreno parlayed his family print shop and Spanish newspaper business into a fortune in outdoor advertising and was a minority partner in the Arizona Diamondbacks prior to purchasing the Angels. He immediately cut ticket and concession prices and shelled out $146 million in long-term contracts for free agent Dominicans Vladimir Guerrero and Bartolo Colón as a means of broadening fan appeal and competing with the market-dominant Dodgers, with their significant Latino following. Venezuelan Francisco Rodriguez, an Angel recruit, set an MLB season record for saves in 2008 before signing a lucrative contract to join the New York Mets. Since drawing 2.2 million in their 2002 world championship year, the Angels' attendance has consistently topped the 3 million mark, although those numbers still lag those posted by the Dodgers. The Angels also are among the top teams in season ticket sales and have dominated the American League West.[111]

Even without minority general or field manager, the Angels' strategy suggests that individual teams increasingly recognize the value of Latinos on the consumption as well as the production side and are doing so in a businesslike rather than a neocolonial manner. The Mets, who also play in a market with a significant Latino population, notably Puerto Rican and Dominican, have Minaya, MLB's only Latino general manager. He has accelerated the focus on the Latino player and consumer markets. In 2001, the Mets appointed a former Dominican shortstop, Rafael Bournigal, director of international scouting to upgrade Caribbean recruiting. In 2004, the team signed defected Cuban and resident Dominican righthander Alay Soler to a three-year $2.8 million contract, stimulating escalation in Latino recruit compensation. Subsequently, in addition to Rodriguez, the Mets have added big-name stars Pedro Martinez (Dominican Republic), Johan Santana (Venezuela), Carlos Delgado (Puerto Rico), and Carlos Beltran (Puerto Rico) as well as several lesser-known Latino players and players from Japan and South Korea as part of an effort to appeal to the multiethnic New York market. Minaya refers to this approach as "a global development plan."[112]

Befitting MLB's racial history, fans and media have criticized Minaya's moves as "Latinizing the Mets." MLB general managers quickly rallied to his defense: according to the New York Yankees' Brian Cashman, "We're required to put the best team on the field, and we're going to be judged on those decisions." Says Minaya, "The sad thing about it is, in 2006, we're talking about issues of race in sports, and there are people who not only keep stats on baseball, but keep stats on race."[113] As a meritocratic system replaces racism in MLB, vestiges of the possessive investment in whiteness remain in the larger community.

While continuing to resist significant subjugation to an external governor, MLB has made progress in the half-century since Robinson's entry, coming closer to providing financial parity and managerial opportunity for people of all races and nationalities at the Major League level. Responding to criticisms and suggestions, MLB is implementing some hard and soft power suggestions to improve conditions for the entities that feed the majors.

HOME PLATE

BASEBALL AS A GLOBAL BUSINESS: BALANCING POWER

Entertainment—not autos, not steel, not financial services—
is fast becoming the driving wheel of the new world economy.
—MICHAEL J. WOLF

This chapter concludes the progressive synthesis of baseball, viewed through MLB, as sport, domestic monopoly, neocolonial power, and global business. Each of those elements is an important part of MLB and is represented in the World Baseball Classic (WBC), an international showcase competition initiated by MLB and MLBPA in 2006 and cosponsored by league organizations of the fifteen other participating countries. A complementary event and emerging counterpoint to the WBC was the Summer Olympics, which terminated baseball participation after the 2008 Beijing games. These events provide insight into MLB's opportunities and challenges in the global arenas. The WBC's continuing success and expansion and the resumption of Olympic baseball are critical factors for MLB's global business success. Discussion of the WBC and the Olympics follows an analysis of MLB's international strategic and operational activity.

GLOBALIZATION

Recent actions by both MLB and individual teams suggest an organizational shift from a neocolonial to a multinational and multiracial business strategy in a global economy. Joseph S. Nye Jr. defines globalization as "the growth of networks of worldwide interdependence." American studies scholar Michael Denning notes that the term *globalization* was first used in 1961 and first included in a book title in 1988. He asserts that the concept, marked by the opening of the Berlin Wall in 1989, redefines modernity and signals the end of the three separate historical culture "worlds"—capitalism, communism, and decolonizing—that were the post–World War II international influences. In Denning's view, the nation-state no longer is the central actor in the new consumption world that features global flows of commodities and communication.[1] As both U.S. and MLB international experiences indicate, however, nationalism seems to be a significant resistant response to globalization, as it has been to neocolonialism.

Walter LaFeber observes that the U.S. multinational corporation (MNC) first emerged in the late nineteenth century to dominate the world market in such commodities as oil (Standard Oil), film (Eastman Kodak), and sewing machines (Singer). Modern MNCs differ from their predecessors in at least five respects: they produce abroad rather than at home, they trade in knowledge and innovation rather than natural resources or industrial products, they depend increasingly on world markets for profit, they require massive advertising to sell product, and they are less accountable to the U.S. government. Nevertheless, modern MNCs follow earlier corporations' lead in seeking to develop foreign revenues well in excess of their domestic business.[2]

While MLB is increasing its international focus, it does not fully conform to that description of a modern MNC. For the foreseeable future, MLB's domestic business will far outweigh its foreign activity despite relative growth abroad. Its products (MLB players and games) are still produced primarily at home, although its global production objective is to secure more potential MLB players abroad and promote international competition. While baseball could be considered an innovation in some foreign countries, it is an old, traditional game that lacks the technological cachet of many MNC products. While MLB's overall profit is just becoming influenced by its growing international revenues, they remain small compared to the domestic portion. As with other consumer businesses in the world entertainment economy, baseball does and will require significant advertising and celebrity endorsement to sell the game. Therefore, the emergence of foreign superstars such as Ichiro Suzuki of Japan or Chien-Ming Wang of Taiwan will be critical to global success. A country's interest in baseball receives significant impetus if a native succeeds in MLB, a process that reinforces Michael J. Wolf's thesis regarding celebrity currency.

MLB's accountability to the U.S. government is unique because of the sport's monopoly status, but as the steroid issue has indicated, government can play a significant role if it chooses to do so. Therefore, MLB is not yet an MNC but is simply trying to develop a fledgling international business. Rather than aspiring to become a typical MNC, MLB seeks to become a smart power leader in developing and influencing an increasing network of national affiliations and games to increase its profitability and appeal. Through media development and player exchanges, MLB seeks to market itself as an international brand.

Some observers contend that globalization of sport, like other cultural forms, initially tends to produce an essentialized homogenous culture. Lynn Hirschberg, an editor at large for the *New York Times Magazine*, observes that the globalization process simplifies stories for movies as U.S. producers seek to reach the widest possible audience. Because they now seek primarily a global rather than a domestic market, many U.S. movies rely more on action or fantasy than on nuances of language or parochial subtleties of comedy. Moviemakers take care in depicting villains or countries for fear of alienating audience segments. The net result, Hirschberg contends, is that U.S. movies have less influence on the art form while increasing audience and revenues.[3] Contradicting this assertion are the 2006 Oscar-nominated movies *Brokeback Mountain*, *Crash*, and *Munich* and the continuing growth of American independent films with messages that tend to refute that argument and influence the international markets. Richard S. Tedlow's market-segmentation proposition and the glocalization concept are viable strategies in movies as well as in MLB's global reach.

Writing in the *Guardian*, John Harris, a British critic of popular music, argues that globalization has also homogenized rock music. He asserts that cultural exchange, which should be part of a global market, has not worked effectively since the Beatles "invaded" America in the 1960s. The result is that American pop has become a hegemonic monolith that rebuffs the influences of European and African music.[4] Yet hip-hop, now more popular than pop or country, the traditional leading genres, reflects Latino and African influences that go beyond the streets of the urban United States. Likewise, after years of hegemonic imposition, U.S. baseball is assimilating Caribbean and Japanese variations of the sport.

McDonald's is often used to represent globalization of consumption because of its worldwide scope and its standardization of product and business practices. Malcolm Waters disagrees with the prevailing "McDonaldization" theory, which suggests that the consumer world is becoming homogenized. Rather, he contends, intrusion of companies such as McDonald's disrupts local homogeneity and replaces it with global diversity. That intrusion produces "flexible specialization" of production and consumption rather than standardization. Although McDonald's seeks to control consumers, it also recognizes that they are potentially autonomous. Respecting their resistant tendencies, the company adjusts to their various tastes in a competitive local market. Waters's globalization theory asserts that international culture is chaotic, not orderly; integrated and relativized, not unified or centralized.[5] Local modification appears to be a critical factor in acceptance of a foreign product, including baseball.

Noting that the "cultural turn" of the latter half of the twentieth century represents a sea change to a world market for cultural forms, Denning observes the growing resistant influence of cultural politics as cultural forms become mass commodities. Arguing for a new way of thinking about cultural forms, Denning contends that sport needs a new perspective. As examples, he cites C. L. R. James and his treatment of the resistant symbolic action of Caribbean cricket players and the feminist movement's enfranchisement of women as sports producers and consumers.[6] These scholarly observations also apply to MLB's experience in the Dominican Republic and elsewhere.

Using the concept of "sporting nationalism," which he links to political nationalism, Alan Bairner notes that globalization provokes national sport resilience. That reaction may be reinforced loyalty to the local sport or greater choice among the globalized sports. Through the glocalization process, a globalized sport outside its home country tends to acquire a national variation, such as *béisbol romántico* in the Dominican Republic. These resistances produce hybrid variations of the sport that the international promoter must respect. Once again, IBM's international strategy, "Think global, act local," proves effective. Bairner concludes, "Sport and globalization have become accomplices in a process whereby the importance of national identity has been ensured despite, or arguably because of, supernationalist tendencies." The Olympics and World Cup events reinforce the importance of nationalism in global sports.

According to Bairner, popular U.S. team sports do not lend themselves easily to international competition and consequently have not spread effectively without explicit organizational promotion. U.S. sports in general and baseball in particular have become a form of domestic "social glue," linked with indigenous mythology to strengthen national identity.[7] As the national pastime, represented by MLB, baseball has to be "sold" in an international business rather than neocolonial environment. A country's political opinion of the United States as a geopolitical entity influences baseball's acceptance in that country. The effectiveness of MLB's soft power attraction in a country depends on U.S. government smart power acceptance there. The waning of U.S. government acceptance presents a challenge to international promotion of its national pastime. Eric Pfanner points out that in certain areas where U.S. hard power foreign policy is not popular, U.S. consumer brands have suffered. William J. Holstein, editor in chief of *Chief Executive*, argues that anti-U.S. sentiment is not new and that it has been building at least since the fall of communism. European and Middle Eastern surveys currently reflect great antipathy toward the United States, though Barack Obama's election as U.S. president has reduced this hostility.[8]

In Iraq, the hard power military policy that resulted in the unilateral U.S. takeover of that country produced both a baseball opportunity and a hard power impediment. In fall of 2003, Ismael Khalil Ismael, a Baghdad shop owner, created what became the Iraqi Baseball and Softball Federation. The federation, which plays in the fall, when the heat subsides, now fields twenty-six men's baseball and fifteen women's softball teams. The National Olympic Committee of Iraq admitted the federation the following year and provides limited financial support. While MLB would likely provide equipment, training, and organizational support in keeping with its soft power international strategy, Ismael has been reluctant to seek help from U.S. sources because of fear of insurgent backlash. The constrained Iraqi baseball situation illustrates the negative effect of hard power geopolitics.[9]

Israel, a country generally friendly with the United States, attempted to develop professional baseball through a six-team Israel Professional League playing a forty-five-game season in 2007, with former MLB players Ron Blomberg, Ken Holtzman, and Art Shamsky managing three of the teams. While the initial rosters were composed primarily of foreign players, the objective was to develop native players. The league incurred substantial debt in its first season and suspended play for 2008. Interested parties are attempting to relaunch a stronger entry.[10]

The U.S. multinational corporations that best withstand political backlash, Holstein contends, use soft power emphasis on local connections and imagery. In a French consumer survey, for example, former U.S. president George W. Bush is considered "least cool," while Levi's jeans are considered the coolest fashion brand. French consumers of Levi's seem either to differentiate between the United States as a global power and such locally attractive U.S. products or to ignore their U.S. connection.[11] Some investment analysts see global brands as increasingly vulnerable to local brands or generic copiers. This vulnerability may stem from general political attitudes or consumer assertion of individuality or, more often, from competitors demonstrating better market sensitivity.

David J. Winters, chief investment officer of Franklin Mutual Advisers, concludes that global brands such as Coca-Cola and Gillette thrive by maintaining their signature characteristics while perpetually refreshing them to appeal to new customers and markets.[12] MLB's principal brand challenge comes from indigenous or previously imported and embraced sports. Since sports tend to be seasonal, a sport's success depends in part on its ability to dominate a season. Like professional soccer in the United States, MLB must contend with an already full sports seasonal calendar in other countries.

In this entertainment economy, "celebrity is the only universal currency." In sport, for example, a star such as Michael Jordan, "the greatest endorser of the 20th century," became a brand himself. Though Jordan never played basketball in China, Nike advertising enabled him to join the late prime minister Zhou Enlai as the greatest figures of the twentieth century according to a survey of Chinese youth. Wolf notes that 40 percent of the entertainment economy revenue stream comes from advertising, which activist Naomi Klein ironically labels an "extreme sport." LaFeber asserts that globalization is "paid for by advertising," which has blown "apart governmental regulation and geographical boundaries." In the battle between capital and culture in a multinational economy, "capital will ultimately win," he concludes.[13]

Advertising and celebrities are prevalent vehicles for soft power initiatives, but both run the risk of being negatively as well as positively received. MLB consciously attempts to showcase its star players from other countries as a way of building brand recognition and revenue in the players' homelands as well as in U.S. ethnic markets. The MLB steroid issue, however, illustrates the negative side of such celebrity-focused marketing.

In his study of early-twentieth-century business history, William Leach observes that the establishment of a capitalist/consumer conception of self still prevails a century later. This conception includes two myths: consumption is freedom and self-fulfillment, and the market is always expanding. Extending those myths, LaFeber sees two central themes of the globalization age: acquiring vast, fresh markets developed by capital, and amassing capital to create markets that absorb U.S. popular culture. MLB's strategy incorporates these two myths. Leach questions whether soft power approaches merely serve as covers for hard power imperialism. Ironically, he contends, U.S.-expanded capitalism in the chaotic global market undermines the order and stability that U.S. citizens love.[14] The disruptive globalization process creates additional risk. MLB appears to have mitigated somewhat its hard power practices in the Caribbean and has not repeated those tactics in more recent international initiatives. It is trying to market the pastoral myth in a glocalized manner.

Describing globalization as currently "America-centric," Nye observes that its influence is diminishing through the spread of technology and other forms of modernization as well as the emergence of national and local resistances and modifications. His view is akin to the popular "flat world" concept promulgated by *New York Times* columnist Thomas J. Friedman. Both Nye and Friedman caution the United States to use its superpower influence judicially lest it "squander ... soft power through a combination of arrogance and indifference"[15] that extends from hard power economic and military strength.

THE IOC AND IBAF

The Summer and Winter Olympics are the most significant global sporting events. Claiming origin in ancient Greece, the modern summer games began appropriately in Athens in 1896. The winter games started in 1924. Despite expansion to worldwide participation, the games' leadership body, the International Olympic Committee (IOC), has been dominated by Europeans throughout its history. With U.S.-European hard power relations reaching perhaps an all-time low, it follows that the IOC has not been supportive of the United States or of its national pastime.

Baseball's Olympic history dates to the 1912 Stockholm Games, when it appeared as an exhibition sport. When the IOC sanctioned the creation of a baseball governing body in 1936, the game appeared again in the Berlin Olympics that year. Two years later, the IOC established the International Baseball Federation (IBAF) to guide the development and expansion of the sport. After World War II, baseball returned as an exhibition sport to the 1952 Helsinki, 1956 Melbourne, and 1964 Tokyo Games. Responding to American pressure, the IOC elevated baseball to a demonstration sport for the 1984 Los Angeles and 1988 Seoul Games and to an official sport for Barcelona in 1992 and subsequent Olympics.

In 2005, however, it decided not to renew baseball's and softball's inclusion after the 2008 games. The stated reasons for baseball's removal included lack of U.S. control of drugs and MLB's refusal to allow its players to leave their teams in midseason, as the National Hockey League does for the Winter Games. The IOC also contended that the U.S. women were too dominant in softball, which had not spread sufficiently throughout the world. U.S. speculation on the reasons for the sports' demotion included the presence of substantial anti-U.S. sentiment on the European-dominated IOC. On February 9, 2006, the IOC reaffirmed its decision following appeals from the two sports, partially because of its conservative unwillingness to reverse a recent earlier position.[16] The 2008 Beijing Olympics was the swan song for baseball and women's softball until at least 2016. In the softball finale, Japan upset the perennially dominant U.S. women's team, which had won all previous gold medals in the sport. South Korea won its first baseball gold medal by defeating Cuba, while the United States won the bronze over Japan. Those results, reflecting how baseball talent has spread across the globe, offer further support for the reinstatement of the two sports. U.S. leadership in those sports, principally represented by USA Baseball but supported by MLB, continues to plead their cases for a 2016 readmission, with a decision due in November 2009. Approval would be more likely if Chicago or Tokyo, two of the leading applicants, were selected to host the 2016 games. Participation in the Olympics, the premier international sports event, remains critical for baseball's successful globalization.

The IBAF consists of 110 regular and 3 provisional member countries. Since 1994, the federation has been headquartered in Lausanne, Switzerland, the Olympic capital. It has organized three senior world tourneys: the biennial Baseball World Cup, the Olympics, and the Intercontinental Cup, an invitational tourney that debuted in 1975. The IBAF also sponsors a junior (maximum age eighteen) and youth (maximum age sixteen) world championship and launched the Women's World Baseball Cup in 2004. Since MLB has not participated in the men's events because of season conflicts, its relationship with the IBAF has been tenuous. With 113 participating countries, however, the IBAF "world" illustrates the scope of the potential international market for MLB, which worked closely with the IBAF to launch the WBC. In 2007, the IBAF elected Harvey Schiller, a former U.S. Air Force general, New York Yankee executive, and U.S. Olympic Committee executive director, to be its president. This move is helping MLB strengthen its international presence. Included in his challenges is reinstatement of baseball (and women's softball) as an Olympic sport for 2016.[17] With an improved drug policy, MLB would next face the hurdle of MLB players' availability, while women's softball needs to demonstrate geographically based skill growth.

IS CANADA "INTERNATIONAL"?

Baseball's "international" element has its roots at the beginning stages of the sport's "American" creation. Baseball's early development in North America included major cities not only of the northeastern United States but also of southern Ontario. The earliest Canadian accounts of ball playing are an April 13, 1803, diary reference by Ely Playter, a tavern owner in what is now Toronto, and an 1878 Belden Atlas notation that a game was played on July 13, 1803, to decide who would pay for dinner following a three-day conference. Both of these documents offer few details of the games played and may not refer to baseball.

The most famous early Canadian account involves a baseball-type game played in Beachville, Ontario, on June 4, 1838, seven years before the Knickerbocker rules were established. Dr. Adam Ford wrote the account in a May 5, 1886, letter while residing in Denver. Since he had been a seven-year-old boy when the game was played, his long-delayed account is distorted by the intervening years and seems unrealistically detailed, indicating some later research. Other reports exist of similar activity during the 1830s and 1840s, however.[18]

William Humber, a Canadian baseball historian, contends that Canadian baseball was a regional variation of the games developing in New York, New England, and Philadelphia during the first half of the nineteenth century. Therefore, he contends, Canadian baseball is the only international version that is not the product of U.S. imperialism. Elsewhere, baseball came with soldiers, sailors, educators, or missionaries who sought to spread the U.S. way of life to other countries. Indigenous development helped baseball to become the most popular game in southern Canada during the nineteenth century. Humber observes, however, that the widely publicized emergence of the game as the U.S. national pastime caused some resentment among nationalistic Canadians and a reduction in its local popularity.[19] MLB's ability to collaborate through soft power initiatives and the receiving country's willingness to accept and customize the game are key factors in the spread of the game.

Bairner asserts that baseball helped Canada as well as the United States counter the sporting hegemony of their former British colonizer. In Canada, baseball became more popular than cricket as a warm-weather team sport, becoming the country's most popular sport in the first two decades of the twentieth century.[20] Because of the nationalistic U.S. attitude, however, baseball may also have indirectly facilitated the emergence of hockey, probably a fast-paced derivative of the Irish game of curling, as Canada's national sport. The southern and westward farm system movement of U.S. baseball in the 1920s also lessened Canadian recruiting for and interest in the U.S. professional game. Canadian football, a derivative of the U.S. game, has become more popular than baseball, which never underwent a specifically Canadian modification, thereby lessening the country's "ownership" commitment.

After World War II, Canadian Minor League baseball boomed when the Canadian Amateur Athletic Union lost its hold on Canadian sports. One highlight was Jackie Robinson's professional baseball debut as a member of the Montreal Royals, the Dodgers' AAA team, in 1946. Branch Rickey was also responsible for hiring the first black manager in organized baseball when, as general manager of the Pittsburgh Pirates in 1951, he named Sam Bankhead to lead their Class C farm team in Farnham, Quebec.[21] Because of its more liberal attitude toward blacks, therefore, Canada facilitated racial integration in U.S. professional baseball.

Ironically, the advent of the MLB in Canada signaled a decline in Minor League baseball there, echoing the process in the southern and western United States in the 1950s and 1960s. MLB expanded to Canada in 1969 with the creation of the National League Montreal Expos; the American League Toronto Blue Jays followed in 1977. While the Toronto franchise has generally met with success, highlighted by back-to-back world championships in 1992–93, the Montreal team ultimately failed despite some good years in the early 1990s. MLB bought the struggling team, renamed the franchise the Nationals and relocated it to Washington, D.C., in 2004, and sold it.

Toronto's relative success results partly from the historical foundation laid by the game in Ontario during the nineteenth and early twentieth century, the close relationship of that area of Canada to the United States, and the strong local business support in establishing and maintaining the franchise. The original owners included Imperial Trust, Labatt Breweries, and the Canadian Imperial Bank of Commerce. These large corporations forged a strong albeit exploitative partnership with the provincial government to build the Sky Dome (subsequently renamed the Rogers Centre), a state-of-the-art domed stadium with a retractable roof, in 1989.[22] Given the substantial costs, collaboration between the public and private sectors is a common requisite for professional baseball success virtually everywhere. The share of public financing for MLB parks has dropped in recent years, reflecting increased public and government resistance to such funding.

In contrast, Montreal lacked both a strong historical involvement in the game and significant local corporate support. Quebec was less urbanized than Ontario and gravitated to other sports alternatives, particularly hockey. The province also lacked a large English-speaking middle class to provide fan support. The French influence included no cultural interest in baseball, as A. G. Spalding discovered during his 1889 tour stop in France. Further, the latter half of the twentieth century witnessed a strong political interest in French nationalism in the province and an accompanying distaste for the United States. With the absence of soft power support and the presence of hard power antipathy, the MLB team could not sustain itself.

The net result is that Canada remains a moderately positive participant in the game, but its role is as an adjunct to the United States, unlike other international participants, which have modified the game. Canada's ongoing professional participation beyond the Blue Jays is relatively modest. An eight-team Canadian Baseball League formed and folded in 2003. Ottawa's AAA team relocated to the United States in 2008, leaving Canada without a Minor League team and with only two teams in the independent Can-Am League. Canada has fielded a WBC team sprinkled with Canadian-born Major Leaguers. High school, college, and amateur programs still serve as a feeder to MLB through its annual draft. With the MLB Blue Jays and draft eligibility, Canada serves more as an extension of U.S. baseball than as a distinct international site.

MLB'S "WORLD"

With a quasi-international source in Canada and an already established nearby international influence in Latin America, MLB is achieving contrasting results in promoting the game in Europe and Asia.

As with many consumer exports, baseball's geographic expansion produces some nationalistic resistance in each country. Nevertheless, a generalized difference between European and Asian acceptance appears to exist. The greater Asian acceptance seems partially to result from both Europe's increasing general resistance to the United States and Asia's historically greater interest in U.S. cultural programs. Further, as a former colonizer of America, Europe seems less willing to accept a U.S. innovation such as baseball than does Asia, which has no history of dominance over America. Other sports are also more pervasive and entrenched in Europe, with its sporting tradition, than in Asian countries, some of which hardly promoted such activity because of educational or religious beliefs that eschewed sports participation.

Adding to that relative difference is the lack of a significant proximate country stimulus in Europe and a strong catalytic support from Japan in Asia. Like Cuba and later the Dominican Republic, Japan has served as an influential bridge to nearby country acceptance of the game. These "translator" countries have facilitated broader regional appeal. The translators culturally modify baseball in a way that more easily enables other countries in the region to accept the game as their own and add their local influences. All Caribbean countries, for example, play a version of the Dominican Republic's *béisbol romántico*. Rather than having a catalytic translator to encourage regional acceptance, European sports leadership—in particular, England and France—discourages other countries from accepting an outside sport in favor of regionally developed sports such as soccer.

Asia seems more accepting of external influence than Europe, which has only recently evolved from separate national to a consolidated regional hard power economic base, the European Community. That still controversial development of a meganation appears to reinforce earlier European consolidation of power in sports in its imagined community as Benedict Anderson defines it. With this expanded nationalism at the continental level, Europe has added another layer of exceptionalism to that which exists in various degrees in each country. That combination serves as a strong counterpoint to the historical exceptionalism demonstrated by the U.S. national pastime. Therefore, the failure of the geopolitically stronger United States to sell baseball to most of Europe is comparable to England's earlier failure to impose cricket on the United States. Both failures have hard power elements compounded by historical differences in perceived superiority. There may even be an element of resistant payback as the prior rejectee (Europe) rejects the prior rejector (the United States). Unlike other U.S. popular culture exports that have been accepted by individual European consumers, sports must also deal with the inherently conservative European and European-controlled sports organizations such as the international soccer governing body, FIFA, and the IOC.

ANGLO-EUROPEAN DEVELOPMENT

North American professional baseball had considered international expansion even before the National League was formed in 1876. Harry Wright, a former British cricketer and at the time owner of the Boston Red Stockings, the best professional team, sponsored a tour of his native England in 1874. He chose Albert Spalding, his star pitcher, to lead the tour, which failed to sway the English to consider baseball as a viable sport. England has yet to embrace the sport, but in the 1990s Ireland launched a modest initiative that is captured in a 2006 documentary film, *The Emerald Diamond*, that shows how baseball served as a sports buffer during the decade's Protestant-Catholic clashes in Northern Ireland. Aided by a development donation from Peter O'Malley, former Dodgers owner, and some recruited Irish-American college players, Ireland won a bronze medal in the 2004 European Championships. O'Malley also contributed funds for a state-of-the-art baseball field in Zimbabwe, continuing O'Malley's interest in globalizing baseball, which he had pursued with the Dodgers.[23]

Spalding undertook a second world tour, from October 1888 to April 1889, that paradoxically reflected both America's tendency toward exceptionalism and its growing desire to spread its culture abroad. Spalding saw the tour as an opportunity to demonstrate his evangelistic moral passion for the sport and his business acumen in promoting his sporting goods. Originally scheduled to visit only Australia, where the first recorded baseball game had occurred in Victoria in 1857, Spalding added stops in Ceylon, Egypt, Italy, France, and the British Isles on the way home, but only the Australian portion proved successful. Spalding asked colleague Harry Simpson to remain there to serve as Australia's "first baseball development officer," promoting the sport and Spalding products.[24] Simpson helped baseball to create a following as a winter game in the mild climate, while British-influenced cricket prevailed as the summer game. Such seasonal subdivision enabled baseball to be played on cricket grounds or soccer fields, and not until 1968, when the Claxton Shield amateur national baseball competition, begun in 1934 and the focal point of Australian baseball, was held in Brisbane, did the country create its first baseball-only grounds.

The 1956 Melbourne Olympics provided a stimulus to international baseball. Although only a demonstration sport, the Melbourne baseball competition significantly enhanced the sport's image in Australia. More than one hundred thousand spectators, the largest baseball crowd in history, watched the U.S.-Australia Olympic contest on December 1. The Australia Baseball Council emerged soon thereafter as the controlling body for the sport and spurred development of junior baseball clubs. In 1968, Australia joined the Baseball Federation of Asia. A Japanese team toured the country that year, and an Australian team toured the Philippines the following year and Japan and South Korea in 1971. In 1978, Australia participated for the first time in the World Baseball Championship, finishing ninth out of eleven teams. Reflecting the country's focus on the amateur game, the youth program continued to grow and now serves as a modest source of talent for MLB teams. An Australian youth team toured the United States in 1979, and the country hosted the World Youth Series in 1988.

Literally befitting Wolf's thesis of celebrity currency, Australian baseball received both an image and a financial boost in the 1990s from Dave Nilsson, a Queensland catcher signed by the Milwaukee Brewers in 1987. In 1999, Nilsson cut short his solid if unspectacular Major League career to return to Australia to prop up the failing International Baseball League of Australia. Although that league folded after 2002, it nevertheless enhanced club-level baseball as well as encouraged MLB interest in supporting the sport Down Under. In 2001, in cooperation with the Australia Sports Commission and the Australia Baseball Federation, MLB created the MLB Australian Academy Program on the Gold Coast. The program develops players under MLB control, much as the individual MLB team academies do in the Caribbean.[25] This soft power initiative is enabling Australia to reactivate professional baseball while developing talent for MLB.

With the additional stimulus of the 2000 Sydney Olympics and Australia's surprising silver-medal performance in the 2004 games, in which MLB permitted a dozen Australian Major and Minor Leaguers to play for their country, Australia continues to progress modestly as a baseball country, fielding teams in the WBC. Australian baseball remains alive 125 years after Spalding and Simpson hatched their vision for the sport, although the country seems to be lacking a strong indigenous cultural impetus to naturalize the sport. Australian sports reflect the legacy of British cricket, soccer, and rugby more than Canada does. The only significant hegemony/resistance sports modification in the country has been the development of Australian football, a local invention derived from soccer and rugby. There is no local version of baseball comparable to the Caribbean's *béisbol romántico*.

Despite baseball's European historical linkages, particularly with Great Britain, MLB has been even less successful than the National Football League and National Basketball Association in establishing its sport in Europe. Soccer clearly remains Europe's sport of choice and from that base has established itself as the premier international sport. Soccer's World Cup is second only to the Olympics in global sports appeal and participation. In an effort to capitalize on mutual brand recognition, the New York Yankees and the best-known European soccer team, Manchester United, now owned by American Malcolm Glazer, have developed a partnership. Tom Hicks, owner of the Texas Rangers, is now a joint owner of the Liverpool soccer team but has yet to cross-market the two enterprises.[26] MLB has conducted Baseball Festivals in Europe and in 2005 established an annual European Baseball Academy.[27] Because of tepid response, however, MLB has not yet set up All-Star tours or regular-season games in Europe, as it has in Latin America and Japan.

The competition at the 1992 Barcelona Olympics provided some general impetus for the sport on the continent. Italy and the Netherlands now have established professional leagues and are participating in the WBC. Russia represents a large, virtually untapped market that is a high priority for MLB. As in China, its other high-priority country, MLB is providing equipment, training, and promotions to build participant and fan foundations in Russia. MLB has expressed a willingness to retrofit soccer fields to accommodate baseball. In large part because of the Barcelona stimulus, Moscow now has some thirty teams of youth between the ages of eight and sixteen. In 2003, defending champion Russia hosted the European Juvenile Baseball Championship (ages ten to twelve), the first time the country had served as host in the half century history of the European Baseball Federation. MLB's soft power approach is beginning to show results.[28]

Italy and the Netherlands, both of which have positive geopolitical attitudes toward the United States, have Europe's best professional baseball leagues.

Baseball in Italy can be traced to Spalding's visit during the 1880s. The country now has an eight-team major league that plays a forty-two-game season as well as a relegation (minor) league. In 2008, San Marino won its first title. Italy participated in the first two WBCs, losing in the first round both times. The Netherlands, the only other European entry in the WBC, has a nine-team Dutch Major League that plays a forty-game season. Amsterdam won the 2008 title, its first since 1990. In 2007, Kinheim won the European Cup. The Dutch national team won the biennial European Championships for the fifth straight time. In 2006, the Dutch defeated Italy in the first European Series. In the 2009 WBC, the Netherlands upset and eliminated the Dominican Republic team before losing in the second round.

For the past century, a British version of baseball has survived in very limited form, confined essentially to Cardiff and Newport in Wales and Liverpool in England. Considered in the 1930s a potential threat to cricket as Britain's summer team sport, the game reflects the sorts of local modifications seen elsewhere. Although the game bears some similarity to cricket—flat bats, two innings in which all players bat, no foul area—it also seems to have been stimulated by the Irish version of rounders. The game has declined in popularity in recent years, but its centennial international (Wales-England) game took place in 2008.[29]

Founded in 2002 to offer MLB broadcasts in Europe, the North American Sports Network, now a subsidiary of ESPN, initially targeted U.S. expatriates. Expanding on its mission to attract European interest in American sports, the network now reaches ten million households in thirty-two countries, showing an increasing variety of U.S. and Canadian sporting events. At one point it showed Major League Soccer games but has ceased doing so because audiences preferred local games.[30] To increase its focus on Europe, MLB has opened an office in London. Guided by Schiller, the IBAF shifted its 2009 World Cup to seven European nations, with the finals held in Rome. It also plans to create a European professional league that will begin play in 2010.[31]

ASIA, BASEBALL'S INTERNATIONAL CENTER

While concepts such as globalization, smart power, and the flat world focus on pervasive geopolitical issues at government and megacorporate levels, they also hold lessons for MLB in its international pursuits. In the 1990s, MLB formulated and began implementing a global strategy designed to build its fan base as well as tap new talent sources. Having established a nearby international outlet in Latin America, it sought to expand an Asian presence beyond the Japanese foundation. Echoing its Latin American strategy and Dominican office, MLB opened an office in Japan to upgrade its focus on the Asian market.

In his history of baseball in Asia, Joseph Reaves observes, "Baseball is an important tool of cultural hegemony and a powerful weapon to fight that hegemony. It can promote acculturation and assimilation, or it can encourage defiance and self-assertion."[32] That comment applies particularly to the development of baseball in Japan but also pertains to China, the Philippines, South Korea, and Taiwan as well as Latin America. Missionaries, teachers, and military personnel served as baseball evangelists throughout Asia.

The 1853 arrival of Commodore Matthew Perry and the "Black Ships" opened Japan to the West. The Meiji Restoration, which began in 1867, strongly encouraged adoption of western practices. A few years later, Horace Wilson came from the United States to teach history at what is now Tokyo University. He also taught his students the fundamentals of baseball, but another U.S.-born teacher, Albert Bates, is credited with organizing Japan's first recorded game, which took place in 1873. Stimulated by university students, the game quickly achieved broader popularity in the country as a by-product of the growing Japanese desire to learn from the West.

In 1878, the Shinbashi Athletic Club Athletics became the first organized team through the efforts of Hiroshi Hiraoka, a railway engineer who had become an ardent Boston Red Stocking fan while studying in the United States. That same year, an English lecturer at Tokyo University, F. William Strange, recorded baseball rules in Japanese, and a visiting University of Wisconsin team defeated Keio University in the first Japanese-American game. In 1884, Albert Spalding, who did not include Japan on his 1888–89 world tour, sent equipment to replace the kendo (bamboo sword fencing) masks used by catchers and the cricket balls used for baseballs. He also sent his *Guide*, which further helped to standardize Japanese baseball rules.[33]

For the next half century, baseball's development in Japan was confined to the university and high school amateur levels, but they provided a solid foundation that became the basis for Japan's professional structure, created in the 1930s. Two national high school championship tournaments, one in the spring and one in the summer, are immensely popular and serve as showcases for potential professionals. International rivalry, a characteristic of the hegemony/resistance pattern, began around the turn of the twentieth century when Japanese school teams played U.S. club or military teams. Ichiko, the primary preparatory school for Tokyo University, swept a Yokohama club team filled with U.S. sailors in a three-game series in 1896. A 1905 poem, "Yakyû Buka," commemorated the victories in national militaristic terms. With that early resistant influence, Japan developed its own "small ball" version of the game, *yakyû*, which contrasts with *besubôru*, the U.S. power game. Also in 1905, a Waseda University team toured the United States, winning nine of twenty-six games against American university teams. In 1924, Waseda hosted the University of Chicago team and defeated it convincingly.[34]

U.S. professional tours of Japan started in 1908 and reached a peak in 1934 when Babe Ruth, playing in his last games in a Yankee uniform, hit fourteen home runs in a sixteen-game sweep of makeshift Japanese teams. (Another Yankee great, Joe DiMaggio, played his last professional games on a Japanese tour in 1951.) Ruth's tour underscored the impact of celebrities in promoting the game. Sponsored by the *Yomiuri Shinbun*, a leading Japanese newspaper, the tour launched professional baseball in Japan. Matsutaro Shoriki, head of the paper, soon formed a professional team that ultimately became the Tokyo Giants. They toured the United States in 1935, winning 93 of 102 games against semipro and Minor League teams. That success led the next year to the formation of a league with eight teams sponsored by various corporations.[35]

Suspended during World War II, Nippon Professional Baseball (NPB) reemerged and expanded to the current two-league, twelve-team structure. During the twentieth century, more than four hundred U.S. citizens played in the Japanese pro leagues. The total accumulated foreign participation now exceeds seven hundred, including players from countries other than the United States. Indicative of the ambivalent relationship between MLB and Japan, U.S. players' participation has strengthened Japanese baseball's attraction to and rivalry with its U.S. cousin. This participation has also created a pattern of U.S.-Asian player movement that has extended throughout the Pacific Rim. In the 1950s, the American players were Nisei Japanese; in the 1960s, they were Minor Leaguers; in the 1970s, Major League has-beens; in the 1980s, active Major Leaguers; and since the 1990s, U.S. Major Leaguers with varying issues, U.S. Minor Leaguers, and increasingly other foreigners.[36] NPB has become attractive for aspiring players from other Asian countries, sometimes as a bridge to MLB and sometimes as a culturally comfortable goal in itself. This trend is reinforcing Japan's position as the center of Asian baseball.

In 1984, when NPB was aggressively recruiting high-caliber foreigners, Warren Cromartie, a thirty-year-old Montreal Expo outfielder in midcareer, signed a three-year guaranteed contract with the Tokyo Giants. He played seven years in Japan, winning a batting title and an MVP award. His book, *Slugging It Out in Japan*, cowritten with Japanese baseball scholar Robert Whiting, provides insights on the similarities and differences between Japanese and American baseball. Cromartie overcame the cultural challenges through active participation in the Japanese system and excelled as a player, offering a sharp contrast to the many U.S. players who resisted and consequently failed on and off the field.[37]

As in the Caribbean winter leagues, U.S. participation provoked Japanese pride. While many more U.S. players in Japan have failed than have succeeded because of cultural, training, and on-field differences, the Japanese have not always welcomed U.S. players' success when it occurred. Most notably, the Japanese have responded negatively when U.S. players have challenged Sadaharu Oh's single-season NPB record of 55 home runs. Though his career total of 868 homers has remained beyond reach, his season record faced serious challenges from former MLB players in 1985 (Randy Bass), 2001 (Tuffy Rhodes), and 2002 (Alex Cabrera). Although the Taiwanese Oh is also a *gaijin* (foreigner) in Japan, his on-field prowess made him a hero in his adopted country. In all three years, he served as manager of the team facing the challenger to his record in the season finale. Bass entered the finale with 54 homers and was walked four times. Rhodes had already tied the record but saw only two strikes among the eighteen pitches thrown his way during the last game. And Cabrera, who also entered the final game with 55 home runs, was walked twice and hit by a pitch. Players later claimed that Oh had ordered his pitchers' evasive actions, although he has repeatedly denied such allegations. An object of xenophobia himself early in his career, Oh apparently practiced it against the Americans. In 2001 and 2002, however, Oh's actions did not receive support from the Japanese press, perhaps because Ichiro Suzuki had been so graciously received in the United States in 2001.

Until recently, the emigration of Japanese players to the United States lagged considerably behind the flow of players in the other direction. Masanori Murakami, a lefthander from the Nankai Hawks, pitched for the San Francisco Giants in 1964 and 1965, but the conditions of his arrangement became the subject of dispute between NPB and MLB, and Murakami then returned to Japan. In 1967, a United States–Japanese Player Contract Agreement was concluded, enabling movement under specifically limited conditions, but MLB teams did not sign another Japanese player until 1995, when the Dodgers reached an agreement with pitcher Hideo Nomo, who "retired" from the Kintetsu Buffaloes at age twenty-five to make himself available. The 1967 agreement had specified that retired players could return only to their former teams in the same country but did not specifically bar players from going to teams in other countries, a loophole that was closed soon after Nomo's departure.[38]

Nomo's signing and initial MLB performance—he made the All-Star Team and was named NL Rookie of the Year in 1995—indicated that good Japanese pitchers could succeed in MLB. Since then, a steadily growing number of Japanese players have come to MLB after becoming free agents under Japanese rules, and that door has opened under similar conditions to other Asian players—in particular, South Koreans and Taiwanese—as well. Nomo's enthusiastic reception in the Japanese and U.S. media contrasted sharply with the virtual absence of publicity associated with the Americans' quest for Oh's home run record. On both sides of the Pacific, "Nomomania" served as an early indicator of baseball's potential international appeal as well as further confirmation of the celebrity thesis. Twenty-four still photographers and fifteen television cameras attended Nomo's Dodger signing. Japanese fans took "Nomo vacations" to see him pitch in the United States. One Japanese radio station created the "Nomocast," broadcasting only the half innings that he pitched. Every game Nomo pitched was televised live in Japan, often on huge outdoor screens. The Dodgers opened a Japanese restaurant in their ballpark.

Sports and cultural critics offered various opinions on the implications of the Nomo phenomenon, seeing it as, among other things, an indication of receding Japanese exclusivity, an example of rising Japanese nationalism, confirmation of superior Japanese baseball technique, a demonstration of international goodwill, and a triumph of American meritocracy over Japanese tradition. These opinions underscore both countries' active ambivalence regarding each other and their games.[39] That dynamic tension has nevertheless strengthened baseball's attractiveness along the Pacific Rim. This tension resembles that in the Caribbean and seems to reflect the international experience.

The Japanese-U.S. baseball relationship climaxed with the Seattle Mariners' 2001 signing of Orix Blue Wave superstar Ichiro Suzuki (befitting celebrity status, he is called only by his first name in both Japan and the United States) and solidified with Hideki "Godzilla" Matsui's 2003 move from the Tokyo Giants to the New York Yankees. The Red Sox's 2007 signing and the subsequent success of Daisuke Matsuzaka affirmed that Japanese pitchers can succeed in MLB. Unlike Nomo, these players were established Japanese icons who shifted when they became eligible to do so under the player agreement.

Whereas the Caribbean features open and at times chaotic competition for players, Japan closely regulates MLB's recruiting in a businesslike manner. First, NPB conducts bidding in which MLB teams seek the signing rights to players who have either become free agents or conformed to the posting process. Winning teams must negotiate with the Japanese teams that hold players' rights before offering contracts to the players themselves. In Ichiro's case, for example, Seattle paid Orix $13.125 million for signing rights before giving him a three-year, $14 million contract. Ichiro, Matsui, and Matsuzaka have had tremendous success in MLB, and the cross-Pacific media attention has increased even further from the days of Nomomania.[40]

It is no coincidence that Ichiro, the first of this wave of Japanese superstar migrants, joined the Mariners, owned primarily by Hiroshi Yamauchi, president of Nintendo, a Japanese manufacturer of computer games. Nintendo purchased the team during a period of strained Japanese-U.S. trade relations and other tensions stirred by the commemoration of the fiftieth anniversary of the attack on Pearl Harbor. The shift in team ownership engendered controversy and accusations of racism, "economic miscegenation," treason, and political weakness.[41] To MLB's soft power credit and continuing benefit, the sale was quickly consummated, and the franchise has prospered, in part because of the area's strong Japanese American fan base. The Seattle experience exemplifies continuing American ambivalence toward Asia in general and Japan in particular.

Gary Okihiro observes that the United States has constructed negative ("yellow peril") and positive ("model minority") concepts to facilitate racially based continental or national summary understandings of Asian Americans. He sees those concepts as curiously connected: "Like those pliant and persistent constructions of Asian culture, the concepts of yellow peril and the model minority, although at apparent disjunction, form a seamless continuum. While the yellow peril threatens white supremacy, it also bolsters and gives coherence to a problematic construction: the idea of a uniting 'white' identity. Similarly, the model minority fortifies white dominance, or the status quo, but it also poses a challenge to the relationship of majority over minority."[42] The Japanese purchase of the Mariners rekindled short-lived thoughts of a yellow peril, while the signing of Ichiro reinforced the model minority concept.

As *béisbol romántico* helped MLB produce a modified, flashier game, so has *yakyû*, the Japanese version, provided MLB with a more balanced model. Like the Japanese teams, the world champion 2005 White Sox, 2006 Cardinals, the 2007 Red Sox, and the 2008 Phillies reflected a blend of pitching, speed, defense, and offense that has been lacking in recent years in MLB, when the home run has been overemphasized. The Japanese formally (and briefly) brought their style to the United States in 2005 when an all-Japanese-born team, the Samurai Bears, was entered in the newly formed independent Golden League. Managed by Cromartie, the team had no home field, playing all ninety of its games on the road. The league's cofounder, Amit Patel, had hoped to add similar teams from China, Taiwan, and South Korea, but Samurai folded and no other Asian teams emerged.[43]

Born also out of nationalistic resistance as well historical tradition, *bushido* (a code of player behavior based on the way of the samurai), emphasizes *wa* (team harmony) as well as loyalty, self-discipline, simplicity, modesty, and unquestioning obedience. A 1992 comparative cultural study of sport in Japan and the United States concluded that Japanese practice "democratic conformity," while Americans practice "reluctant conformity." Japanese players demonstrate control over their wills by moving toward consensus, while Americans focus on fulfillment of individual potential and responsibilities. Other Asian countries follow the Japanese model more closely than the American pattern.[44]

The Japanese code reflects a hegemony/resistance pattern. The Meiji Restoration initially emphasized, perhaps overly so, absorption of anything western to overcome Japan's centuries of isolation and to modernize as quickly as possible. As Japan experienced subsequent exploitation by the West, it sought to recapture its traditional values. Reflective of that sequence, the Japanese initially called baseball *besubôru*, a form of the U.S. term, but have since called it *yakyû*, an indigenous term, especially when resistance has spiked—late in the Meiji period and during World War II. Early in the twentieth century, Ichiko, the premier prep school feeder to Imperial University (now Tokyo University), developed the concept of *seishin yakyû* (spirit baseball), which essentially turned the game into a form of martial arts drawing on *bugei* (military training). In his memoir, Cromartie endorses the Japanese approach, although he objects to its obsessive degree, which leaves little room for the individual modification that Americans prefer.[45] He appreciates a blending of the cultural variations.

An effective blend of American and Japanese approaches bore fruit in Japan as the Chiba Lotte Marines won the Pacific League and Japan Series titles in 2005. Leading them was Bobby Valentine, a former MLB player and manager who had managed in Japan ten years earlier, spent several years at the helm of the New York Mets, and then returned to Japan with an American *besubôru*-style approach in 2004. The same year NPB introduced interleague play, following MLB's lead. NPB also created its first expansion team, the Tohoku Rakuten Golden Eagles, which filled the spot vacated by the merger of two Kobe area teams, the Osaka Kintetsu Buffaloes and Orix Blue Wave, into the Orix Buffaloes, as a result of financial problems.[46]

During 2007, four of the twelve NPB teams had turned to a *gaijin kantoku* (foreign manager). The American managers fared well, with Trey Hillman's Pacific League champion Nippon Ham Fighters losing to the Chunichi Dragons in the Japan Series. Hillman adjusted his American style to include some of the Japanese training and small ball tactics, causing one Japanese sportscaster to observe, "Hillman-san is the first American manager ever to make the switch from *bésubôru* to *yakyû*." He retained a blended approach after returning to the United States as the manager of the Kansas City Royals in 2008.[47]

The departure of superstars Ichiro, Matsui, and Matsuzaka as well as a growing list of lesser players has caused NPB concern. Tohoku manager Katsuya

Nomura laments, "If this keeps up, Japanese baseball is truly finished." Whiting notes, however, that most Japanese fans do not resent their stars' departure but continue to identify with them and expand their baseball interest to include MLB. More significantly, Whiting asserts that conservative NPB marketing and player development are major problems. Continuing dominance by the Yomiuri Giants and the team's leader, Tsuneo Watanabe, has restrained NPB from adopting creative revenue-producing schemes and expanding player recruiting and development. Whiting also argues that the Japanese players union needs to demand higher salaries, which more aggressive marketing would make possible.[48] These problems mirror those MLB experienced thirty years earlier and subsequently reduced, if not resolved.

Both the Latino and Japanese approaches to the game suggest baseball margin examples of Okihiro's mainstream/margin thesis of cultural development:

> The core values and ideals of the nation emanate not from the mainstream but from the margins—from among Asian and African Americans, Latinos and American Indians, women, gays and lesbians.... And despite its authorship of the central tenets of democracy, the mainstream has been silent on the publication of its creed. In fact, the margin has held the nation together with its expansive reach; the margin has tested and ensured the guarantees of citizenship; and the margin has been the true defender of American democracy, equality, and liberty. From that vantage, we can see the margin as the mainstream.[49]

In Asia, the marginal Japanese game is becoming the mainstream as Japan asserts its influence over South Korea, Taiwan, and to a lesser extent China, which currently is utilizing U.S. support. Those marginal countries may in turn influence mainstream Japan as they develop. These four major Asian baseball countries have participated in a season-ending Asian Series, comparable to the Caribbean Series, since 2004, a soft power collaborative effort to promote the game and reinforce national pride.

Frank P. Jozsa observes that the South Koreans consider baseball Japanese rather than American despite the two Asian countries' long, vitriolic history. Their baseball relationship exemplifies soft power collaboration. Korean players aspire to play in NPB and are permitted to do so under the NPB foreign-player roster restrictions. (Each team is permitted up to four foreigners on its roster, with no more than three being either pitchers or position players.) Since baseball has been deeply intertwined with volatile national politics in Korea since its 1905 introduction by missionary Philip J. Gillet, the sport's persistence is perhaps a tribute to the game's soft power element there. Japan and Korea spent most of the twentieth century as military and/or economic enemies. Baseball appears to provide a means of cultural conciliation and amelioration of their hard power differences. Reaves observes that baseball serves as a public outlet for venting frustration and student unrest in Korea. As in the hard power global economic arena, Korean baseball is following closely behind the Japanese version of the sport and developing a soft power rivalry that reaches to the United States. While the 2008 MLB Opening Day rosters included sixteen Japanese players but only two Koreans, several other Koreans played in the Majors during the season.[50] In addition, the Korean baseball team took the gold medal in the 2008 Beijing Olympics, further boosting Korea's status as an international baseball force.

The Korean Baseball Organization is a league with a 132-game season and eight professional teams sponsored by large corporations, as in Japan. In 2008, the SK Wyverns, managed by Lee Man-soo, voted Korea's all-time most popular player, won their second consecutive Korean Series. In 2004, a scandal involving military service recalled MLB's activity to minimize player military service during the Vietnam War. The Korean version involved player use of brokers to learn how to feign kidney ailments to avoid the country's requirement for twenty-six months of military service. Like MLB in the Vietnam era, the Korean Baseball Organization avoided addressing the issue until it was widely publicized but then resolved it quietly.[51]

Hard power politics has played a generally negative role throughout the international expansion of baseball. In the Philippines, for example, Americans introduced the sport in 1894, and the military promoted it during the Spanish-American War and subsequent occupation. By 1910, baseball was well established at the school level, and the sport subsequently benefited from international exchanges. During World War II, however, the country's infrastructure collapsed, and the Philippines have subsequently been beset by political turmoil. Reaves observes that baseball reflects the country's social and cultural confusion, although a Philippine team won the Little League World Series in 1992. While the sport continues to operate at the school level, it has not progressed to organized professional status.[52] Lacking higher-level competition, the Philippines do not participate in the WBC.

According to Reaves, Shanghai was the birthplace of baseball in Asia. William Henry Boone, who had moved there with his parents in the late 1840s, returned to the United States to complete medical school and serve in the Civil War before crossing the Pacific again as a medical missionary and baseball devotee in 1863. By then, the Shanghai Base Ball Club was in existence, supported by the city's several hundred American residents. Boone and others helped to promote the sport as part of the government's "self-strengthening movement," which encouraged the adoption of western practices. China, however, did not embrace these practices as much or as quickly as Japan did. After World War II, the Communists, who took over the country, specifically promoted anti-Americanism, and baseball consequently remained only a minor novelty until the last quarter of the twentieth century.

In 1872, the Chinese Educational Mission program began sending elite students to the United States for scientific, engineering, and military study. Contrary to their passive Confucian upbringing, they quickly gravitated to American sports, most notably baseball. This new love of sports ultimately provoked a government cancellation of the program in 1881. During that time, however, the students formed a baseball team and used baseball, as had immigrants before and since, as a means of assimilation. Henry Lees Kingman, the son of a missionary, became the first Chinese-born Major Leaguer when he appeared briefly with the New York Yankees in 1914 before returning to China as a missionary and subsequently serving as coach of the Chinese baseball team in the Far Eastern Olympics. Chinese revolutionary Sun Yat-sen learned baseball as a student in Hawaii and formed a baseball team to aid his military training. He and subsequent militarists considered throwing a baseball good practice for hurling hand grenades; no Chinese sport offered similar training.

Chinese baseball received a boost in 1905 when Chinese students flocked to Japan in the aftermath of the Russo-Japanese War. Baseball had already become Japan's most popular intercollegiate sport. The 1931 Japanese invasion of Manchuria reinforced baseball's popularity in China. Communist revolutionaries played baseball in the 1930s and 1940s, and U.S. troops promoted it where they were stationed during World War II. Popularity continued through the 1950s. In 1959, thirty teams competed for China's national baseball championship. During the Cultural Revolution of the 1960s and 1970s, however, baseball, like other western practices, all but disappeared, only to be resurrected in the 1980s and 1990s as part of the "friendship first, competition second" strategy that encouraged cultural exchanges with other countries.[53]

Japan has had a greater baseball influence than the United States on China and on other Asian areas. The Chinese strategy, in baseball as in more significant economic and geopolitical areas, appears to be one of friendly absorption with limited return to the supplier. While China's economy continues to grow significantly, producing a surplus with the United States of more than two hundred billion dollars, the country is trying to build a soft power relationship with both MLB and NPB. On November 23, 2003, the China Baseball

Association (ChBA) and MLB agreed jointly to promote baseball in anticipation of the 2008 Beijing Olympics. The two organizations have engineered coaching exchanges, and MLB has begun scouting Chinese players. Former Major League player and manager Jim Lefebvre and former MLB pitcher and coach Bruce Hurst led the Chinese national team, derived mostly from the China Baseball League (which at the time had four teams and played a twenty-four-game season), in the 2003 Asian championships. Both men continued their roles with the Chinese entry in the initial World Baseball Classic. In 2007, MLB hosted the team in spring training in Arizona, where it played games against Minor League teams and some players participated in extended spring training with nine MLB teams in Arizona and Florida.[54] The China Baseball League expanded to a two-division, six-team league in 2007. The Tiangin Lions won their third consecutive title in 2008.

In February 2007, the New York Yankees, which have contractual ties to Britain's world-renowned Manchester United soccer team and the Yomiuri Giants in NPB, executed a memorandum of understanding with the ChBA to develop players and exchange coaching personnel. The following June, the Yankees became the first MLB team to sign Chinese players, doing so with the approval of the ChBA. The club also entered into a marketing deal with a Chinese dairy company, the first MLB-related sponsorship arrangement in that country.[55]

The ChBA hosted the two-game exhibition series between the Los Angeles Dodgers and San Diego Padres in Beijing on March 15–16, 2008. The series promoted the sport among the locals and increased interest in the baseball segment of the Beijing Olympics held later in the year. The Chinese team defeated Taiwan for its only win in the games, further stimulating interest in baseball. MLB's Play Ball program had grown to 120 schools in five cities in the country. MLB and ChBA have entered into discussions about a season-opening MLB series in China in the near future.

Taiwan has had "a proud and sorry" baseball history, notes Jozsa. Since the 1949 Communist coup, baseball has grown more rapidly on Taiwan than on the mainland. Geopolitically, Taiwan sought to demonstrate affinity for the United States, which became the island's principal protector. Its spectacular success in Little League international competition—seventeen championships between 1969 and 1995—has been tainted at the professional level by periodic gambling issues that included a nationwide 1998 scandal, the 2007 banning of six players from the Chinatrust team for fixing games, and the 2008 expulsion of the Dmedia T-Rex team and three of its players as well as the Chinatrust Whales. . Taiwan's Chinese Professional Baseball League, reduced to four teams after the scandal, currently provides feeder talent to NPB and MLB as well as talent for Taiwan's WBC entry. Pitcher Chien-Ming Wang's success with the New York Yankees provides the celebrity currency to attract and develop talent and fans. In 2008, the President Lions won their second straight title.[56]

Complementing the professional game are Little League and high school baseball, with the latter culminating in the annual Golden Dragon tournament, established in 1995. "Both Japan and the United States have claimed baseball as their national game. In Taiwan, the game is more than that. At times, baseball is nothing short of the national passion," concludes Reaves. Baseball has positively reinforced Taiwan's political ties with the United States and Japan but has also contributed to the country's continuing gambling problem.[57] To survive, the Chinese Professional Baseball League needs to expunge gambling.

WORLD BASEBALL CLASSIC

On May 11, 2005, MLB and the MLBPA jointly announced that the inaugural WBC, a sixteen-nation tournament in which the world's best players represent their home countries, would be held on March 3–20, 2006. MLB and the MLBPA scheduled the event during spring training to avoid conflicting with the regular season (as the Olympics do) and to avoid extending the number of months during which players are competing. Many MLB players and teams would have preferred to hold the tournament in the fall, after the World Series, but some countries disagreed with that idea.[58] Scheduling is but one of the soft power challenges for this international showcase. The final two rounds feature a single-elimination format, which shortens the WBC tournament but leaves the championship vulnerable to fluke upsets.

In the spring, virtually all MLB pitchers build arm strength gradually and so are not in regular-season form, necessitating pitch limits for protection. Many players use spring training to transition from injury rehabilitation to game readiness, while others use the time to work on specific skills. Further, some teams withheld players for various reasons, while Yankee owner George Steinbrenner publicly complained about supplying five players to the U.S. team. Therefore, MLB participation in and the overall quality of the initial WBC were less than they would have been if the tournament were held in midseason. Although MLB player participation increased somewhat in 2009, it was uneven among the teams, prompting Commissioner Selig to urge teams "to put the best interests of the game ahead of your own selfish, provincial interests."[59] MLB must find a way to balance WBC, team owner, and player desires.

Although MLB consulted NPB before initiating the event and assumed the financial risks accompanying the WBC, it was created without official NPB approval, a move that offended the protocol-conscious Japanese. To their mutual credit, MLB and NPB reached an accord: MLB made some concessions, and more importantly, the competition received the endorsements of Ichiro, who agreed to play for Japan, and Oh, who agreed to manage the Japanese entry. The first WBC therefore provided a valuable cultural learning experience for MLB.

With cooperating sponsors, the NPB, the Korean Baseball Organization, their respective player organizations, and professional leagues in other participating countries, the WBC received sanction from the IBAF. Perhaps not coincidentally, the WBC was announced one week after the IOC voted to remove baseball and softball from the Games after 2008.[60] In addition to the United States, Japan, and South Korea, countries participating in the WBC included Australia, Canada, China, Cuba, the Dominican Republic, Italy, Mexico, the Netherlands, Panama, Puerto Rico, South Africa, Taiwan (competing as Chinese Taipei, as it did in the Olympics), and Venezuela.

Players with ties to several countries (as a result of birth, citizenship or qualification for citizenship or passport, residency, or parental birth, citizenship, or residency) could choose which one to represent. MLB stars therefore populated most of the rosters. These liberal guidelines enhanced the global connection and soft power appeal of baseball as well as spread MLB talent beyond the U.S. team to strengthen the overall competition. Ichiro represented Japan, Mike Piazza played for Italy, Jason Bay played for Canada, Bobby Abreu played for Venezuela, and Albert Pujols played for the Dominican Republic.

The format consisted of four pools, initially located in Arizona, Florida, Japan, and Puerto Rico, each of which included four teams that faced each other in a round-robin format. The top two teams from each pool moved on to the second round, which was divided into pools in California and Puerto Rico. Once again, the top two teams from each pool moved on, and the format switched to single-elimination. The semifinals and finals were held at PETCO Park, home of the San Diego Padres. Japan took home the championship, defeating Cuba 10–6 in the final. All participating countries received compensation, however, with the stipulation that they use the money to enhance baseball. Exhibition games preceded the tourney in Japan and the United States, with NPB and MLB teams providing opposition for the national teams.[61]

Since the United States was eliminated in the second round, domestic television ratings of the last two rounds were lower than expected but still doubled the average spring training game audience. With two Latin American and two Asian teams competing in the semifinals and Japan and Cuba in the final, the

WBC enhanced foreign national interest and served its international marketing pursuits. While MLB players raised the overall quality of play by participating on many teams, the final game included only two MLB players (for Japan), thereby demonstrating that quality baseball extends beyond the United States.

The WBC provided a critical showcase and challenge for MLB's smart power strategy as well as a modest diplomatic test for the U.S. government. The WBC accentuates MLB's already shaky relationship with the IOC but also provides an opportunity for MLB to build its relationship with the IBAF, particularly with regard to the subject of Cuba. Would the soft power value of sports competition outweigh the U.S. government's hard power anti-Castro position, which is influenced by Cuban American political factions in South Florida? Cuba has been a perennial winner in international baseball competition, but political constraints have restricted head-to-head competition between the two countries and prevented MLB from directly recruiting Cuban players while indirectly encouraging Cuban players to defect. The U.S. government initially barred Cuba from participating in the WBC because it would provide income to Cuba and thus violate the embargo.

Cuba's Major League consists of sixteen teams that play a 90-game season and a brief Super League season that follows the Serie National (Cuban national championship series) in June. Cuba's national team won 152 straight international tournament games in the early to mid-1990s.[62] It won 11 straight games in 2005 en route to the sixteen-team World Cup championship, which it has dominated for a decade. In 2007, it won its tenth straight Pan-American Games title. In the Olympics, Cuba won three gold and two silver medals in the five Olympic competitions. Before its second-round elimination in the 2009 WBC, Cuba had participated in thirty-eight consecutive international tournament finals.

Because Cuba has dominated international baseball competition over the past two decades, its absence from the WBC would have severely hampered the tournament's on-field objective of selecting the best national team in the world. The U.S. government's original hard power position would also have hurt MLB's chances to use the goodwill generated by the WBC to promote baseball internationally. On January 20, 2006, seven weeks before the tourney, the parties reached a compromise that allowed the United States to approve participation and the IBAF to maintain its sanction. Cuba agreed to have its share of WBC profits donated directly to a Hurricane Katrina relief fund. President George W. Bush, former managing partner of the Texas Rangers, used soft power to influence the outcome. The compromise regarding Cuba reinforces the value of soft power over hard power in the international arena. MLB is working to reestablish an ongoing relationship with Cuban baseball as that country's government undergoes leadership transition.

The 2009 WBC included the same sixteen teams, but its twelve-member steering committee featured more balanced leadership—four U.S. representatives, three from Japan, two from Korea, two from the IBAF, and one from Australia. In contrast to 2006, all first-round play was double-elimination rather than round-robin and occurred entirely outside the United States, as MLB sought more collaborative involvement and fan participation from other nations.[63] Japan, South Korea, the United States, and Venezuela participated in the final two rounds at Dodger Stadium, with Japan winning its second consecutive title in an extra-inning all-Asian title game.

Paul Archey Jr., MLB's senior vice president, International Operations, situates the WBC within MLB's overall global strategy to develop both participation and fan interest worldwide, with particular emphasis on certain countries, such as China. He notes that MLB has no interest in expanding its long-established World Series to include other countries, as Little League has done, but asserts that the WBC can serve a similar purpose with more balanced competition because of the opportunity to distribute MLB players among nations. He cites MLB's primary objective for the WBC as stimulating global marketing of MLB-related products and services, thereby reinforcing MLB's profit-oriented global business strategy.[64]

The percentage of foreign-born MLB players stands at slightly below 30 percent and seems to have stabilized at that level. The mix of countries from which those players originate is likely to change, however, reflecting somewhat greater non-Latino participation as other countries develop their baseball talent and Latino recruiting costs continue to rise. With MLB games now televised in more than 220 countries and the number of international commercial sponsors exceeding fifty, Archey argues that MLB can leverage its international mix of players to take advantage of their celebrity currency in their home countries. The WBC thus fits strategically well within MLB's international revenue focus on television, sponsorships, licensing, and staged events. The tournament enhances opportunities to make deals with local entities in the participating countries.[65] The WBC's success will be a significant determinant of MLB's future global strategy. Allan Klein notes that the WBC is "global in form, but national in essence."[66] MLB's ability to balance the global and the national is a soft power challenge on the road to development of collaborative support for the game.

FINAL SCORE

Baseball is baseball wherever it is played. The only difference is the game.
—FRANK P. JOZSA

Exemplified by the World Baseball Classic (WBC), Major League Baseball (MLB) is a composite of a sport, a domestic monopoly, a neocolonial power, and an international business. The WBC represents the blend of myth and reality that MLB strives to balance in pursuing its international strategy. MLB's "smart power" implementation of the WBC represents a merger of its soft power cultural and celebrity attraction to co-opt participating countries and their fans with the hard power economic leverage to induce countries to follow its leadership.

Although baseball generally meets Allen Guttmann's definition of a modern sport, with its organized and measured elements and its urban influence, it has created and still retains through MLB a primordial morality and fantasy that provide participants and spectators a quasi-religious spiritual connection with the game. Embedded in its Cooperstown "immaculate conception," open time frame and venue, traditional rules and rituals, and seasonal progression, baseball re-creates a mythical agrarian imagined community that unites those who play and/or watch the game. From its early professional history, the baseball community embraced the sports media, which used their increasing soft power leverage to promote and further mythologize the sport. As both general and specific baseball history have shown, however, such a community runs the risk of exclusivity and therefore diminished popular appeal. Throughout most of MLB's existence, its leaders shunned players and fans of color, as did white society, which practiced similar prejudice in day-to-day life. As MLB expanded internationally, it also found that its strong national identity provoked resistance and game modification abroad. Accommodating local influence has been and will remain a critical factor in broadening the baseball market, as in other global consumer ventures.

As baseball evolved in the latter half of the nineteenth century, it linked its mythology with the United States as the national pastime. From that connection, MLB reinforced a patriotic aspect and an expanded presence in national popular culture and language. With such enhanced visibility, however, came risk of negative exposure, as experienced in the Black Sox scandal and subsequent issues such as player strikes and illegal drug use. Generally, however, MLB has withstood the short-term consequences of these negative events and recaptured popularity, although that popularity has steadily declined in the face of increasing competition and of more critical media in an expanding entertainment economy that both worships and castigates celebrities.

With the creation of the National League in 1876, what would become MLB commodified itself as a domestic business that leveraged its mythical appeal. It used celebrity attraction and product licensure to expand its revenue beyond the ballpark. Reinforced by an illogical Supreme Court decision declaring it a legal monopoly in 1922, MLB operated with virtual immunity for another half century. Its business progression, however, trailed the history of U.S. consumer marketing. Its management skills also lagged because of the antitrust protection and owners' reluctance to hire, develop, and delegate to professional management. Like other seats of abnormal power, MLB leaders abused their power by exploiting players, fans, and local governments to increase profits, thereby complicating and contradicting its mythical stature as a moral sport. Its hard power monopoly status, however, enabled it to control its labor costs unilaterally and to establish local market exclusivity. But it also removed a competitive challenge that in a free market forces businesses to improve their practices. By allowing team owners' significant latitude, MLB compounded its business development problem. It lacked critical elements of organizational control and consistency that could have avoided or mitigated subsequent resistant responses.

Such excessive dominance begets resistance and counterforces. In the last quarter of the twentieth century, MLB saw the emergence of a powerful players union, government constraints, alternative entertainment outlets, and public backlash that demanded stronger management and marketing. While MLB has responded to those pressures, it has not always done so with adroit soft power tactics. Its bilateral monopoly relationship with the MLBPA produced a hard power economic cold war fraught with continuing hostility. Their Collective Bargaining Agreement negotiations provide periodic and visible megatests that determine whether the parties can complement their independent hard power goals with soft power collaboration toward smart power mutual success.

Increased sponsorships, licensing relationships, and luxury box sales from corporate America have helped to increase the revenue base but have also made MLB more vulnerable to economic downturns. "I used to think we were recession-proof," Commissioner Selig said in March 2009, but "this is different." . With the new model of higher-priced seats in smaller ballparks, teams may suffer disproportionately from reduced disposable corporate and individual income during tough economic times. In early 2009, Bank of America ended talks about becoming the elite sponsor of the new Yankee Stadium, thereby costing the team at least ten million dollars annually.[1] The steroid issue, which resulted in an embarrassing congressional intervention, served as a wake-up call for both players and management although they did not receive conclusive public condemnation from a sports citizenry that has come to overemphasize performance at the expense of conformance to rules and laws.

As a mirror of U.S. society, MLB used its monopoly economic leverage to reinforce racial bias at home and abroad for most of its history. That bias first excluded minority talent and then included but exploited it as MLB began to lose its unilateral hold on white players. Although justly applauded for signing Jackie Robinson in 1945, MLB continued its prejudice more subtly, albeit less consistently. Now a virtual meritocracy on the playing field, MLB still lags in persuading all its owners to take affirmative action in management hiring. It is, however, increasing its soft power marketing efforts, with limited success, to try to win back African American athletes and fans migrating to basketball and football.

In the Caribbean, MLB's first international center, neocolonialism quickly became the operating norm. Leveraging the already established U.S. government and corporate dominance in the region, MLB teams exploited Latino youths with romantic promises of a better life, thereby enabling teams to mitigate the effects of rising domestic player acquisition and salary costs. Within the past decade, however, MLB has substantially increased the controls on teams' practices in the Caribbean. While hard power economics prevails, MLB increasingly blends it with soft power collaboration in relationships with countries and their representatives. With a relatively loose confederation of teams, however, MLB leaders must also rely heavily on soft power persuasion within the organization.

MLB's business history in the Caribbean has provided some experience for dealing in larger, more complicated international markets, although much of the learning must be country-specific and often takes place through trial and error. Through its increasing use of soft power attraction and collaboration at home and in the Caribbean, MLB is developing a business skill set that augurs well for further international expansion of its player recruiting and consumer marketing. While generally unsuccessful in Europe because of that continent's more established sports' dominance and general antipathy toward the United States, MLB is making modest but uneven progress across the Atlantic while achieving more positive results in several Asian countries.

The emergence of Japanese MLB stars has fostered a broader celebrity appeal not only among Asian Americans but also among Asians. Largely because of that appeal, Japan is by far the largest source of MLB's international revenue. As the quality of the Japanese game improves and as its influence grows among other Asian countries, MLB faces stronger competition for players and fans. An accompanying risk, however, is that MLB will attract more of the premier talent in Japan, jeopardizing Nippon Professional Baseball, and in other countries as their talent pools develop. So far, however, the soft power collaborative relationship with Japan appears to be a win-win model for expanded implementation.

The initial World Baseball Classic provided an international showcase that enhanced baseball's image in the participating countries. While the U.S. team's second-round elimination dampened the WBC's domestic appeal, the Asian-Caribbean semifinals and final enhanced its international attraction. The first WBC also provided a learning opportunity for MLB to observe which tactics work in the international marketplace and which do not. As a result of that experience, MLB made the second WBC governance more multilateral. The U.S. team's greater success in the 2009 tourney also increased domestic interest. Participation by only sixteen countries, with significantly different skill levels, in the first two WBCs illustrates not only that baseball is far from a global sport but also that it has a positive future well beyond the national pastime. The IBAF's 113 member countries indicate the market potential for MLB's international pursuits. Successful continuation of the WBC and reinstatement of baseball in the Olympics would reinforce MLB's global mission.

MLB will need to implement further strategies to enhance itself at home and abroad:

1. build on Major League Baseball Advanced Media's current successes in Internet marketing and joint ventures by expanded use of and further developing technology on an international platform;
2. strengthen marketing/operational support for Minor League Baseball and learn from diverse, innovative business experiences in the Minors;
3. pursue cooperation with and/or Minor League Baseball absorption of independent leagues to help protect and enhance the game's brand;

4. directly and/or collaboratively provide more junior-college baseball scholarships to avoid some competition with four-year colleges that favor football and basketball and often cut back on baseball scholarships to meet Title IX goals, since MLB's extensive farm system makes it less dependent on four years of collegiate development than other sports;
5. use increased scholarships and expanded Revitalizing Baseball in Inner Cities–type programs to attract and develop minority players, particularly from urban areas;
6. increase multilateral control of Caribbean recruiting and development practices and develop more balanced partnerships with national governments and local businesses;
7. leverage the WBC success and Washington connections into closer relations with Cuban baseball as that country's government transitions;
8. increase the number of WBC participants through increased development support in other countries, such as Russia, and enhance fan acceptance through marketing activities;
9. and strengthen the possibility of baseball's return to the Olympics by collaborating with the IBAF and USA Baseball and by arranging Major League player participation to balance teams and minimize regular-season disruption.

While each of these smart power initiatives possesses both hard and soft power elements, they depend significantly on multilateral, collaborative actions reflecting judicious use of soft power. Hardball is the game, but smart ball is increasingly the business of baseball.

Let's play smart ball.

NOTES

AT BAT
1. Nye, *Soft Power*, 2.
2. Nye, *Paradox*, xii.
3. Nye, *Soft Power*, x.
4. Nye, *Paradox*, 9, 11.
5. Ibid., 67, xiii.
6. Nye, *Bound to Lead*, 29–32.
7. Nye, *Paradox*, 5, 12.
8. Casey Tefertiller, "A's Extra Effort Lands Inoa," *Baseball America*, July 28–August 10, 2008, 3.

FIRST BASE
1. Block, *Baseball*, 94, xx, 101–8, 75. Block's work is the most comprehensive investigation of the sport's origins.
2. For further explanation of Cartwright's diminished role in rules documentation and in spreading the game west, see Nucciarone, *Alexander Cartwright*.
3. Rossi, *National Game*, 4.
4. Barthes, *Mythologies*, 144, 130, 143. While unrelated to baseball, as one would expect of a French work, Barthes's theses correlate very closely with MLB's development and promotion of its mythology.
5. Spalding, *America's National Game*, 19.
6. Pope, *Patriotic Games*, 66.
7. Spalding, *America's National Game*, 20; Harrington E. Crissey Jr., "Baseball and the Armed Services," in *Total Baseball*, ed. Thorn et al., 2513.
8. Bill Francis, "Doubleday Field: A Diamond in the Pasture," *Memories and Dreams* 27:3 (Fall 2005): 14–16.
9. Block, *Baseball*, xv, 1.

10. Bill Pennington, "Baseball's Origins: They Ain't Found till They're Found," *New York Times*, September 12, 2004. This Pittsfield discovery indirectly reinforces Block's conclusion that baseball's origin most likely derived from an evolutionary confluence of Anglo-American "town ball" games.
11. Springwood, *Cooperstown to Dyersville*, 9–10, 54.
12. Barthes, *Mythologies*, 129.
13. Good, *Diamonds*, 71.
14. Nathan, *Saying It's So*, 20, 11.
15. Riess, *Touching Base*, 213. Riess effectively describes this late-nineteenth-century juxtaposition of baseball's promoted mythology and the advent of urban-influenced reality that continues to characterize MLB.
16. Gehring, *Mr. Deeds*, 118–21, 151.
17. Wood and Pincus, *Reel Baseball*, 88–90, 93–94.
18. Clifford, *Predicament of Culture*, 92, 14, 16.
19. Susman, *Culture as History*, 288. Susman's generally described tension is applicable to MLB's mythology-reality tension.
20. Clifford, *Predicament of Culture*, 106.
21. Greenberg, *Celebrant*, 8, 4–5.
22. Anderson, *Imagined Communities*, 6.
23. Goldstein, *Playing for Keeps*, 2.
24. Mandelbaum, *Meaning of Sports*, 41.
25. Smith, *Storied Stadiums*, 4.
26. Christopher Hawthorne, "Now Taking the Field: Bold Stadium Designs," *New York Times*, July 27, 2003.
27. Associated Press, "Robinson's Legacy Set in Stone at Citi Field," *Sporting News*, April 15, 2008.
28. Bruce Schoenfeld, "The Empire's New Kingdom," *Sporting News*, September 1, 2008; Richard Sandomir, "New Stadiums: Prices, and Outrage, Escalate," *New York Times*, August 26, 2008.
29. John Branch, "Yankee Grass Is Now a Brand," *New York Times*, March 22, 2009.
30. Alan Ross, "Little League Baseball: It's a Hit from Williamsport, Pa., to Fields across America," *American Profile*, July 7–13, 2005, 6–7.
31. Scully, *Market Structure*, 319.
32. Quirk and Fort, *Hard Ball*, 3.
33. Zingg, *Sporting Image*, 354.
34. Barthes, *Mythologies*, 143.
35. Zoss and Bowman, *Diamonds*, xii.
36. Guttmann, *From Ritual to Record*, 3.
37. Mandelbaum, *Meaning of Sports*, 4.
38. Guttmann, *From Ritual to Record*, 4–7, 16–55, 116. Guttmann's description of modern sport is the general standard. His characteristic of secularism, however, needs to recognize degrees of ritualism and "religion." As later noted by other authors, all sports have at least a quasi-religious element. Baseball has perhaps the most such elements.
39. Riess, *City Games*, 1, 253.
40. Danielson, *Home Team*, 66.
41. Frederick L. Paxson, "The Rise of Sport," in *Sporting Image*, ed. Zingg, 60.
42. John R. Betts, "The Technological Revolution and the Rise of Sport, 1850–1900," in ibid., 171.
43. Pope, *Patriotic Games*, 3; Leifer, *Making the Majors*, 26.
44. Powers, *Business of Baseball*, 117.

45. Riess, *Touching Base*, 27–30, 213–19; Dizikes, *Sportsmen and Gamesmen*. Dizikes contends that all of American sport evolved from a foundation of Jacksonian values.
46. Goldstein, *Playing for Keeps*, 5, 23, 155.
47. Riess, *Sport*, 166.
48. Guttmann, *From Ritual to Record,*, 91.
49. Leifer, *Making the Majors*, 155.
50. Bryan Curtis, "The National Pastime(s), *New York Times*, February 1, 2009.
51. Guttmann, *From Ritual to Record,*, 116.
52. Leifer, *Making the Majors*, 265.
53. Gehring, *Mr. Deeds*, 123.
54. Coakley, *Sport in Society*, 479–89, 98–101, 494. The "muscular Christianity" movement of the late nineteenth century interlocked sports and religion as man treated his body as a temple.
55. Zoss and Bowman, *Diamonds*, 77; Barzun, *God's Country*, 162, 160.
56. Burk, *Never Just a Game*, xi, 2.
57. Ted Vincent, *Rise and Fall*, 108.
58. Skolnik, *Baseball*, 60.
59. Mandelbaum, *Meaning of Sports*, 4.
60. Crepeau, *Baseball*, 39–46.
61. Michael Kimmel, "Baseball and the Reconstitution of American Masculinity 1880–1920," in *Baseball History*, ed. Dreifort, 49, 55–56, 61.
62. Riess, *Touching Base*, 132. West to east is still the prevailing direction of new ideas as less institutionalized areas tend to spawn alternatives to convention. One can project a modification of that tendency as the West becomes more established and therefore conventional.
63. Ibid., 136–53, 155.
64. Evans and Herzog, *Faith*, xiii, 9, xix, 3–10, 182, 242.
65. Giamatti, *Take Time*, 36–48, 66.
66. Hyman S. Baras, "Moses at the Bat in the Big Inning," *Smithsonian*, June 2008, 104.
67. Anderson, *Imagined Communities*, 6.
68. Pope, *Patriotic Games*, 14, 72.
69. Mandelbaum, *Meaning of Sports*, 77, 101–3.
70. Thorn, *Total*, 2514–15.
71. *World Almanac*, 542; Ron Briley, "Baseball and Dissent: The Vietnam Experience," *Nine: A Journal of Baseball History and Culture* 17:1 (Fall 2008): 61.
72. Briley, *Class at Bat*, 7. While never a replacement for war, increased global sports competition in baseball and other sports enhances international relations among countries.
73. Rossi, *National Game*, 144.
74. Gehring, *Mr. Deeds*, 40.
75. Thorn, *Total*, 2517–19.
76. Briley, "Baseball and Dissent," 3.
77. Gehring, *Mr. Deeds*, 179.
78. Thorn, *Total*, 2520.
79. Briley, "Baseball and Dissent," 68–69, 4, 65–66.
80. Michener, *Sports in America*, 468, 471.
81. Ned Martel, "Learning after 9/11 That There Is a Balm to Baseball," *New York Times*, September 14, 2004; Briley, "Baseball and Dissent," 1–2.
82. Mandelbaum, *Meaning of Sports*, 128.

83. George Carlin, "Carlin: The Difference between Baseball and Football," www.foxsports.com, June 23, 2008.
84. Brandon Harris, "Reds Join in Welcoming Back Veterans," MLB.com, July 4, 2008.
85. Mickey Herskowitz, "Take Me Out to the Museum," *Houston Chronicle*, May 27, 2005; Samantha Carr, "Baseball as America comes Home," *Memories and Dreams* 30:5 (Fall 2008): 25–26.
86. McGimpsey, *Imagining Baseball*, 5–6. Although McGimpsey may be literally correct that baseball is not culturally unique, the combination of its emphasis on pastoral populist values and its pervasive popularity has enabled it to become more prevalent on the U.S. cultural landscape than any other sport.
87. Powers, *Business of Baseball*, 6.
88. Gehring, *Mr. Deeds*, 92–98.
89. Marshall G. Most and Robert Rudd, "Designated Heroes: Cinematic Reflections of Baseball's Cultural Ideology," in *Reel Baseball*, ed. Wood and Pincus, 75–76, 200; White, *Creating*, 200.
90. John Thorn, "Take Me into the Ballgame," *New York Times*, June 2, 2006.
91. Terrence Rafferty, "Baseball on the Screen: Some Hits, Many Errors," *New York Times*, April 2, 2006.
92. Schaaf, *Sports, Inc.*, 159, 69.
93. Rader, *In Its Own Image*, 5, 201, 200.
94. Eitzen, *Fair and Foul*, 4.
95. Dizikes, *Sportsmen and Gamesmen*, 311.
96. Schaaf, *Sports, Inc.*, 343.
97. Eitzen, *Sport*, 307.
98. Eitzen, *Fair and Foul*, 3.
99. Helyar, *Lords*, 1.

SECOND BASE

1. Dizikes, *Sportsmen and Gamesmen*, 305.
2. Zirin, *What's My Name, Fool?* 17.
3. Abrams, *Money Pitch*, xiii.
4. Powers, *Business of Baseball*, 4.
5. Tedlow, *New and Improved*, xxii. Tedlow's historical phases correlate closely with MLB's evolution as a marketer.
6. Schaaf, *Sports, Inc.*, 314.
7. McCraw, *American Business*, 187.
8. Tedlow, *New and Improved*, xxiii.
9. Riess, *Touching Base*, 7.
10. Fizel, Gustafson, and Hadley, *Baseball Economics*, 4.
11. Abrams, *Money Pitch*, 5.
12. William J. Morgan, "Baseball and the Search for American Moral Identity," in *Baseball and Philosophy*, ed. Bronson, 159.
13. Abrams, *Money Pitch*, xv. While exaggerated, this disparity correlates with the separation of top level and average or bottom level salaries in American business.
14. Alfred D. Chandler Jr., *Visible Hand*.
15. Alan Schwarz, "Fighting to Get In," *Baseball America*, December 19, 2005–January 15, 2006, 10.
16. "Slow to Change but Change It Has," *Baseball America*, March 1–7, 2006, 9; en.wikipedia.org/wiki/Fantasy_sports#size_of_hobby.

17. McGregor, *Human Side*, 33–57.
18. Richard J. Puerzer, "From John McGraw to Joe Torre: Industrial Management Styles Applied throughout the History of Major League Baseball," in *Baseball and American Culture*, ed. Rielly, 137–49.
19. Levine, *A. G. Spalding*, xi, xiv.
20. Spalding, *America's National Game*, 119, 126.
21. Roberta Newman, "Here's the Pitch: Baseball and Advertising," in *Baseball and American Culture*, ed. Rielly, 129.
22. Levine, *A. G. Spalding*, 17–19, 21–22, 75–76, 78–79; Abrams, *Money Pitch*, 11.
23. Newman, "Here's the Pitch," 131, 129; Abrams, *Money Pitch*, 1–2, 11–12.
24. Newman, "Here's the Pitch," 128–29.
25. Wolf, *Entertainment Economy*, 28.
26. Schaaf, *Sports, Inc.*, 79–82; Bloom, *House of Cards*, 17–18; Elizabeth Lesly, "A Bubble Burst at Topps," *Business Week*, August 23, 1993, 74.
27. John Kimelman, "New Game Is Played Online at Topps," *New York Times*, May 5, 2002; Eric A. Taub, "Webcam Brings 3-D to Topps Sports Cards," *New York Times*, March 9, 2009.
28. Ken Bensinger, "Collectors Favor Older Baseball Items," *Minneapolis Star Tribune*, October 2, 2005.
29. Miriam Horn, "Baseball Beauties," *U.S. News and World Report*, July 5, 1993, 11.
30. John Odell, "Curator's Corner: Of Bobbleheads and Ballplayers," *Memories and Dreams* 27:4 (Winter 2005): 22–23.
31. Szymanski and Zimbalist, *National Pastime*, 32–33.
32. Burk, *Never Just a Game*, 92, xiii.
33. Zimbalist, *Baseball and Billions*, 143.
34. Lears, *Fables of Abundance*, 10–11, 382, 385.
35. McCraw, *American Business*, 22.
36. Michelle Kaufman, "Baseball Debate: To Replay or Not," *Albuquerque Journal*, October 26, 2005.
37. Burk, *Never Just a Game*, 171, 157, 161–68, 188–93.
38. Although the formation of the Continental League, headed by Branch Rickey in 1960, provoked MLB's first team expansion, it never coalesced as a competitive playing league.
39. Burk, *Never Just a Game*, 188–95, 200–203, 243, 206–9, 212–16, 240.
40. Pietruska, *Judge and Jury*, 78–89, 119.
41. Zimbalist, *In the Best Interests*, 39–40, 174.
42. Dick Thornburgh, foreword to Pietruska, *Judge and Jury*, vii.
43. Zimbalist, *In the Best Interests*, 33.
44. Moffi, *Conscience*, 39.
45. Pietruska, *Judge and Jury*, 387; Rader, *Baseball*, 110.
46. Pietruska, *Judge and Jury*, 431.
47. Powers, *Business of Baseball*, 49, 45.
48. Braudy, *Frenzy of Renown*, 573–74.
49. Abrams, *Money Pitch*, 74; Scot Mondore, "100 Years of Player Endorsements: Honus Wagner and Louisville Slugger," *Memories and Dreams* 27:4 (Winter 2005): 31.
50. Kristen Jones, "'And Here's the Pitch': Advertising Long Part of National Game," *Memories and Dreams* 27:4 (Winter 2005): 25.
51. Burk, *Much More than a Game*, 23.
52. Szymanski and Zimbalist, *National Pastime*, 125.
53. Powers, *Business of Baseball*, 50–52.

54. Schaaf, *Sports, Inc.*, 83–86.
55. Screen Actors Guild Awards, Turner Broadcasting System, January 29, 2006.
56. Szymanski and Zimbalist, *National Pastime*, 126.
57. Richard Sandomir, "ESPN Increases Budget in a Deal with Baseball," *New York Times*, September 15, 2005; Richard Sandomir, "Waiting on Deck in the Rights Lineup," *New York Times*, March 24, 2006; Richard Sandomir, "Smart Play for Baseball and N.F.L. in Sirius Deals," *New York Times*, February 11, 2009; Brad Stone, "MLB.TV Adds Enhanced Video and User-Selected Replays," *New York Times*, March 24, 2009; Barry M. Bloom, "MLBAM, ESPN Expand Agreement," MLB.com, August 21, 2008.
58. Richard Sandomir, "A Network to Satisfy the Appetite of Baseball-Hungry Fans," *New York Times*, October 3, 2008; John Consoli, "A Network Takes Us Out to a Ballgame," *New York Times*, March 24, 2009.
59. Tim Arango, "Online Piracy Menaces Pro Sports," *New York Times*, December 29, 2008.
60. Szymanski and Zimbalist, *National Pastime*, 126; Newman, "Here's the Pitch," 124–25.
61. Linda Greenhouse, "No Ruling Means No Change for Fantasy Baseball Leagues," *New York Times*, June 3, 2008.
62. "MLB Advanced Media and National Association of Professional Baseball Leagues Announce Major Partnership Agreement," MLB.com, January 13, 2005; Matt Richtel, "Pro Baseball and Take-Two Make a Deal," *New York Times*, February 1, 2005; Jerry Crasnick, "Power Brokers: A New Look at the People at the Top of Baseball's Power Structure Reveals a Wealth of Changes," *Baseball America*, March 28–April 10, 2005, 22.
63. Mark Newman, "WBC to Be Spoken during Super Bowl," MLB.com, February 3, 2006.
64. Stuart Elliott, "Baseball Makes a Play for the Super Bowl Audience," *New York Times*, January 22, 2004; Stuart Elliott, "In New Ads for Baseball, the Fans Are the Stars," *New York Times*, March 14, 2005.
65. LEXIS-NEXIS Academic 259 U.S. 200; 42 S.Ct. 465; 66 L.Ed. 898; 1922 U.S. LEXIS 2475; 26 A.L.R. 357, 5.
66. Carter, *Reason and Law*, 70.
67. Zimbalist, *Baseball and Billions*, 15.
68. Duquette, *Regulating*, 76.
69. Abrams, *Legal Bases*, 69.
70. Lowenfish, *Imperfect Diamond*, 202.
71. William W. Wright and Mick Cochrane, "The Uses of History in Baseball Labor Disputes," in *Diamond Mines*, ed. Staudohaur, 67.
72. Miller, *Whole Different Ball Game*, 293, 75.
73. Kuhn, *Hard Ball*, 157–58.
74. Miller, *Whole Different Ball Game*, 293, 301.
75. Kuhn, *Hard Ball*, 346, 77, 79–80.
76. Miller, *Whole Different Ball Game*, 106, 91.
77. Studs Terkel, foreword to Miller, *Whole Different Ball Game*, x.
78. Zimbalist, *In the Best Interests*, 92–95.
79. Duquette, *Regulating*, 136.
80. Paul D. Staudohaur, "The Baseball Strike of 1994–95," in *Diamond Mines*, ed. Staudohaur, 55–56, 49.
81. Zimbalist, *In the Best Interests*, 150–52, 144–45, 178, 199.
82. Fay Vincent, *Last Commissioner*, 186.

83. Zimbalist, *Baseball and Billions*, 212.
84. Kuhn, *Hard Ball*, 412.
85. Moffi, *Conscience*, 101.
86. Zimbalist, *Baseball and Billions*, 159; Zimbalist, *In the Best Interests*, 144–45.
87. Paul White, "Baseball Has Made Progress in Decade of Labor Peace," *USA Today Sports Weekly*, February 1–7, 2006.
88. Gennaro, *Diamond Dollars*, 238.
89. Tony Lima, Leo Kahane, and Nan L. Maxwell, "A Game Theoretic Analysis of Owner-Player Relations," in *Diamond Mines*, ed. Staudohaur, 122–40.
90. Bryant, *Juicing the Game*, 267, 135–38.
91. Lisa Winston, "Minor League Report," *USA Today Sports Weekly*, June 8–14, 2005.
92. Bryant, *Juicing the Game*, 256, 271–73, 303–16, 331–32, 388–97.
93. Jerry Crasnick, "Ban on 'Greenies' Could Change Look," *Baseball America*, February 13–26, 2006, 4.
94. George J. Mitchell, "Report to the Commissioner of Baseball of an Independent Investigation into the Illegal Use of Steroids and Other Performance Enhancing Substances by Players in Major League Baseball," MLB.com, December 13, 2007.
95. Allan H. Selig, Press Conference, New York, MLB.com, December 13, 2007.
96. Associated Press, "MLB Establishes Investigations Unit," foxsports.com, January 11, 2008.
97. "MLB Joins Forces in Fight against Drugs," MLB.com, January 10, 2008.
98. Rosen, *Erosion*. Rosen provides a comprehensive review and analysis of the increasingly negative influence of competition on the traditional moral values of sport.

THIRD BASE

1. Deloria, *Playing Indian*. Deloria provides a comprehensive historical analysis of cultural abuse of Native Americans.
2. Ellen J. Staurowsky, "An Act of Honor or Exploitation? The Cleveland Indians' Use of the Louis Francis Sockalexis Story," *Sociology of Sport Journal* 15:4 (December 1998): 299–316. As a result of Staurowsky's published research, Cleveland removed its specific linkage of Sockalexis to the nickname, although the team has continued to publicize his brief tenure with the club.
3. Young, *Postcolonialism*, 47.
4. Samuel O. Regalado, "Latin Players on the Cheap: Professional Baseball Recruitment in Latin America and the Neocolonialist Tradition," *Indiana Journal of Global Legal Studies* 8:1 (Fall 2000): 11–12.
5. San Juan, *Beyond Postcolonial Theory*, 156.
6. Spivak, *Critique*, 373.
7. Balibar and Wallerstein, *Race, Nation, Class*, 37, 53, 58–59, 96, 105.
8. Said, *Culture and Imperialism*, 291, 300.
9. Young, *Postcolonialism*, 47.
10. Guttmann, *Games and Empires*, 172–78.
11. C. L. R. James, *Beyond a Boundary*, xi–xv.
12. John Monteleone, introduction to Rickey, *Branch Rickey's Little Blue Book*, 15.
13. Lowenfish, *Branch Rickey*, 547.
14. Tygiel, *Past Time*, 95.
15. Polner, *Branch Rickey*, rev. ed., 93.

16. John Wesley, "The Use of Money," Sermon 50, in *Works*, 2:267–79.
17. Lowenfish, *Branch Rickey*, 325; Simon, *Jackie Robinson*, 83.
18. Chalberg, *Rickey and Robinson*, 6.
19. Monteleone, introduction, 14.
20. J. G. Taylor Spink, *Judge Landis*, 232.
21. Monteleone, introduction, 122.
22. William James, "The Moral Equivalent of War," in *Memories and Studies*, 267–96.
23. Lowenfish, *Branch Rickey*, 181.
24. Duncan J. Watts, "Is Justin Timberlake a Product of Cumulative Advantage?" *New York Times*, April 15, 2007.
25. Billet and Formwalt, *America's National Pastime*, 17.
26. Bjarkman, *Baseball*, 5.
27. Burk, *Never Just a Game*, 34; Lipsitz, *Possessive Investment*, vii.
28. Regalado, "Latin Players," 11–12.
29. Ruck, *Tropic of Baseball*, 100.
30. Bréton and Villegas, *Away Games*, 41.
31. Wendel, *New Face*, 70.
32. Burk, *Much More than a Game*, 81–86.
33. Balibar and Wallerstein, *Race, Nation, Class*, 130. Wallerstein points out that this outcome contradicts the capitalist desire to minimize production costs, including wages, to maximize profits.
34. Polner, *Branch Rickey*, rev. ed., 133; Simon, *Jackie Robinson*, 82.
35. Chalberg, *Rickey and Robinson*, 24–25.
36. Mann, *Branch Rickey*, 214–15.
37. Lowenfish, *Branch Rickey*, 365–68.
38. Tygiel, *Baseball's Great Experiment*, 65.
39. Peter M. Rutkoff, "Introduction—Jackie Robinson: Baseball, Brooklyn, and Beyond," in Hall and Rutkoff, *Cooperstown Symposium*, 10, 20.
40. Anthony R. Patranis and Marlene E. Turner, "Nine Principles of Successful Affirmative Action: Branch Rickey, Jackie Robinson, and the Integration of Baseball," in ibid., 152–70.
41. Jules Tygiel, "The Grand Experiment Fifty Years Later," in ibid., 259.
42. Cockroft, *Latinos in Baseball*, 16.
43. Powers, *Business of Baseball*, 257.
44. Burk, *Much More Than a Game*, 300; Mark Newman, "Robinson to Be Honored Annually," MLB.com, March 3, 2004.
45. Tom Verducci, "Blackout: The African American Baseball Player Is Vanishing: Does He Have a Future?" *Sports Illustrated*, July 7, 2003, 58; Associated Press, "Number of Black Baseball Players Drops," sportingnews.com, April 15, 2008.
46. "The 50 Most Powerful African Americans in Sports," *Black Enterprise*, March 2005, 88–108.
47. Burk, *Much More Than a Game*, 96; Helyar, *Lords*, 46–47. Rickey's business acumen later proved shortsighted in one area when he resisted televising Dodger games.
48. Peggy Beck, "Working in the Shadows of Rickey and Robinson: Bill Veeck, Larry Doby, and the Advancement of Black Players in Baseball," in Hall and Rutkoff, *Cooperstown Symposium*, 110.
49. Powers, *Business of Baseball*, 163.
50. Burk, *Much More Than a Game*, 135. According to Burk, Robinson's peak salary came in 1957, although his last playing year was 1956.

51. Bruce K. Johnson, "Team Racial Composition and Players' Salaries," in *Diamonds Are Forever*, ed. Sommers, 192.
52. Roediger, *Wages of Whiteness*, 8–13. Roediger objects to the Marxist reduction of race issues to those of class. He contends that whiteness is a "wage" for white workers. In Johnson's view, this psychic wage translates into dollars.
53. Gerald W. Scully, "Discrimination: The Case of Baseball," in *Sport*, comp. Eitzen, 365.
54. Ibid., 381–86; Hoose, *Necessities*, 132–33.
55. Burk, *Much More Than a Game*, 136; Eric Eide and Daraius Irani, "Positional Segregation in Major League Baseball: 1961–1990," in *Baseball Economics*, ed. Fizel, Gustafson, and Hadley, 179–89.
56. Burk, *Much More Than a Game*, 136.
57. Briley, *Class at Bat*, 84–90.
58. Burk, *Much More Than a Game*, 129; Threston, *Integration of Baseball*, 81.
59. Ruck, *Tropic of Baseball*, 12; Bjarkman, *Baseball*, 119.
60. "Cuban Baseball Legacy Rich in American Heritage," *Memories and Dreams* 28:3 (July–August 2006): 9.
61. Regalado, "Latin Players," 12; Bjarkman, *Baseball*, 102.
62. Bréton and Villegas, *Away Games*, 102.
63. Bjarkman, *Baseball*, 13–14, 124; Kerrane, *Dollar Sign*, 94, 233.
64. Bjarkman, *Baseball*, 13–14.
65. Hoose, *Necessities*, 95.
66. Ben Badler, "Landmark Year Wraps up Internationally," *Baseball America*, October 20–November 2, 2008, 16; Kevin Baker, "Dominican Bonuses Draw Attention of Federal Agents," *Baseball America*, July 28–August 10, 2008, 5; Casey Tefertiller, "A's Extra Effort Lands Inoa," *Baseball America*, July 28–August 10, 2008, 3; Alex Speier, "Sox Fire Top D.R. Scout as MLB Probe Widens," *Baseball America*, August 25–September 10, 2008, 5; *Baseball America*, September 8–21, 2008, 5; Lacy Lusk, "Nats Force Out Bowden, Rijo," *Baseball America*, March 23–April 5, 2009, 3.
67. Alan Schwarz, "Pressure Building for Draft of Players from Outside U.S.," *New York Times*, July 13, 2008.
68. Burk, *Much More Than a Game*, 300; Alan M. Klein, "Coming of Age in North America: Socialization of Dominican Baseball Players," in *Inside Sports*, ed. Coakley and Donnelly, 96–103.
69. Edna Bonacich, "Class Approaches to Ethnicity and Race," in *Majority and Minority*, ed. Yetman, 64–65.
70. Tim Weiner, "Low-Wage Costa Ricans Make Baseballs for Millionaires," *New York Times*, January 25, 2004.
71. Bjarkman, *Baseball*, 69.
72. Alan M. Klein, *Sugarball*, 151–52.
73. Said, *Culture and Imperialism*, 291.
74. Bréton and Villegas, *Away Games*, 18; Alan M. Klein, *Sugarball*, 14.
75. Krich, *El Béisbol*, 110.
76. Cockroft, *Latinos in Baseball*, 116.
77. Tom Farrey, "Dominican Gold Rush," *Outside the Lines* (ESPN), May 4, 2004.
78. Krich, *El Béisbol*, 111.
79. Lowe, *Immigrant Acts*, 8, 182–83 n. 19.
80. Bréton and Villegas, *Away Games*, 9; Alan M. Klein, *Sugarball*, 42; Regalado, "Latin Players," 18.

81. Krich, *El Béisbol*, 156; Bréton and Villegas, *Away Games*, 47.
82. Mehmet, *Westernizing*, 11.
83. Alan M. Klein, *Sugarball*, 3; *USA Today Sports Weekly*, March 2–8, 2005.
84. Bréton and Villegas, *Away Games*, 191, 195.
85. Alan M. Klein, *Sugarball*, 47, 111–14.
86. Gandhi, *Postcolonial Theory*, 17.
87. Bréton and Villegas, *Away Games*, 79–80, 82.
88. Alan M. Klein, *Sugarball*, 1.
89. Ibid., 154; Gandhi, *Postcolonial Theory*, 156.
90. Arturo Marcano and David J. Fidler, "The Globalization of Baseball: Major League Baseball and the Mistreatment of Latin American Baseball Talent," *Indiana Journal of Global Legal Studies* 6:2 (Spring 1999): 513.
91. Jerry Crasnick, "Cracking Down on an Age-old Problem," *Baseball America*, April 1–14, 2002, 20.
92. Marcano and Fidler, "Globalization of Baseball," 543–45, 547, 555–61.
93. Angel Vargas, "The Globalization of Baseball: A Latin American Perspective," *Indiana Journal of Global Legal Studies* 8:1 (Fall 2000): 34–35.
94. Said, *Culture and Imperialism*, 276.
95. Gandhi, *Postcolonial Theory*, 218–26.
96. Marc Fisher and John Jeter, "The Home Run in Black and White: McGwire, Sosa Draw Diverse Fans," *Washington Post*, September 5, 1998.
97. Sosa and Bréton, *Sosa*, 1.
98. George Vecsey, "Sports of the Times: McGwire and Sosa Just Keep Going," *New York Times*, September 28, 1998.
99. Benjamin G. Rader, "The Home Run Mystique Involves the Power of One Dramatic Blast to Pull a People Together," *Christian Science Monitor*, October 1, 1998.
100. Joe Connor, "Baseball Festival Courts Fans," MLB.com, December 1, 2003.
101. *USA Today*, March 9, 2001.
102. Crasnick, "Cracking Down," 20.
103. Richard Sandomir, "Better Late Than Never to Fix Latino Promotion," *New York Times*, September 1, 2005.
104. "Baseball! Béisbol! to Explore Latino Baseball," *Memories and Dreams* 28:1 (March–April 2006): 5.
105. Ron Draper, "Hispanic Museum Getting Close to Home," MLB.com, January 27, 2006.
106. Alan Schwarz, "Miller Brings Baseball Back to the City," *Baseball America*, February 13–26, 2006, 7.
107. Lorraine Cwelich, "Urban Academy Event Gives Players a Chance," *Baseball America*, August 25–September 7, 2008, 50.
108. George Vecsey, "Sports of The Times: Taking a Seat With the Guys Again," *New York Times*, February 28, 2006; Jack Curry, "Woman among 17 Elected to Hall of Fame," *New York Times*, February 28, 2006.
109. Barry Bloom, "Diversity Producing Key Leaders," MLB.com, May 15, 2003.
110. Murray Chass, "Diversity Is Missing from Management," *New York Times*, February 19, 2006; Jim Salisbury, "Phillies Tab Amaro as GM," *Baseball America*, December 1–14, 2008, 3.
111. Harvey Araton, "The Honcho with the Midas Touch," *New York Times*, October 6, 2005.
112. Marty Noble, "Mets Make Quick Push into Latin America," *Baseball America*, November 21–December 4, 2005, 11.

114. Murray Chass, "Mets' Signing of Latin Players Stirs Debate," *New York Times*, January 29, 2006.

HOME PLATE

1. Nye, *Paradox*, xiii; Denning, *Culture*, 17–22.
2. LaFeber, *Michael Jordan*, 55–57.
3. Lynn Hirschberg, "What Is an American Movie Now?" *New York Times*, November 14, 2004.
4. John Harris, "The Bland Played on: Rock 'n' Roll Is the Latest Victim of Corporate Globalization—and It Shows," *Guardian*, May 8, 2004.
5. Malcolm Waters, "McDonaldization and the Culture of Consumption," in *McDonaldization*, ed. Ritzer, 213–21.
6. Denning, *Culture*, 2–3, 7, 113–14.
7. Bairner, *Sport*, 17, 173, 6, 1, 176, 91, 95, 102.
8. Eric Pfanner, "Foreign Policy and Marketing," *New York Times*, January 20, 2004; William J. Holstein, "Erasing the Image of the Ugly American," *New York Times*, October 23, 2005.
9. Kirk Semple, "Baseball in Iraq: As Pastimes Go, It's Anything But," *New York Times*, September 7, 2005.
10. Murray Chass, "Whither the Game? Just Asking," *New York Times*, December 20, 2007; Chetwood, *Baseball in Europe*, 210–13.
11. Holstein, "Erasing the Image."
12. Conrad De Aenlle, "Famous Brands Can Bring Benefit, or a Backlash," *New York Times*, October 19, 2003.
13. Wolf, *Entertainment Economy*, 21; LaFeber, *Michael Jordan*, 21, 27, 69–71, 134; Naomi Klein, *No Logo*, 85.
14. Leach, *Land of Desire*, 386–88; LaFeber, *Michael Jordan*, 156.
15. Nye, *Paradox*, 80, 96, 98, xvi.
16. "Baseball, Softball Get the Boot," *Albuquerque Journal*, February 10, 2006.
17. "New Leader for the IBAF," in *Baseball America 2008 Almanac*, 397.
18. William Humber, "It's Our Game, Too, Neighbour," in *Dominionball*, ed. Dorward, 4–5.
19. Humber, *Diamonds*, 3, 4, 34.
20. Bairner, *Sport*, 117.
21. Christian Trudeau, "Integration in Quebec: More Than Jackie," in *Dominionball*, ed. Dorward, 23–24.
22. Humber, *Diamonds*, 168–71.
23. Levine, *A. G. Spalding*, 17–20; Jack Curry, "It's a Whole New Ballgame in Ireland, and a Movie, Too," *New York Times*, February 10, 2006; Chetwood, *Baseball in Europe*, 206–10; Marty Appel, "Zimbabwe and Israel: Two Nations of Growth," *Memories and Dreams* 28:3 (July–August 2006): 28.
24. Levine, *A. G. Spalding*, 99–106.
25. Clark, *History*, ix, 18, 53, 61, 65–67, 71–72, 76–77, 90–91, 120, 132.
26. Joe Nocera, "It's a Bloody Takeover," *New York Times*, September 14, 2008.
27. "Major League Baseball International to Conduct European Baseball Academy July 27–August 18 in Italy," MLB.com, July 21, 2006.
28. Jozsa, *Sports Capitalism*, 39–40; Kim Palchikoff, "Russia Discovers Another Pastime," *New York Times*, July 6, 2003.
29. Andrew Weltch, "British Baseball: How a Curious Version of the Game Survives in Parts of England and Wales," *National Pastime: A Review of Baseball History* 28 (2008): 30–33.

30. Bruce Crumley, "Baseball in Belgium," *Time*, September 17, 2007, Global 6.
31. "IBAF Announces Plan for European League," *Baseball America*, July 28–August 10, 2008, 5.
32. Reaves, *Taking*, 3.
33. Ibid., 13–14, xv; Obojski, *Rise*, 3; Savuri Guthrie-Shimizu, "For the Love of the Game: Baseball in Early U.S.-Japanese Encounters and the Rise of a Transnational Sporting Fraternity," *Diplomatic History* 28:5 (November 2004): 649, 652.
34. Reaves, *Taking*, 50; Whiting, *Meaning*, 56–57.
35. Whiting, *Meaning*, 58–59.
36. Jerome Holtzman, "Bittersweet Travels," MLB.com, March 15, 2000; Masaru Ikei, "Baseball, Besuboru, Yakyu: Comparing the American and Japanese Games," *Indiana Journal of Global Legal Studies* 8:1 (Fall 2000): 78–79.
37. Cromartie and Whiting, *Slugging It Out*.
38. Whiting, *Meaning*, 154–60, 74–80, 97, 103–6.
39. Ibid., 106–12.
40. Bob Nightengale, "Far East Stars Rise in the West," *USA Today Baseball Weekly*, March 14–20, 2001.
41. Kent A. Ono, "... America's Apple Pie: Baseball, Japan-Bashing, and the Sexual Threat of Economic Miscegenation," in *Out of Bounds*, ed. Baker and Boyd, 81–101.
42. Okihiro, *Margins and Mainstreams*, 141.
43. "Samurai Baseball," *Minor Trips Newsletter*, January 2006, 3.
44. Whiting, *Chrysanthemum*, 37–38; Whiting, *Meaning*, 51–52.
45. Whiting, *Meaning*, 53; Cromartie and Whiting, *Slugging It Out*, 35, 273–74.
46. Wayne Graczyk, "Valentine Win Highlights Season," in *Baseball America 2006 Almanac*, 356.
47. Robert Whiting, "Foreign Managers Change the Face of Japanese Game," *Asian Baseball Committee Journal*, July 2007, 11 (originally published in *Japan Times*, April 2007).
48. Robert Whiting, "Is MLB Destroying Japan's National Pastime?" *Asian Baseball Committee Journal*, July 2007, 8–10; "NPB Needs Major Reforms, Vision to Prosper Like MLB," *Asian Baseball Committee Journal*, July 2007, 13–15; "NPB Players in Need of Strong Union Like MLBPA," *Asian Baseball Committee Journal*, July 2007, 15–17 (all originally published in *Japan Times*, April 2007).
49. Okihiro, *Margins and Mainstreams*, ix, 175.
50. Jozsa, *Baseball, Inc.*, 114–36; Reaves, *Taking*, 16; Murray Chass, "Major Leagues Take a Few Hefty Cuts at the Trade Deficit," *New York Times*, April 10, 2005; "Opening Day Rosters Feature 239 Players Born Outside the 50 United States," MLB.com, April 1, 2008.
51. Thomas St. John, "Wyverns Win Back-to-Back Titles," in *Baseball America 2009 Almanac*, 423; Thomas St. John, "Controversy Hits Korean Season," in *Baseball America 2005 Almanac*, 365.
52. Jozsa, *Baseball, Inc.*, 88–110; Reaves, *Taking*, 16.
53. Reaves, *Taking*, 27–31, 18–24, 37–44; Howard W. French, "China Warms Up and Practices for a Future in Baseball," *New York Times*, May 24, 2004.
54. Greg Boeck, "Baseball Takes Small Steps into China, *USA Today*, November 6, 2007.
55. "Yankees Tap China Market," *Baseball America*, February 26–March 11, 2007, 3; "Yankees Ink Chinese Players," *Baseball America*, July 16–29, 2007, 3.
56. Ben Chen, "Lions Repeat as Taiwan Champion," in *Baseball America 2009 Almanac*, 424; Will Lingo, "Plenty of Action to Follow in Other Countries, Too," *Baseball America*, December 1–14, 2008, 20.
57. Reaves, *Taking*, 149–55.

58. "WBC Is Riddled with Logistical Problems," *Baseball America*, February 27–March 12, 2006, 46.
59. Kevin Kernan, "Hey GMs, WBC Isn't Going Anywhere," *New York Post*, March 22, 2009.
60. "Inaugural World Baseball Classic to Be Played in March 2006," MLB.com, May 11, 2005.
61. Matt Myers, "Carpetbaggers Create Complaints and Confusion," *Baseball America*, February 27–March 12, 2006, 40.
62. Lisa Winston, "Cuba's International Reputation Is on the Line," *Baseball America*, March 1–7, 2006, 27.
63. "World Baseball Classic, Inc. Approves Final Eight Invitations for March 2009 Tournament," MLB.com, February 19, 2008.
64. Paul Archey Jr., telephone interview by author, February 26, 2004.
65. Ibid. George Vecsey, "When the Game Absorbs the Globe," *New York Times*, April 1, 2007.
66. Alan M. Klein, *Growing the Game*, 247.

FINAL SCORE
1. Richard Sandomir and Ken Belson, "In Economic Downturn, Corporate Ties Put Bind on Sports," *New York Times*, March 22, 2009.

BIBLIOGRAPHY

Aaron, Hank, and Lonnie Wheeler. 1991. *I Had a Hammer: The Hank Aaron Story*. New York: HarperCollins.
Abrams, Roger I. 1998. *Legal Bases: Baseball and the Law*. Philadelphia: Temple University Press.
———. 2000. *The Money Pitch: Baseball Free Agency and Salary Arbitration*. Philadelphia: Temple University Press.
Alexander, Charles C. 1988. *John McGraw*. Lincoln: University of Nebraska Press.
Altherr, Thomas L., ed. 1992–2004. *Sports in North America: A Documentary History*. 10 vols. Gulf Breeze, Fla.: Academic International.
Anderson, Benedict R. O'G. 1991. *Imagined Communities: Reflections on the Origin and Spread of Nationalism*. New York: Verso.
Angus, Jeff. 2006. *Management by Baseball: The Official Rules for Winning Management in Any Field*. New York: HarperCollins.
Ashe, Arthur. 1993. *A Hard Road to Glory: A History of the African-American Athlete*. New York: Amistad.
Bairner, Alan. 2001. *Sport, Nationalism, and Globalization*. Albany: State University of New York Press.
Baker, Aaron, and Todd Boyd, eds. 1997. *Out of Bounds: Sports, Media, and the Politics of Identity*. Bloomington: Indiana University Press.
Baldassaro, Lawrence, and Dick Johnson. 2002. *The American Game: Baseball and Ethnicity*. Carbondale: Southern Illinois University Press.
Balibar, Etienne, and Immanuel Maurice Wallerstein. 1991. *Race, Nation, Class: Ambiguous Identities*. New York: Verso.
Barthes, Roland. 1984. *Mythologies*. Selected and trans. Annette Lavers. New York: Hill and Wang.
Barzun, Jacques. 1954. *God's Country and Mine: A Declaration of Love Spiced with a Few Harsh Words*. Boston: Little, Brown.
Baseball America 2005 Almanac. 2005. Durham, N.C.: Baseball America.
Baseball America 2006 Almanac. 2006. Durham, N.C.: Baseball America.

Baseball America 2008 Almanac. 2008. Durham, N.C.: Baseball America.
Baseball America 2009 Almanac. 2009. Durham, N.C.: Baseball America.
Billet, Bret L., and Lance J. Formwalt. 1995. *America's National Pastime: A Study of Race and Merit in Professional Baseball.* Westport, Conn.: Praeger.
Bjarkman, Peter C. 1994. *Baseball with a Latin Beat: A History of the Latin American Game.* Jefferson, N.C.: McFarland.
Block, David. 2005. *Baseball before We Knew It: A Search for the Roots of the Game.* Lincoln: University of Nebraska Press.
Bloom, John. 1997. *A House of Cards: Baseball Card Collecting and Popular Culture.* Minneapolis: University of Minnesota Press.
Bouton, Jim. 1970. *Ball Four.* Ed. Leonard Schector. New York: World.
Boyd, Brendan C., and Fred C. Harris. 1973. *The Great American Baseball Card Flipping, Trading, and Bubble Gum Book.* Boston: Little, Brown.
Bradbury, J. C. 2007. *The Baseball Economist.* New York: Dutton.
Braudy, Leo. 1997. *The Frenzy of Renown: Fame and Its History.* New York: Vintage.
Bréton, Marcos, and José Luis Villegas. 1999. *Away Games: The Life and Times of a Latin Baseball Player.* New York: Simon and Schuster.
Briley, Ron. 2003. *Class at Bat, Gender on Deck, and Race in the Hole: A Line-Up of Essays on Twentieth Century Culture and America's Game.* Jefferson, N.C.: McFarland.
Bronson, Eric, ed. 2004. *Baseball and Philosophy: Thinking Outside the Batter's Box.* Chicago: Open Court.
Bryant, Howard. 2005. *Juicing the Game: Drugs, Power, and the Fight for the Soul of Major League Baseball.* New York: Viking.
Burgos, Adrian, Jr. 2007. *Playing America's Game: Baseball, Latinos, and the Color Line.* Berkeley: University of California Press.
Burk, Robert F. 1994. *Never Just a Game: Players, Owners, and American Baseball to 1920.* Chapel Hill: University of North Carolina Press.
———. 2001. *Much More than a Game: Players, Owners, and American Baseball since 1921.* Chapel Hill: University of North Carolina Press.
Cagan, Joanna, and Neil DeMause. 1998. *Field of Schemes: How the Great Stadium Swindle Turns Public Money into Private Profit.* Monroe, Maine: Common Courage.
Carter, Lief H. 1998. *Reason in Law.* 5th ed. New York: Longman.
Chalberg, John C. 2000. *Rickey and Robinson: The Preacher, the Player, and America's Game.* Wheeling, Ill.: Harlan Davidson.
Chandler, Albert B. (Happy), with Vance H. Trimble. 1989. *Heroes, Plain Folks, and Skunks: The Life and Times of Happy Chandler: An Autobiography.* Chicago: Bonus.
Chandler, Alfred D., Jr. 1977. *The Visible Hand: The Managerial Revolution in American Business.* Cambridge: Belknap Press of Harvard University Press.
Chetwood, Josh. 2008. *Baseball in Europe: A Country by Country History.* Jefferson, N.C.: McFarland.
Clark, Joe. 2003. *A History of Australian Baseball: Time and Game.* Lincoln: University of Nebraska Press.
Clifford, James. 1988. *The Predicament of Culture: Twentieth-Century Ethnography, Literature, and Art.* Cambridge: Harvard University Press.
Coakley, Jay J. 1978. *Sport in Society: Issues and Controversies.* St. Louis: Mosby.
Coakley, Jay J., and Peter Donnelly, eds. 1999. *Inside Sports.* New York: Routledge.

Cockroft, James D. 1996. *Latinos in Baseball.* New York: Watts.
Coover, Robert. 1968. *The Universal Baseball Association, Inc., J. Henry Waugh, Prop.* New York: Random House.
Crepeau, Richard C. 1980. *Baseball, America's Diamond Mind, 1919–1941.* Orlando: University Presses of Florida.
Cromartie, Warren, and Robert Whiting. 1991. *Slugging It Out in Japan: An American Major Leaguer in the Tokyo Outfield.* New York: Kodansha.
Dam, Kenneth W. 2001. *The Rules of the Global Game: A New Look at U.S. International Economic Policymaking.* Chicago: University of Chicago Press.
Danielson, Michael N. 1997. *Home Team: Professional Sports and the American Metropolis.* Princeton: Princeton University Press.
DeLillo, Don. 1997. *Underworld.* New York: Scribner.
Deloria, Philip J. 1998. *Playing Indian.* New Haven: Yale University Press.
Denning, Michael. 2004. *Culture in the Age of Three Worlds.* New York: Verso.
Dickson, Paul, comp. 1991. *Baseball's Greatest Quotations.* New York: Burlingame.
Dizikes, John. 1981. *Sportsmen and Gamesmen:* Boston: Houghton Mifflin.
Dorward, Jane Finnan. 2005. *Dominionball: Baseball above the 49th.* Cleveland: Society for American Baseball Research.
Dreifort, John E., ed. 2001. *Baseball History from Outside the Lines: A Reader.* Lincoln: University of Nebraska Press.
Duquette, Jerold J. 1999. *Regulating the National Pastime: Baseball and Antitrust.* Westport, Conn.: Praeger.
Dyja, Thomas. 1997. *Play for a Kingdom.* New York: Harcourt Brace.
Eitzen, D. Stanley, comp. 1984. *Sport in Contemporary Society: An Anthology.* 2nd ed. New York: St. Martin's.
———. 2003. *Fair and Foul: Beyond the Myths and Paradoxes of Sport.* 2nd ed. Lanham, Md.: Rowman and Littlefield.
Elias, Robert. 2001. *Baseball and the American Dream: Race, Class, Gender, and the National Pastime.* Armonk, N.Y.: Sharpe.
Evans, Christopher H., and William R. Herzog II, eds. 2002. *The Faith of Fifty Million: Baseball, Religion, and American Culture.* Louisville, Ky.: Westminster John Knox.
Fizel, John, Elizabeth Gustafson, and Lawrence Hadley, eds. 1996. *Baseball Economics: Current Research.* Westport, Conn.: Praeger.
Foer, Franklin. 2004. *How Soccer Explains the World: An Unlikely Theory of Globalization.* New York: HarperCollins.
Fox, Richard Wightman, and T. J. Jackson Lears. 1983. *The Culture of Consumption: Critical Essays in American History.* New York: Pantheon.
Frommer, Harvey. 1982. *Rickey and Robinson: The Men Who Broke the Color Barrier.* New York: Macmillan.
Gandhi, Leela. 1998. *Postcolonial Theory: A Critical Introduction.* New York: Columbia University Press.
Gehring, Wes D. 2004. *Mr. Deeds Goes to Yankee Stadium: Baseball Films in the Capra Tradition.* Jefferson, N.C.: McFarland.
Gennaro, Vince. 2007. *Diamond Dollars: The Economics of Winning in Baseball.* Hingham, Mass.: Maple Street.
Giamatti, A. Bartlett. 1989. *Take Time for Paradise: Americans and Their Games.* New York: Summit.

Gmelch, George, ed. 2006. *Baseball without Borders: The International Pastime*. Lincoln: University of Nebraska Press.
Goldstein, Warren Jay. 1989. *Playing for Keeps: A History of Early Baseball*. Ithaca: Cornell University Press.
Good, Howard. 1997. *Diamonds in the Dark: America, Baseball, and the Movies*. Lanham, Md.: Scarecrow.
Greenberg, Eric Rolfe. 1983. *The Celebrant: A Novel*. New York: Everest.
Guttmann, Allen. 1978. *From Ritual to Record: The Nature of Modern Sports*. New York: Columbia University Press.
———. 1988. *A Whole New Ball Game: An Interpretation of American Sports*. Chapel Hill: University of North Carolina Press.
———. 1994. *Games and Empires: Modern Sports and Cultural Imperialism*. New York: Columbia University Press.
Hall, Alvin, and Peter M. Rutkoff, eds. 2000. *The Cooperstown Symposium on Baseball and American Culture, 1997*. Jefferson, N.C.: McFarland.
Harris, Mark. 1953. *The Southpaw*. Indianapolis: Bobbs-Merrill.
Helyar, John. 1994. *Lords of the Realm: The Real History of Baseball*. New York: Villard.
Hoose, Phillip M. 1989. *Necessities: Racial Barriers in American Sports*. New York: Random House.
Hughson, John, David Ingers, and Marcus Free. 2005. *The Uses of Sport: A Critical Study*. New York: Routledge.
Humber, William. 1995. *Diamonds of the North: A Concise History of Baseball in Canada*. Toronto: Oxford University Press.
Jamail, Milton H. 2000. *Full Count: Inside Cuban Baseball*. Carbondale: Southern Illinois University Press.
James, C. L. R. 1993. *Beyond a Boundary*. Durham, N.C.: Duke University Press.
James, William. 1924. *Memories and Studies*. New York: Longmans, Green.
Jozsa, Frank P. 2004. *Sports Capitalism: The Foreign Business of American Professional Leagues*. Burlington, Vt.: Ashgate.
———. 2006. *Baseball, Inc.: The National Pastime as Big Business*. Jefferson, N.C.: McFarland.
Kaplan, Amy, and Donald E. Pease, eds. 1993. *Cultures of United States Imperialism*. Durham, N.C.: Duke University Press.
Kerrane, Kevin. 1999. *Dollar Sign on the Muscle: The World of Baseball Scouting*. Lincoln: University of Nebraska Press.
Kinsella, W. P. 1983. *Shoeless Joe*. New York: Ballantine.
Klein, Alan M. 1991. *Sugarball: The American Game, the Dominican Dream*. New Haven: Yale University Press.
———. 2006. *Growing the Game: The Globalization of Major League Baseball*. New Haven: Yale University Press.
Klein, Naomi. 2000. *No Logo: Taking Aim at the Brand Bullies*. Toronto: Knopf Canada.
Krich, John. 1989. *El Béisbol: Travels through the Pan-American Pastime*. New York: Prentice Hall.
Kuhn, Bowie. 1997. *Hard Ball: The Education of a Baseball Commissioner*. Lincoln: University of Nebraska Press.
LaFeber, Walter. 1999. *Michael Jordan and the New Global Capitalism*. New York: Norton.
Lapchick, Richard E. 1996. *Sport in Society: Equal Opportunity or Business as Usual?* Thousand Oaks, Calif.: Sage.
———. 2001. *Smashing Barriers: Race and Sport in the New Millennium*. Lanham, Md.: Madison.

Lardner, Ring. 1960. *You Know Me Al: A Busher's Letters.* New York: Scribner.
Leach, William. 1993. *Land of Desire: Merchants, Power, and the Rise of a New American Culture.* New York: Vintage.
Lears, T. J. Jackson. 1994. *Fables of Abundance: A Cultural History of Advertising in America.* New York: Basic Books.
Leifer, Eric. M. 1995. *Making the Majors: The Transformation of Team Sports in America.* Cambridge: Harvard University Press.
Levine, Peter. 1985. *A. G. Spalding and the Rise of Baseball: The Promise of American Sport.* New York: Oxford University Press.
Lipsitz, George. 1998. *The Possessive Investment in Whiteness: How White People Profit from Identity Politics.* Philadelphia: Temple University Press.
Lowe, Lisa. 1996. *Immigrant Acts: On Asian American Cultural Politics.* Durham, N.C.: Duke University Press.
Lowenfish, Lee. 1991. *The Imperfect Diamond: A History of Baseball's Labor Wars.* New York: Da Capo.
———. 2007. *Branch Rickey: Baseball's Ferocious Gentleman.* Lincoln: University of Nebraska Press.
MacCambridge, Michael. 2004. *America's Game: The Epic Story of How Pro Football Captured a Nation.* New York: Random House.
Maguire, Joseph. 1999. *Global Sport: Identities, Societies, Civilizations.* Malden, Mass.: Blackwell.
Malamud, Bernard. 1952. *The Natural.* New York: Harcourt, Brace.
Mandelbaum, Michael. 2004. *The Meaning of Sports: Why Americans Watch Baseball, Football, and Basketball, and What They See When They Do.* New York: Public Affairs.
Mandell, Richard D. 1994. *Sport: A Cultural History.* New York: Columbia University Press.
Mann, Arthur. 1957. *Branch Rickey: American in Action.* Boston: Houghton Mifflin.
Markovits, Andrei S., and Steven L. Hellerman. 2001. *Offside: Soccer and American Exceptionalism.* Princeton: Princeton University Press.
Maslow, Abraham. 1957. *Motivation and Personality.* 3rd ed. New York: Longman.
McCraw, Thomas K. 2000. *American Business, 1920–2000: How It Worked.* Wheeling, Ill.: Harlan Davidson.
McGregor, Douglas. 1960. *The Human Side of Enterprise.* New York: McGraw-Hill.
McGimpsey, David. 2000. *Imagining Baseball: America's Pastime and Popular Culture.* Bloomington: Indiana University Press.
McKelvey, G. Richard. 2001. *For It's One, Two, Three, Four Strikes You're Out at the Owners' Ball Game: Players versus Management in Baseball.* Jefferson, N.C.: McFarland.
Mehmet, Ozay. 1999. *Westernizing the Third World: The Eurocentricity of Economic Development Theories.* 2nd ed. New York: Routledge.
Michener, James A. 1976. *Sports in America.* New York: Random House.
Miller, Marvin. 1991. *A Whole Different Ball Game: The Sport and Business of Baseball.* Secaucus, N.J.: Carol.
Moffi, Larry. 2006. *The Conscience of the Game: Baseball's Commissioners from Landis to Selig.* Lincoln: University of Nebraska Press.
Mrozek, Donald J. 1983. *Sport and American Mentality, 1880–1910.* Knoxville: University of Tennessee Press.
Myrdal, Gunnar. 1944. *An American Dilemma.* New York: Harper.
Nathan, Daniel A. 2003. *Saying It's So: A Cultural History of the Black Sox Scandal.* Urbana: University of Illinois Press.

Nucciarone, Monica. *Alexander Cartwright: The Life behind the Baseball Legend*. Lincoln: University of Nebraska Press, 2009

Nye, Joseph S., Jr. 1990. *Bound to Lead: The Changing Nature of American Power*. New York: Basic Books.

———. 2002. *The Paradox of American Power: Why the World's Only Superpower Can't Go It Alone*. New York: Oxford University Press.

———. 2004. *Soft Power: The Means to Succeed in World Politics*. New York: Public Affairs.

Obojski, Robert. 1975. *The Rise of Japanese Baseball Power*. Radnor, Pa.: Chilton.

Ogden, David, and Joel Nathan Rosen, eds. Forthcoming. *Fallen from Grace*. Jackson: University Press of Mississippi.

Okihiro, Gary Y. 1994. *Margins and Mainstreams: Asians in American History and Culture*. Seattle: University of Washington Press.

Peterson, Harold. 1973. *The Man Who Invented Baseball*. New York: Scribner's.

Peterson, Robert W. 1970. *Only the Ball Was White*. Englewood Cliffs, N.J.: Prentice-Hall.

Pietruska, David. 1998. *Judge and Jury: The Life and Times of Judge Kenesaw Mountain Landis*. South Bend, Ind.: Diamond.

Polner, Murray. 1982. *Branch Rickey: A Biography*. New York: Atheneum.

———. 2007. *Branch Rickey: A Biography*. Rev. ed. Jefferson, N.C.: McFarland.

Pope, S. W. 1997. *Patriotic Games: Sporting Traditions in the American Imagination, 1876–1926*. New York: Oxford University Press.

———, ed. 1997. *The New American Sport History: Recent Approaches and Perspectives*. Urbana: University of Illinois Press.

Powers, Albert Theodore. 2003. *The Business of Baseball*. Jefferson, N.C.: McFarland.

Quirk, James P., and Rodney D. Fort. 1992. *Pay Dirt: The Business of Professional Team Sports*. Princeton: Princeton University Press.

———. 1999. *Hard Ball: The Abuse of Power in Pro Team Sports*. Princeton: Princeton University Press.

Rader, Benjamin G. 1983. *American Sports: From the Age of Folk Games to the Age of Spectators*. Englewood Cliffs, N.J.: Prentice-Hall.

———. 1992. *Baseball: A History of America's Game*. Urbana: University of Illinois Press.

———. 1999. *In Its Own Image: How Television Has Transformed Sports*. Upper Saddle River, N.J.: Prentice Hall.

Reaves, Joseph A. *Taking in a Game: A History of Baseball in Asia*. Lincoln: University of Nebraska Press.

Rickey, Branch. 2004. *Branch Rickey's Little Blue Book: Wit and Strategy from Baseball's Last Wise Man*. Ed. John Monteleone. Toronto: Sport Classic.

Rielly, Edward J., ed. 2003. *Baseball and American Culture: Across the Diamond*. New York: Haworth.

———, ed. 2006. *Baseball in the Classroom: Essays on Teaching the National Pastime*. Jefferson, N.C.: McFarland.

Riess, Steven A. 1989. *City Games: The Evolution of American Urban Society and the Rise of Sports*. Urbana: University of Illinois Press.

———. 1995. *Sport in Industrial America, 1850–1920*. Wheeling, Ill.: Harlan Davidson.

———, ed. 1997. *Major Problems in American Sport History: Documents and Essays*. Boston: Houghton Mifflin.

———. 1999. *Touching Base: Professional Baseball and American Culture in the Progressive Era.* Urbana: University of Illinois Press.

———, ed. 2006. *Encyclopedia of Major League Baseball Clubs.* Vol. 1, *National League.* Vol. 2, *American League.* Westport, Conn.: Greenwood.

Ritzer, George, ed. 2002. *McDonaldization: The Reader.* Thousand Oaks, Calif.: Pine Forge.

Roberts, Randy, and James Stuart Olson. 1989. *Winning Is the Only Thing: Sports in America since 1945.* Baltimore: Johns Hopkins University Press.

Roediger, David R. 1991. *The Wages of Whiteness: Race and the Making of the American Working Class.* New York: Verso.

Rogosin, Donn. 1983; 1995. *Invisible Man: Life in Baseball's Negro Leagues.* New York: Kodansha.

Rosen, Joel Nathan. 2007. *The Erosion of the American Sporting Ethos: Shifting Attitudes toward Competition.* Jefferson, N.C.: McFarland.

Rosentraub, Mark S. 1997. *Major League Losers: The Real Cost of Sports and Who's Paying for It.* New York: Basic Books.

Rossi, John P. 2000. *The National Game: Baseball and American Culture.* Chicago: Dee.

Ruck, Rob. 1999. *The Tropic of Baseball: Baseball in the Dominican Republic.* Lincoln: University of Nebraska Press.

Said, Edward W. 1994. *Culture and Imperialism.* New York: Vintage.

San Juan, E. 1998. *Beyond Postcolonial Theory.* New York: St. Martin's.

Sassen, Saskia. 1996. *Losing Control? Sovereignty in an Age of Globalization.* New York: Columbia University Press.

Schaaf, Phil. 2004. *Sports, Inc.: 100 Years of Sports Business.* Amherst, N.Y.: Prometheus.

Scully, Gerald W. 1989. *The Business of Major League Baseball.* Chicago: University of Chicago Press.

———. 1995. *The Market Structure of Sports.* Chicago: University of Chicago Press.

Seymour, Harold. 1989. *Baseball.* New York: Oxford University Press.

Silk, Michael, David L. Andrews, and C. L. Cole, eds. 2005. *Sport and Corporate Nationalisms.* New York: Berg.

Simon, Scott. 2002. *Jackie Robinson and the Integration of Baseball.* Hoboken, N.J.: Wiley.

Skolnik, Richard. 1994. *Baseball and the Pursuit of Innocence: A Fresh Look at the Old Ball Game.* College Station: Texas A & M University Press.

Smith, Curt. 2001. *Storied Stadiums: Baseball's History through Its Ballparks.* New York: Carroll and Graf.

Sommers, Paul M., ed. 1992. *Diamonds Are Forever: The Business of Baseball.* Washington, D.C.: Brookings Institution.

Sosa, Sammy, and Marcos Brétón. 2000. *Sosa: An Autobiography.* New York: Warner.

Spalding, A. G. 1992. *America's National Game: Historic Facts Concerning the Beginning, Evolution, Development, and Popularity of Base Ball, with Personal Reminiscences of Its Vicissitudes, Its Victories, and Its Votaries.* Lincoln: University of Nebraska Press.

Spink, Alfred H. 2000. *The National Game.* Carbondale: Southern Illinois University Press.

Spink, J. G. Taylor. 1947. *Judge Landis and Twenty-five Years of Baseball.* New York: Crowell.

Spivak, Gayatri Chakravorty. 1999. *A Critique of Postcolonial Reason: Toward a History of the Vanishing Present.* Cambridge: Harvard University Press.

Springwood, Charles Fruehling. 1996. *Cooperstown to Dyersville: A Geography of Baseball Nostalgia.* Boulder, Colo.: Westview.

Staudohar, Paul D., ed. 2000. *Diamond Mines: Baseball and Labor*. Syracuse, N.Y.: Syracuse University Press.
Stiglitz, Joseph E. 2002. *Globalization and Its Discontents*. New York: Norton.
Susman, Warren. 1984. *Culture as History: The Transformation of American Society in the Twentieth Century*. New York: Pantheon.
Szymanski, Stefan, and Andrew S. Zimbalist. 2005. *National Pastime: How Americans Play Baseball and the Rest of the World Plays Soccer*. Washington, D.C.: Brookings Institution.
Tedlow, Richard S. 1990. *New and Improved: The Story of Mass Marketing in America*. New York: Basic Books.
Thorn, John, Pete Palmer, Michael Gershman, and David Pietrusza, with Matthew Silverman and Sean Lahman, eds. 1999. *Total Baseball*. 2nd ed. New York: Total Sports.
Threston, Christopher. 2003. *The Integration of Baseball in Philadelphia*. Jefferson, N.C.: McFarland.
Tygiel, Jules. 1997. *Baseball's Great Experiment: Jackie Robinson and His Legacy*. New York: Oxford University Press.
———. 2002. *Past Time: Baseball as History*. New York: Oxford University Press.
Umphlett, Wiley Lee. 1985. *American Sport Culture: The Humanistic Dimension*. Lewisburg, Pa.: Bucknell University Press.
Vail, James. 2001. *The Road to Cooperstown: A Critical History of Baseball's Hall of Fame Selection Process*. Jefferson, N.C.: McFarland.
Veblen, Thorstein. 1979. *The Theory of the Leisure Class: An Economic Study of Institutions*. Franklin Center, Pa.: Franklin Library.
Vincent, Fay. 2002. *The Last Commissioner: A Baseball Valentine*. New York: Simon and Schuster.
Vincent, Ted. 1994. *The Rise and Fall of American Sport: Mudville's Revenge*. Lincoln: University of Nebraska Press.
Ward, Geoffrey, and Ken Burns. 1994. *Baseball: An Illustrated History*. New York: Knopf.
Wendel, Tim. 2003. *The New Face of Baseball: The One-Hundred Year Rise and Triumph of Latinos in America's Favorite Sport*. New York: Rayo.
Wesley, John. 1985. *The Works of John Wesley*. Ed. Albert C. Outler. Nashville, Tenn.: Abington.
Westerbeek, Hans, and Aaron Smith. 2003. *Sport Business in the Global Marketplace*. New York: Palgrave Macmillan.
White, G. Edward. 1996. *Creating the National Pastime: Baseball Transforms Itself, 1903–1953*. Princeton: Princeton University Press.
Whiting, Robert. 1977. *The Chrysanthemum and the Bat: Baseball Samurai Style*. New York: Dodd, Mead.
———. 1990. *You Gotta Have Wa*. New York: Vintage.
———. 2004. *The Meaning of Ichiro: The New Wave from Japan and the Transformation of Our National Pastime*. New York: Warner.
Wolf, Michael J. 1999. *The Entertainment Economy: How Mega-Media Forces Are Transforming Our Lives*. New York: Times Books.
Wood, Stephen C., and J. David Pincus, eds. 2003. *Reel Baseball: Essays and Interviews on the National Pastime*. Jefferson, N.C.: McFarland.
The World Almanac 2002. 2002. New York: World Almanac Books.
Yetman, Norman R., ed. 1991. *Majority and Minority: The Dynamics of Race and Ethnicity in American Life*. 5th ed. Boston: Allyn and Bacon.
Young, Robert. 2001. *Postcolonialism: An Historical Introduction*. Malden, Mass.: Blackwell.

Zimbalist, Andrew S. 1992. *Baseball and Billions: A Probing Look inside the Big Business of Our National Pastime*. New York: Basic Books.

———. 2003. *May the Best Team Win: Baseball Economics and Public Policy*. Washington, D.C.: Brookings Institution.

———. 2006. *In the Best Interests of Baseball: The Revolutionary Reign of Bud Selig*. Hoboken, N.J.: Wiley.

Zingg, Paul J., ed. 1988. *The Sporting Image: Readings in American Sport History*. Lanham, Md.: University Press of America.

Zirin, Dave. 2005. *What's My Name, Fool? Sports and Resistance in the United States*. Chicago: Haymarket.

Zoss, Joel, and John Stewart Bowman. 1996. *Diamonds in the Rough: The Untold History of Baseball*. Chicago: Contemporary Books.

INDEX OF MAJOR LEAGUE BASEBALL NAMES

Aaron, Hank, 83
Abreu, Bobby, 130
Alexander, Grover Cleveland, 32
Allen, Mel, 34
Almeida, Rafael, 87
Alou, Felipe, 92
Alvarez Lugo, Carlos David (Esmailyn Gonzalez), 89
Amaro, Ruben, 101
Archey, Paul, Jr., 132

Bankhead, Sam, 112
Bass, Randy, 121
Bay, Jason, 130
Bell, Cool Papa, 79
Bellan, Enrique, 79
Beltran, Carlos, 102
Bender, Chief, 79
Blomberg, Ron, 108
Bonds, Barry, 67–68, 99
Bournigal, Rafael, 102
Bouton, Jim, 29
Bowden, Jim, 89
Bunning, Jim, 67

Burke, Michael, 20
Bush, George W., 8, 30, 108, 131

Cabrera, Alex, 121
Cambria, Joe, 87, 90
Campanella, Roy, 84
Caray, Harry, 34
Cartwright, Alexander, 10
Cashman, Brian, 103
Castro, Louis, 79
Chandler, Happy, 29, 40
Chase, Hal, 59
Clemente, Roberto, 87, 100
Cobb, Ty, 53
Colon, Bartolo, 102
Comiskey, Charles, 12, 49
Cromartie, Warren, 120, 123–24

Dean, Dizzy, 34
Delgado, Carlos, 30, 102
DiMaggio, Joe, 120
Doby, Larry, 84
Doubleday, Abner, 11, 27, 31, 41

164 INDEX OF MAJOR LEAGUE BASEBALL NAMES

DuPuy, Bob, 64
Durocher, Leo, 41

Eckert, William, 29
Evans, Billy, 40

Fehr, Donald, 62, 67
Flood, Curt, 60, 63, 84
Frazee, Harry, 53
Freedman, Andrew, 49
Fultz, David, 50–51

Gaffney, James, 71
Gehrig, Lou, 28
Giamatti, Bart, 25
Giambi, Jason, 67
Gibson, Josh, 79
Graham, Archie, 13
Griffith, Clark, 86–87
Guerrero, Vladimir, 102
Guillen, Ozzie, 85

Haak, Howard, 87
Hicks, Tom, 117
Hillman, Trey, 124
Holtzman, Ken, 108
Hulbert, William, 39, 42, 46
Hurst, Bruce, 128

Jackson, Joe, 12–13, 31
James, Bill, 20
Johnson, Ban, 48, 52

Kuhn, Bowie, 29, 60–62, 64, 84

Lajoie, Napoleon, 59, 71
Landis, Kenesaw Mountain, 14, 28, 31, 49, 51–53, 55, 59, 61, 75, 77, 80
Lefebvre, Jim, 128

Mack, Connie, 41
Manley, Effa, 101
Marichal, Juan, 92
Mariner, Jonathan, 101
Maris, Roger, 66, 98
Marsans, Armando, 87

Martin, Billy, 41
Martin, Pepper, 79
Martinez, Pedro, 102
Mathewson, Christy, 14–15
Matsui, Hideki, 122, 124
Matsuzaka, Daisuke, 122, 124
McGraw, John, 40–41, 49
McGwire, Mark, 66–69, 98–99
McHale, John, 64
McNally, Dave, 61
Messersmith, Andy, 61
Miller, Marvin, 6, 60–62
Mills, A. G., 11
Minaya, Omar, 101–3
Mitchell, George, 64, 68
Moreno, Arturo, 102
Mota, Manny, 95
Murakami, Masanori, 121

Newcombe, Don, 84
Nilsson, Dave, 116
Nomo, Hideo, 121–22

O'Doul, Lefty, 29
O'Malley, Peter, 115
O'Malley, Walter, 38, 53, 61

Paige, Satchel, 79, 92
Palmiero, Rafael, 67–68
Parrot, Harold, 71
Payne, Ulice, 101
Pena, Willy Mo, 89
Perez, Rafael, 99
Piazza, Mike, 130
Piniella, Lou, 41
Pond, Arlie, 27
Pujols, Albert, 130

Reagins, Tony, 101
Reichardt, Rick, 88
Reinsdorf, Jerry, 101
Reynolds, Allie, 79
Rhodes, Tuffy, 121
Rickey, Branch, 38, 40, 52, 72, 75–76, 78, 81–84, 87, 94, 112
Ripken, Cal, Jr., 98

Robinson, Frank, 85
Robinson, Jackie, 7, 17, 29, 72, 74, 81–85, 101, 112, 135
Rodriguez, Alex, 69
Ruth, Babe, 6, 16, 44, 51, 53–55, 59, 79, 98, 120

Santana, Johan, 102
Schiller, Harvey, 111, 118
Selig, Bud, 47, 62–64, 66–68, 129, 135
Shamsky, Art, 108
Sheffield, Gary, 67
Sockalexis, Louis, 71
Soler, Alay, 102
Solomon, Jimmie Lee, 101
Sosa, Sammy, 66–68, 98–99
Spalding, Albert, 10–11, 21, 24, 38, 41–43, 45, 49, 54, 113, 115–16
Speaker, Tris, 53
Steinbrenner, George, 38, 129
Stengel, Casey, 38
Suzuki, Ichiro, 105, 121–24, 130

Tejada, Miguel, 89
Todt, Phil, 52
Toolson, George, 59
Torre, Joe, 41
Trost, Lonn, 17

Uberroth, Peter, 62, 64

Valentine, Bobby, 124
Veeck, Bill, 38, 45, 84
Vincent, Fay, 63–64
Virgil, Ozzie, 92

Wagner, Honus, 36, 44, 54
Wang, Chien-Ming, 105, 129
Ward, John Montgomery, 39
Watson, Bob, 101
Weaver, Earl, 41
Williams, Ken, 85, 101
Williams, Ted, 79
Wilpon, Fred, 31, 101
Wright, Harry, 42–43, 115
Wrigley, William, Jr., 57

Yamauchi, Hiroshi, 103
Ynoa, Michel, 7, 89
Young, John, 100

www.ingramcontent.com/pod-product-compliance
Lightning Source LLC
Chambersburg PA
CBHW030344240426
43661CB00052B/1742